Developing, Using, and

Analyzing Rubrics in

Language Assessment with

Case Studies in Asian and

Pacific Languages

NFLRC Monographs is a refereed series sponsored by the National Foreign Language Resource Center at the University of Hawai'i under the supervision of the series editor, Richard Schmidt. NFLRC Monographs present the findings of recent work in applied linguistics that is of relevance to language teaching and learning, with a focus on the less commonly-taught languages of Asia and the Pacific.

Research Among Learners of Chinese as a Foreign Language
   Michael E. Everson & Helen H. Shen ((Editors), 2010
   ISBN 978-0-9800459-4-9

Toward Useful Program Evaluation in College Foreign Language Education
   John M. Norris, John McE. Davis, Castle Sinicrope, Yukiko Watanabe (Editors), 2009
   ISBN 978-0-9800459-3-2

Second language teaching and learning in the Net Generation
   Raquel Oxford & Jeffrey Oxford (Editors), 2009
   ISBN 978-0-9800459-2-5

Case studies in foreign language placement: Practices and possibilities
   Thom Hudson & Martyn Clark (Editors), 2008
   ISBN 978-0-9800459-0-1

Chinese as a heritage language: Fostering rooted world citizenry
   Agnes Weiyun He & Yun Xiao (Editors), 2008
   ISBN 978-0-8248328-6-5

Perspectives on teaching connected speech to second language speakers
   James Dean Brown & Kimi Kondo-Brown (Editors), 2006
   ISBN 978-0-8248313-6-3

ordering information at nflrc.hawaii.edu

Developing, Using, and Analyzing Rubrics in Language Assessment with Case Studies in Asian and Pacific Languages

edited by
JAMES DEAN BROWN

NATIONAL FOREIGN LANGUAGE RESOURCE CENTER
University of Hawai'i at Mānoa

 2012 James Dean Brown

Some rights reserved. See: http://creativecommons.org/licenses/by/3.0/

Manufactured in the United States of America.

The contents of this publication were developed in part under a grant from the U.S. Department of Education (CFDA 84.229, P229A100001). However, the contents do not necessarily represent the policy of the Department of Education, and one should not assume endorsement by the Federal Government.

ISBN: 978–0–9835816–1–1

Library of Congress Control Number: 2011942953

 All wood product components used in interior of this book are Sustainable Forestry Initiative® (SFI®) certified.

book design by Deborah Masterson

distributed by
National Foreign Language Resource Center
University of Hawai'i
1859 East-West Road #106
Honolulu HI 96822–2322
nflrc.hawaii.edu

About the National Foreign Language Resource Center

THE NATIONAL FOREIGN LANGUAGE RESOURCE CENTER, located in the College of Languages, Linguistics, & Literature at the University of Hawai'i at Mānoa, has conducted research, developed materials, and trained language professionals since 1990 under a series of grants from the U.S. Department of Education (Language Resource Centers Program). A national advisory board sets the general direction of the resource center. With the goal of improving foreign language instruction in the United States, the center publishes research reports and teaching materials that focus primarily on the languages of Asia and the Pacific. The center also sponsors summer intensive teacher training institutes and other professional development opportunities. For additional information about center programs, contact us.

Janes Dean Brown, Director
National Foreign Language Resource Center
University of Hawai'i at Mānoa
1859 East-West Road #106
Honolulu, HI 96822–2322

email: nflrc@hawaii.edu
website: nflrc.hawaii.edu.

NFLRC Advisory Board 2010–2014

Robert Blake
University of California, Davis

Mary Hammond
East-West Center

Madeline Spring
Arizona State University

Carol Chapelle
Iowa State University

Contents

Section I:
Introduction

1 Introduction to Rubric-Based Assessment
   James Dean Brown 1

Section II:
Developing, using, and analyzing rubric-based assessment

2 Developing Rubrics for Language Assessment
   James Dean Brown 13

3 Assessing Student Language Performance: Types and Uses of Rubrics
   Larry Davis & Kimi Kondo-Brown 33

4 Issues in Analyzing Rubric-Based Results
   James Dean Brown & Catherine (Katarina) Anne Edmonds 57

Section III:
Case studies in Asian and Pacific languages

5 Māori Language Proficiency in Writing: The Kaiaka Reo Year Eight Writing Test
   Catherine (Katarina) Anne Edmonds 87

6 The Hawaiian Oral Language Assessment: Development and Effectiveness of the Scoring Rubric
   Alohalani Housman, Kaulana Dameg, Māhealani Kobashigawa, & James Dean Brown 131

7 Rubric-Based Scoring of Japanese Essays: The Effects on Generalizability of Numbers of Raters and Categories
   James Dean Brown & Kimi Kondo-Brown 169

Section IV:
Conclusion

8 Conclusions on Rubric-Based Assessment
   James Dean Brown 187

Section I:
Introduction

Introduction to Rubric-Based Assessment

James Dean Brown
University of Hawai'i at Mānoa

Introduction

The term *rubric* has existed in English for more than 600 years and, during some of that time, it has meant a set of "printed rules or instructions" (*Encarta Encyclopedia*, 2004). However, more recently, rubric has come to be used widely in education. In the classroom, rubric may mean a set of categories, criteria for assessment, and the gradients for presenting and evaluating learning. When grading a student's essay, for example, a teacher may apply a rubric for its quality of organization, giving a 3 for *Advanced Proficient*, 2 for *Proficient*, and a 1 for *Partially Proficient* (Cooper & Gargan, 2009, p. 54).

A *rubric in language teaching* is typically a grid set up in one of two ways (a) with scores along one axis of the grid and language behavior descriptors inside the grid for what each score means in terms of language performance (see Table 1) or (b) with language categories along one axis and scores along the other axis and language behavior descriptors inside the grid for what each score within each category means in terms of language performance (see Table 2). [For more formal discussions of the differences between these two types of rubrics, see Chapters 2 and 3.] As such, a rubric is a tool that any language teacher can use for scoring students' language abilities and, perhaps more importantly, for giving them feedback on their progress in learning those language abilities. More specifically, rubrics can be used to assess students' abilities to use productive language skills (speaking or writing), or to use productive skills in interactions to perform well-defined tasks like writing an essay, giving directions on a map, filling out a form, etc.

Brown, J. D. (2012). Introduction to rubric-based assessment. In J. D. Brown, (Ed.), *Developing, using, and analyzing rubrics in language assessment with case studies in Asian and Pacific languages* (pp. 1–9). Honolulu: University of Hawai'i, National Foreign Language Resource Center.

Table 1. Rubric for scoring written reports with scores on one axis

score	description
4	information clearly relates to the main topic information includes several supporting details and/or examples information is very organized with well-constructed paragraphs and subheadings all paragraphs include introductory sentence, explanations or details, and concluding sentence no grammatical, spelling or punctuation errors all sources (information and graphics) are accurately documented in the desired format.
3	information clearly relates to the main topic information provides 1–2 supporting details and/or examples information is organized with well-constructed paragraphs most paragraphs include introductory sentence, explanations or details, and concluding sentence almost no grammatical, spelling or punctuation errors all sources (information and graphics) are accurately documented, but a few are not in the desired format.
2	information clearly relates to the main topic no details and/or examples are given information is organized, but paragraphs are not well-constructed paragraphs included related information but were typically not constructed well a few grammatical, spelling, or punctuation errors all sources (information and graphics) are accurately documented, but many are not in the desired format.
1	information has little or nothing to do with the main topic information appears to be disorganized paragraphing structure was not clear and sentences were not typically related within the paragraphs many grammatical, spelling, or punctuation errors some sources are not accurately documented.

Table 2. Rubric for scoring written reports with language categories on one axis scores on the other[1]

category	4	3	2	1
quality of information	information clearly relates to the main topic information includes several supporting details and/or examples.	information clearly relates to the main topic information provides 1–2 supporting details and/or examples.	information clearly relates to the main topic no details and/or examples are given.	information has little or nothing to do with the main topic.
organization	information is very organized with well-constructed paragraphs and subheadings.	information is organized with well-constructed paragraphs.	information is organized, but paragraphs are not well-constructed.	information appears to be disorganized.

[1] The rubric in Table 2 was generated online using Rubistar (http://rubistar.4teachers.org/); the rubric in Table 1 was adapted from Table 2 by using *Excel*™.

paragraph construction	all paragraphs include introductory sentence, explanations or details, and concluding sentence.	most paragraphs include introductory sentence, explanations or details, and concluding sentence.	paragraphs included related information but were typically not constructed well.	paragraphing was not clear and sentences were not typically related within the paragraphs.
mechanics	no grammatical, spelling or punctuation errors.	almost no grammatical, spelling or punctuation errors.	a few grammatical spelling, or punctuation errors.	many grammatical, spelling, or punctuation errors.
sources	all sources (information and graphics) are accurately documented in the desired format.	all sources (information and graphics) are accurately documented, but a few are not in the desired format.	all sources (information and graphics) are accurately documented, but many are not in the desired format.	some sources are not accurately documented.

A number of books and articles have been written that can help language professionals develop rubrics. For example, general education books on developing rubrics include Arter and McTighe (2001), Campbell Hill and Ekey (2010), Glickman-Bond and Rose (2006), and Hutson-Nechkash (2003). To my knowledge no book has been devoted entirely to helping language professionals develop rubrics. However, one book by Buttner (2007) does include rubrics along with other activities and assessment strategies. Generic education articles that might be useful to language teachers and testers interested in rubrics include Popham (1997), and three articles that are available free of charge on line: Mertler (2001), Moskal (2000), and Tierney and Simon (2004).

In my search for articles that would be useful for language professionals who want to develop and use rubrics, most of the articles I found focused on technical aspects of developing rubrics for large-scale, high-stakes purposes. North and Schneider (1998, p. 221) summarize much of that literature as follows:

> Whilst an intuitive approach may be appropriate in the development of scales for use in a low-stakes context in which a known group of assessors rate a familiar population of learners, it has been criticized in relation to the development of national framework scales (e.g., Skehan, 1984; Fulcher, 1987 1993 in relation to the [British] English Language Testing Service [ELTS]; Brindley 1986 1991; Pienemann Johnston, 1987 in relation to the Australian Second Language Proficiency Ratings [ASLPR]; Bachman Savignon, 1986; Lantolf Frawley, 1985 1988 1992; Spolsky, 1986 1993 in relation to the American Council of the Teaching of Foreign Languages [ACTFL] Proficiency Guidelines).

Note in this quote the number of instances where there are relationships between large-scale proficiency scales/frameworks and rubrics. These relationships point to the fact that rubrics are not only important to teachers in classrooms and administrators in language programs, but also to the development of the entire language teaching profession.

Additional sources describe how to design rubrics specifically for language assessment including one chapter in a book and one article (Brown, 2005; Upshur & Turner, 1995, respectively). Other modules describe developing and using rubrics in language classrooms for specific purposes (e.g., Arnold, 1998; Blankmann, 1998; Ho, 1998; Johnson, 1998; Russ, 1998; and Shimazaki, 1998) or simply describe the development of rubrics for language assessment and provide examples in the process of doing rubrics-based research (e.g., Brown, & Bailey, 1984; Brown, Hudson, Norris, & Bonk, 2002; Douglas, 1994; Jacobs, Zinkgraf, Wormuth, Hartfiel, & Hughey, 1981; Mullis, 1980; Norris, Brown, Hudson, & Bonk, 2002; and Norris, Brown, Hudson, & Yoshioka, 1998). Sections of two books show a number of examples of rubrics for speaking (Luoma, 2004, pp. 59–95 226–255) and writing/portfolios (Weigle, 2002, pp. 140–171, 190–196, 222–227). Those same books provide considerable information that is otherwise germane to the development and use of speaking and writing assessments.

As imposing as the above rubric-related literature may seem, I have long waited for a book that is designed specifically for language teachers and testers, explaining the basics of developing and using rubrics, as well as analyzing rubric-based scores, while providing numerous samples of language-related rubrics. Tired of waiting, I have edited this book to fill that gap. I hope you will find it useful.

What does this book cover?

One of the reviewers of this book pointed out that there are two types of edited collections of articles: one like a *buffet meal* and the other a *fixed-menu meal*. This seems like an apt set of metaphors to frame the nature and organization of this book. In the buffet collection, readers find a range of choices they can select from, but they are not likely to eat everything. In the fixed-menu collection, the chapters are planned to bolster and supplement each other with the goal of producing a unified and complete reading experience. This volume can be viewed as both types of meals combined. It is fixed-menu in the sense that it offers *how-to* chapters in Section II that are unified, sequenced, and interrelated. Similarly, it provides a fixed-menu of case studies that exemplify the current state statistical analysis in research that uses rubrics for empirical investigations of both writing and speaking skills. However, this book is also a bit of a buffet in the sense that Section II may best suit the appetites of novice rubric developers and users most interested in applying them in their classrooms and language programs, while Section III may be more suitable for the appetites of researchers looking for models of rubric studies that will help them with their own empirical investigations. It is certainly the case that such researchers may also benefit from the basic information provided in Section II. Some novice rubric users may only read Section II and then put the book on their shelf only to come back to it when they later need to see example rubrics, or the examples of rubric-based research provided in Section III. So, just to make sure I have sufficiently over-used this metaphor, let me summarize by saying that this book might best be characterized as a buffet made up of two fixed-menu meals from which the reader is not expected to eat everything–though some will no doubt over-eat. Hopefully, all readers will at least find enough sustenance.

As the next four headings indicate, this book is divided into four sections: an introduction section, two main sections, and a conclusion section.

Section I: Introduction

As should be clear by now, the first section consists of Chapter 1 which provides a brief review of the rubrics-based assessment literature as well as an overview of what the chapters of this book contain. Books on rubrics in the general education literature are abundant, so I cite some of the more useful ones. Books on rubrics specifically designed for language teachers do not exist as far as I know. However, I did find a number of articles using or discussing rubrics in second language studies. I was able to categorize and cite those. This chapter will close by giving an overview of what the present book covers.

Section II: Developing, using, and analyzing rubric-based assessment

Chapter 2 examines a variety of issues and strategies involved in developing rubrics, revising them, and using them to assess students' language performances. In order to do so, the chapter addresses three central questions: (a) What is the difference between holistic and analytic rubrics? (b) What are the steps in the rubric development process (including planning; designing the rubric; planning the assessment procedures and using the rubric; evaluating the reliability/fairness of the rubric; evaluating the quality of the rubric; as well as planning feedback and revising for pedagogically useful ratings)? And (c) what resources can help in creating rubrics (especially online resources)?

Chapter 3 provides further information about the types of rubrics used for language performance assessment (holistic and analytic rubrics, task-dependent and task-independent rubrics, primary-trait rubrics, and rubric-like instruments) and explains the primary uses of rubrics in language instruction (including ways to improve consistency and efficiency in grading, providing feedback and support for student learning, guiding instruction, keeping student achievement records, and communicating with others). The chapter ends with three case studies that illustrate different types of rubrics and uses. Each case study is described in terms of the context, the rubric itself, as well as the assessment results and implications.

Chapter 4 addresses the many issues that arise in doing basic statistical analyses that can help in developing, using, and analyzing rubric-based assessments. It begins by looking at the different kinds of scales that rubrics use (nominal, ordinal, or interval). The chapter also covers classical test theory descriptive and correlational statistics, as well as reliability estimates and the standard error of measurement. In addition, the chapter provides information that will help in understanding more advanced statistical procedures that are also useful for developing, revising, analyzing, and interpreting rubric-based assessments. These advanced statistical analyses include generalizability theory (complete with generalizability and decision studies for relative and absolute decisions, phi(lambda), and signal-to-noise ratios) and multifaceted Rasch measurement (including fit statistics, vertical rulers, probability curves, and bias analysis). The conclusion pulls all of this information together into a chart that you can be used to decide what sorts of analyses are appropriate for answering different types of questions that often arise in analyzing, using, and reporting rubric-based assessment results.

Section III: Case studies in Asian and Pacific languages

Chapter 5 examines the reliability and validity of the Kaiaka Reo Year Eight Māori language writing proficiency test administered to year eight students in Level One in Māori immersion schools in New Zealand. The performances of 40 year eight students were assessed and analyzed by a group of Māori medium educators using an analytical rubric created especially for this project. The chapter explains how the rubric and assessment procedures were developed. Then, multifaceted Rasch analysis was performed with students, raters, and categories as facets. The ratings were given by ten teacher raters in five categories (Organization and Ideas; Grammar and Accuracy; Punctuation, Spelling and Mechanics; Style and Quality of Expression, and Māori Discourse Intelligibility). The results are discussed in terms of the reliability and validity of the Kaiaka Reo Year Eight test as a means of determining the Māori language writing proficiency of year eight students in

Māori medium settings. This project set out to develop a test under the philosophy *by Māori, for Maori, in te reo Maori* and to investigate its reliability and validity by internationally accepted forms of test analysis.

Chapter 6 reports on the development of a set of rubric-based Hawaiian oral language assessment procedures. The participants were 270 students from seven Hawaiian Language Immersion Program schools located on four different islands. The chapter explains how the rubric and assessment procedures were developed, piloted, and revised. The resulting procedures included an Introduction interview and two picture-story tasks, as well as a short oral response subtest with subsets of items on Nouns, Demonstrative Pronouns, Locatives, Marker Verbs, and Pronouns. The rubric was based on seven proficiency domains: communicative skill, vocabulary, grammar, pronunciation, fluency, language steadfastness, and cultural and linguistic authenticity. The chapter goes on to describe the five raters and how they did their ratings based on the rubric. The statistical analyses include descriptive statistics, item analyses, correlation coefficients, and the multifaceted Rasch analyses. Ultimately, the chapter focuses on questions of what the most important aspects of oral language development are for these students, what their Hawaiian oral language proficiency levels are, and what can be done to improve their Hawaiian language proficiency levels.

Chapter 7 reports on a study that applies generalizability theory (G-theory) analysis to the rubric-based scores of three raters who independently assessed 234 Japanese-as a second language (L2) compositions in five language categories (content, organization, vocabulary, language use, and mechanics). The statistical analyses included descriptive statistics, classical test theory reliability estimates (inter-rater), and G-theory analyses included a generalizability study (G-study) with analysis of the attendant variance components and a decision study (D-study) with the generalizability coefficients for relative decisions (i.e., norm-referenced decisions) for various combinations of numbers of raters and categories. The classical test theory analyses revealed the relatively high reliability of these scores and the suitability of the rubric for these students in terms of difficulty and dispersion. The G-study analysis showed the relative importance of the estimated variance components for persons, raters, categories, and their interactions for the Japanese composition scores, as well as the degree to which those facets and their interactions contributed to the dependability of the scores. The D-study results allowed, from a practical perspective, for deciding what numbers of raters and categories would be most effective given the circumstances in a particular institution.

Section IV: Conclusion

The fourth section consists solely of Chapter 8 which briefly summarizes the book and then provides much more detailed information in several areas. First a table is presented and discussed that shows all the rubrics-related topics covered in this book along with which chapter it appears in. A second table then shows and briefly explains where the statistics covered in this book can be found, both in terms of which chapters provide explanations and which contain examples of their use in rubrics-based studies. A table is also shown and briefly discussed that lists all 22 of the example rubrics provided in this book in terms of where they can be found and their characteristics. After reading the book, readers may find these tables useful, particularly when they are returning to the book later to find specific material that they want to review.

Conclusion

In this chapter, I have tried to start the book off on a sound footing by defining what a rubric is and showing two examples. I then provided a brief review of the rubrics-based assessment books in general education as well as four articles and categorized and briefly discussed the articles on rubrics in second language studies. My only hope at this point is that you will learn as much from reading this book as I did by co-authoring some of the articles and editing the book.

Rubrics are an essential tool for all language teachers in this age of communicative and task-based teaching and assessment—a tool that allows us to efficiently communicate to our students what we are looking for in the productive language abilities of speaking and writing and then effectively assess those abilities when the time comes for giving students feedback, for grading, for placement into new courses, and so forth.

References

Arnold, S. L. (1998). Observation, feedback, and individual goal setting. In J. D. Brown (Ed.), *New ways of classroom assessment* (pp. 317–319). Washington, DC: Teachers of English to Speakers of Other Languages.

Arter, J., & McTighe, J. (2001). *Scoring rubrics in the classroom: Using performance criteria for assessing and improving student performance*. Thousand Oaks, CA: Corwin/Sage.

Bachman, L. F., & Savignon, S. J. (1986). The evaluation of communicative language proficiency: A critique of the ACTFL oral interview. *Modern Language Journal, 70*, 380–390.

Blankmann, J. (1998). Oral presentations: How did I do? In J. D. Brown (Ed.), *New ways of classroom assessment* (pp. 87–89). Washington, DC: Teachers of English to Speakers of Other Languages.

Brindley, G. (1986). *The assessment of second language proficiency: Issues and approaches*. Adelaide: National Curriculum Resource Centre.

Brindley, G. (1991). Defining language ability: The criteria for criteria. In S. Anivan (Ed.), *Current developments in language testing* (pp. 139–164). Singapore: Regional Language Centre.

Brown, J. D. (2005). *Testing in language programs: A comprehensive guide to English language assessment* (New edition). New York: McGraw-Hill.

Brown, J. D., & Bailey, K. M. (1984). A categorical instrument for scoring second language writing skills. *Language Learning, 34*(4), 21–42.

Brown, J. D., Hudson, T., Norris, J. M., & Bonk, W. (2002). *Investigating second language performance assessments*. Honolulu, HI: Second Language Teaching & Curriculum Center, University of Hawai'i Press.

Buttner, A. (2007). *Activities, games, assessment strategies, and rubrics: For the foreign language classroom*. Larchmont, NY: Eye on Education.

Campbell Hill, B., & Ekey, C. (2010). *The next-step guide to enriching classroom environments: Rubrics and resources for self-evaluation and goal setting for literacy coaches, principals, and teacher study groups, K–6*. Portsmouth, NH: Heinemann.

Cooper, B. S., & Gargan, A. (2009). Rubrics in education: Old term, new meanings. *Phi Beta Kappan, 19*(1), 54–55

Douglas, D. (1994). Quantity and quality in speaking test performance. *Language Testing, 11*(2), 125–144.

Encarta Encyclopedia. (2004). Redmond, WA: Microsoft.

Fulcher, G. (1987). Tests of oral performance: The need for data-based criteria. *ELT Journal, 41*, 287–291.

Fulcher, G. (1993). *The construction and validation of rating scales for oral tests in English as a foreign language.* PhD thesis, University of Lancaster.

Glickman-Bond, J., & Rose, K. (2006). *Creating and using rubrics in today's classrooms: A practical guide.* Norwood, MA: Christopher-Gordon.

Ho, B. (1998). How well did I communicate? In J. D. Brown (Ed.), *New ways of classroom assessment* (pp. 97–98). Washington, DC: Teachers of English to Speakers of Other Languages.

Hutson-Nechkash, P. (2003). *Help me write: Frames and rubrics for classroom writing success.* Greenville, SC: Thinking Publications.

Jacobs, H. L., Zinkgraf, S. A., Wormuth, D. R., Hartfiel, V. F., & Hughey, J. B. (1981). *Testing ESL composition: A practical approach.* Rowley, MA: Newbury House.

Johnson, J. (1998). So how did you like my presentation. In J. D. Brown (Ed.), *New ways of classroom assessment* (pp. 67–69). Washington, DC: Teachers of English to Speakers of Other Languages.

Lantolf, J., & Frawley, W. (1985). Oral proficiency testing: A critical analysis. *Modern Language Journal, 69,* 337–345.

Lantolf, J., & Frawley, W. (1988). Proficiency, understanding the construct. *Studies in Second Language Acquisition, 10,* 181–196.

Lantolf, J., & Frawley, W. (1992). Rejecting the OPI again: A response to Hagen. *ADFL Bulletin, 23,* 34–37.

Luoma, S. (2004). *Assessing speaking.* Cambridge, UK: Cambridge University.

Mertler, C. A. (2001). Designing scoring rubrics for your classroom. *Practical Assessment, Research & Evaluation,7*(25). Retrieved October 26, 2010 from http://PAREonline.net/getvn.asp?v=7&n=25 .

Moskal, B. M. (2000). Scoring rubrics: What, when and how? *Practical Assessment, Research & Evaluation, 7*(3). Retrieved October 26, 2010 from http://PAREonline.net/getvn.asp?v=7&n=3 .

Mullis, I.V.S. (1980). *Using the primary trait system for evaluating writing.* Manuscript No. 10–W–51. Princeton, NJ: Educational Testing Service.

Norris, J. M., Brown, J. D., Hudson, T. D., & Bonk, W. (2002). Examinee abilities and task difficulty in task-based second language performance assessment. *Language Testing, 19*(4), 396–418.

Norris, J. M., Brown, J. D., Hudson, T., & Yoshioka, J. (1998). *Designing second language performance assessments.* Honolulu, HI: Second Language Teaching & Curriculum Center, University of Hawai'i Press.

North, B., & Schneider, G. (1998). Scaling descriptors for language proficiency scales. *Language Testing, 15*(2), 217–263.

Pienemann, M., & Johnston, M. (1987). Factors influencing the development of language proficiency. In D. Nunan (Ed.), *Applying second language acquisition research* (pp. 89–94). Adelaide: National Curriculum Resource Centre.

Popham, W. J. (1997). What's wrong – and what's right – with rubrics. *Educational Leadership, 55*(2), 72–75.

Russ, R. (1998). Let me explain. In J. D. Brown (Ed.), *New ways of classroom assessment* (pp. 153–155). Washington, DC: Teachers of English to Speakers of Other Languages.

Shimazaki, R. (1998). Guess what my favorite animal is. In J. D. Brown (Ed.), *New ways of classroom assessment* (pp. 354–355). Washington, DC: Teachers of English to Speakers of Other Languages.

Skehan, P. (1984) Issues in the testing of English for specific purposes. *Language Testing, 1,* 202–220.

Spolsky, B. (1986). A multiple choice for language testers. *Language Testing, 3,* 147–158.

Spolsky, B. (1993). Testing and examinations in a national foreign language policy. In K. Sajavaara, S. Takala, D. Lambert, & C. Morfit (Eds), *National foreign language policies: Practices and prospects* (pp. 194–214). Jyväskylä, Finland: University of Jyväskylä, Institute for Education Research.

Tierney, R., & Simon, M. (2004). What's still wrong with rubrics: Focusing on the consistency of performance criteria across scale levels. *Practical Assessment, Research & Evaluation, 9*(2). Retrieved January 9, 2011 from http://PAREonline.net/getvn.asp?v=9&n=2.

Upshur, J. A., & Turner, C. E. (1995). Constructing rating scales for second language tests. *ELT Journal, 49*(1), 3–12.

Weigle, S. C. (2002). *Assessing writing.* Cambridge, UK: Cambridge University.

Section II:
Developing, using, and analyzing rubric-based assessment

Developing Rubrics for Language Assessment

James Dean Brown
University of Hawai'i at Mānoa

Introduction

Chapter 1 provided a definition of what a rubric is in language teaching and assessment: "a grid set up in one of two ways: (a) with scores along one axis of the grid and language behavior descriptors inside the grid for what each score means in terms of language performance…, or (b) with language categories along one axis and scores along the other axis and language behavior descriptors inside the grid for what each score within each category means in terms of language performance." The focus of this chapter will be on providing strategies for developing rubrics for making decisions about students' language performance for high- or low-stakes decisions. This chapter will therefore be applicable to criterion-referenced assessment done at the classroom level for diagnostic, progress, and achievement testing (where the purpose is to find out how much of the material or skills the students have mastered), as well as to norm-referenced assessment, which is used primarily for larger-scale, higher-stakes decisions like proficiency and placement testing (where it is crucial to spread students out along a relatively wide continuum of abilities).

In order to accomplish all of the above, the following questions will be addressed and serve as the organizational framework for this chapter:

What is the difference between holistic and analytic rubrics?

What are the steps in the rubric development process?

What resources can help in creating rubrics?

Brown, J. D. (2012). Developing rubrics for language assessment. In J. D. Brown, (Ed.), *Developing, using, and analyzing rubrics in language assessment with case studies in Asian and Pacific languages* (pp. 13–31). Honolulu: University of Hawai'i, National Foreign Language Resource Center.

What is the difference between holistic and analytic rubrics?

Sometimes the two different types of rubrics described as (a) and (b) (in the definition at the top of this chapter) are also called holistic and analytic rubrics. The rubric labeled (a) and shown in Table 1 results from using a holistic approach, which involves using a single general scale to give a single global rating for each student's language production. Scoring holistically results in a single rating or score. Holistic rubrics are therefore often easier and quicker to use than analytic rubrics, but holistic rubrics are not very useful for providing detailed feedback to students. As a result, holistic scoring is most often used in proficiency testing (for purposes of admitting student to a program) or placement testing (for purpose of placing students into levels of study) because, in both cases, time is of the essence and detailed feedback to students is not a priority.

In contrast, the rubric labeled (b) and shown in Table 2 represents the *analytic approach*, which involves giving separate ratings for different aspects (or categories) of language for each student's language production. A teacher using an analytic rubric may give three, four, five, six or more scores, each of which provides a different piece of information. Analytic rubrics are often more time-consuming to use than holistic rubrics, but they are typically more useful for providing detailed feedback to students. Hence, analytic scoring is most often used for classroom diagnostic, progress, and achievement assessment, where teachers may find it worth taking the time necessary to give detailed feedback to students.

Note that the difference between holistic and analytic rubrics seems to be more about format than it is about the content of the grids. Tables 1 and 2 illustrate this fact. Notice that the content of the two grids is exactly the same. I simply block-copied the words in the second column (the one labeled: 20–18 *Excellent to Good*) of Table 2 and pasted them into the descriptor for a score of 5 in Table 1. The same is true for each of the subsequent columns in Table 2. The resulting difference in format changes the purpose and utility of the rubric fundamentally as described above. The choice between developing a holistic or analytic rubric affects everything else about the scoring process, so deciding on the format should be done early and taken seriously.

Table 1. Holistic version of the scale for rating composition tasks (adapted from Brown & Bailey, 1984, pp. 39–41)

score	descriptors
5	appropriate title, effective introductory paragraph, topic is stated, leads to body; transitional expressions used; arrangement of material shows plan (could be outlined by reader); supporting evidence given for generalizations; conclusion logical & complete. essay addresses the assigned topic; the ideas are concrete and thoroughly developed; no extraneous material; essay reflects thought. native-like fluency in English grammar; correct use of relative clauses, prepositions, modals, articles, verb forms, and tense sequencing; no fragments or run-on sentences; correct use of English writing conventions; left & right margins, all needed capitals, paragraphs indented, punctuation & spelling; very neat. precise vocabulary usage; use of parallel structures; concise; register good.

4	adequate title, introduction, & conclusion; body of essay is acceptable but some evidence may be lacking, some ideas aren't fully developed; sequence is logical but transitional expressions may be absent or misused. essay addresses the issues but misses some points; ideas could be more fully developed; some extraneous material is present. advanced proficiency in English grammar; some grammar problems don't influence communication, although the reader is aware of them; no fragments or run-on sentences. some problems with writing conventions or punctuation; occasional spelling errors; left margin correct; paper is neat and legible; attempts variety; good vocabulary; not wordy; register ok; style fairly concise.
3	Mediocre or scant introduction, or conclusion; problems with the order of ideas in body; the generalizations may not be fully supported by the evidence given; problems of organization interfere. development of ideas not complete or essay is somewhat off the topic; paragraphs aren't divided exactly right ideas getting through to the reader, but grammar problems are apparent and have a negative effect on communication; run-on sentences or fragments present. uses general writing conventions but has errors; spelling problems distract reader; punctuation errors interfere with ideas. some vocabulary misused; lacks awareness of register; may be too wordy.
2	shaky or minimally recognizable introduction; organization can barely be seen; severe problems with ordering of ideas; lack of supporting evidence; conclusion weak or illogical; inadequate effort at organization. ideas incomplete; essay does not reflect careful thinking or was hurriedly written; inadequate effort in area of content. numerous serious grammar problems interfere with communication of the writer's ideas; grammar review of some areas clearly needed; difficult to read sentences serious problems with format of paper; parts of essay not legible; errors in sentence-final punctuation; unacceptable to educated readers. poor expression of ideas; problems in vocabulary; lacks variety of structure.
1	absence of introduction or conclusion; no apparent organization of body; severe lack of supporting evidence; writer has not made any effort to organize the composition (could not be outlined by reader). essay is completely inadequate and does not reflect college level work; no apparent effort to consider the topic carefully. severe grammar problems interfere greatly with the message; reader can't understand what the writer is trying to say; unintelligible sentence structure. complete disregard for English writing conventions; paper illegible; obvious capitals missing, no margins, severe spelling problems. inappropriate use of vocabulary; no concept of register or sentence variety.

Table 2. Analytic scale for rating composition tasks (adapted from Brown & Bailey 1984, pp. 39–41)

language categories	20–18 excellent to good	17–15 good to adequate	14–12 adequate to fair	11–6 unacceptable	5–1 not college-level work
organization: introduction, body & conclusion	appropriate title, effective introductory paragraph, topic is stated, leads to body; transitional expressions used; arrangement of material shows plan (could be outlined by reader); supporting evidence given for generalizations; conclusion logical & complete	adequate title, introduction, & conclusion; body of essay is acceptable but some evidence may be lacking, some ideas aren't fully developed; sequence is logical but transitional expressions may be absent or misused	mediocre or scant introduction, or conclusion; problems with the order of ideas in body; the generalizations may not be fully supported by the evidence given; problems of organization interfere	shaky or minimally recognizable introduction; organization can barely be seen; severe problems with ordering of ideas; lack of supporting evidence; conclusion weak or illogical; inadequate effort at organization	absence of introduction or conclusion; no apparent organization of body; severe lack of supporting evidence; writer has not made any effort to organize the composition (could not be outlined by reader)
logical development of ideas: content	essay addresses the assigned topic; the ideas are concrete and thoroughly developed; no extraneous material; essay reflects thought	essay addresses the issues but misses some points; ideas could be more fully developed; some extraneous material is present	development of ideas not complete or essay is somewhat off the topic; paragraphs aren't divided exactly right	ideas incomplete; essay does not reflect careful thinking or was hurriedly written; inadequate effort in area of content	essay is completely inadequate and does not reflect college level work; no apparent effort to consider the topic carefully

language categories	20–18 excellent to good	17–15 good to adequate	14–12 adequate to fair	11–6 unacceptable	5–1 not college-level work
grammar	native-like fluency in English grammar; correct use of relative clauses, prepositions, modals, articles, verb forms, and tense sequencing; no fragments or run-on sentences	advanced proficiency in English grammar; some grammar problems don't influence communication, although the reader is aware of them; no fragments or run-on sentences	ideas getting through to the reader, but grammar problems are apparent and have a negative effect on communication; run-on sentences or fragments present	numerous serious grammar problems interfere with communication of the writer's ideas; grammar review of some areas clearly needed; difficult to read sentences	severe grammar problems interfere greatly with the message; reader can't understand what the writer is trying to say; unintelligible sentence structure
punctuation, spelling, & mechanics	correct use of English writing conventions; left & right margins, all needed capitals, paragraphs indented, punctuation & spelling; very neat	some problems with writing conventions or punctuation; occasional spelling errors; left margin correct; paper is neat and legible	uses general writing conventions but has errors; spelling problems distract reader; punctuation errors interfere with ideas	serious problems with format of paper; parts of essay not legible; errors in sentence-final punctuation; unacceptable to educated readers	complete disregard for English writing conventions; paper illegible; obvious capitals missing, no margins, severe spelling problems
style & quality of expression	precise vocabulary usage; use of parallel structures; concise; register good	attempts variety; good vocabulary; not wordy; register ok; style fairly concise	some vocabulary misused; lacks awareness of register; may be too wordy	poor expression of ideas; problems in vocabulary; lacks variety of structure	inappropriate use of vocabulary; no concept of register or sentence variety

What are the steps in the rubric development process?

Developing a rubric can involve a few steps or it can involve many steps. I will provide a more or less comprehensive list of the steps that can be taken in developing a rubric here on the theory that readers are more likely to benefit from finding too much detail and cutting it down than from finding too little detail and having to make it up as they go along. A comprehensive list of the steps involved in rubric development will be easier to understand if it is broken up into major stages and the minor steps that are part of each stage so I will present them in stages and steps as shown in Table 3.

Table 3. Suggested stages and steps in the rubric development process

stage		step
1: planning	1.1	Define your goal.
	1.2	Go to the source material.
	1.3	Brainstorm.
	1.4	Analytic or holistic?
	1.5	Decide the categories.
	1.6	Decide the range of scores your want to use.
2: designing the rubric	2.1	Put scores on one axis.
	2.2	Put the categories on the other axis.
	2.3	Fill in the rubric descriptors for each score level.
3: planning the assessment procedures and using the rubric	3.1	Decide on the stimulus formats.
	3.2	Decide on the response formats.
	3.3	Write clear instructions.
	3.4	Make sure the instructions and stimulus materials are ready.
	3.5	Arrange for the mechanics of assessment.
	3.6	Actually do the assessment.
	3.7	Train raters to use the rubric.
4: evaluating the reliability/ fairness of your rubric		
5: evaluating the quality of your rubric	5.1	Evaluate the validity of your rubric.
	5.2	Evaluate the usability of your rubric.
6: planning feedback and revise for pedagogically useful ratings	6.1	Plan for student and teacher feedback.
	6.2	Set up a cycle of revision and improvement.

Stage 1: Planning

Step 1.1: Define your goal.

Before doing anything else, it is worthwhile to sit down and think through why you want to do the assessment that you are contemplating and what your goals are in doing the assessment. If your answer is that you want to place your students into the appropriate level of study in your program at least in part on the basis of a written essay, that decision will entail one set of issues. If your answer is that you want to give students useful pedagogical feedback in your speaking course, that process involves quite another set of issues. So it is important to think your goals through before doing anything else, especially when using rubrics, because you will typically have less control over the range of possible responses that your students will produce in such open-ended assessment, and therefore, you will need to be very clear, yourself, about what it is you are looking for (i.e., what your goal is).

Step 1.2: Go to the source material.

One way to clarify your goals is to go directly to your basic source materials. Typically, this means looking at your goals and objectives, at your materials, and your other assessment materials, and so forth. Your rubric and the associated assessment procedures can then be designed to reflect as closely as appropriate the teaching and learning that the students have experienced. In many respects, doing this step, even though it may involve extra work, will start you down the path to creating a reasonably valid form of assessment. The alternatives (i.e., taking a rubric off the shelf or just making something up) can lead to a mismatch between what the students have experienced in the classroom and the assessment procedures. In technical terms, such a mismatch is likely to create a negative washback effect from the assessments on the learning process.

Step 1.3: Brainstorm.

One source of information that we often forget to use is the knowledge of our colleagues and students. In designing rubrics, two heads are definitely better than one. So, it is often wise to work together with other teachers on such a project. It may even help to bring students into the process. For one thing, involving other teachers (and students) in some sort of brainstorming activity should help in creating teacher/student buy-in to the rubric and the whole assessment process. For another thing, brainstorming is a terrific way to generate new ideas. Yes, two heads are better than one because a second or third person will have different perspectives and ideas. In addition, the very process of brainstorming can help individuals think of and add ideas (for what sorts of categories to include, for ways to describe the behavior in a particular category at a particular score level, etc.).

If you find yourselves out of ideas, it may pay to take a break, turn to the literature on the topic, and create a list of possibilities from the literature so that the list can then serve as the basis for further brainstorming.

In more formal terms, Fulcher (1996, p. 212) talks about the issue of getting expert judges to work together on a rubric: "Alderson (1991) [a document I have never been able to track down] describes the process of the use of expert judges in drafting descriptors, and using marking bands to extract 'key features' from actual interviews." Thus Fulcher is pointing not only to the benefits of professionals working together but also the value of basing their discussions of key features on data derived from an original sources (i.e., the interviews in this case).

Step 1.4: Analytic or holistic?

One of the first things you will need to do whether you are working alone or brainstorming with others is to decide whether an analytic or holistic approach will best suit your purposes.

As discussed above, because it requires multiple ratings for each examinee, analytic scoring is typically more useful in classroom situations where giving feedback to the students is important and the amount of time required to do the ratings is less of an issue. In contrast, holistic scoring, which is more efficient in terms of time, but provides much less feedback, is typically more appropriate for larger scale assessment like proficiency and placement testing. An early part of your brainstorming may need to be about this issue. Once the analytic vs. holistic decision is made, your path will be much clearer.

Step 1.5: Decide the categories.

If you have decided to do analytic scoring, the next obvious step will be to decide on which categories of language behavior you want to assess. For holistic scales you may want to skip this step. However, even in designing holistic scales, you will need to think about what aspects of the language you will describe in your descriptors for each score level.

Analytic rubrics are by definition based on the idea of providing separate scores for each of multiple categories of linguistic content or language behaviors. The problem for rubric designers is that there are many such possible categories. For example, any of the following could be included:

1. pronunciation accuracy or level used
2. stress timing, rhythm, intonation
3. grammar accuracy or level used
4. vocabulary accuracy or level used
5. collocations
6. appropriateness of kinesics, proxemics, facial expressions, or gestures
7. use of downgraders
8. pragmatics with regard to degree of power difference, social distance, imposition, etc.
9. fluency
10. organization
11. logical development of ideas
12. topic coverage
13. getting meaning across
14. mechanics (capitalization, punctuation, etc.)
15. coherence
16. cohesion
17. register
18. style
19. successful task completion
20. amount of language produced

These twenty categories (each of which could be broken down into separate ratable subcategories) took me less than ten minutes to generate. Imagine what a group of teachers at your institution could come up with.

The central exercise in choosing categories essentially involves being aware of the possibilities and then narrowing down from the many options to three, four, five, or whatever number of categories the teachers/raters will find useful in the particular institution or classroom involved. That is why I say that deciding on language categories will tend to be based on their relative pedagogical and political importance. If a proper needs analysis has been performed recently in your institution or class, the information needed to make such selections may be readily available. But decisions about which categories of language to include in a rubric can also be made at a single meeting if the relevant teachers and administrators are of good will and can meet, brainstorm, and make the decisions.

For example, the analytic rubric shown in Table 2 was developed while I was teaching ESL at UCLA. The instructors teaching the highest level course decided that essays should be rated on the basis of an analytical rubric. After a good deal of discussion, we decided that there should be five distinct scores, one each for organization; logical development of ideas; grammar; punctuation, spelling and mechanics; and style and quality of expression as shown in Table 2. Thus we had agreed on (or rather *compromised* on) five categories of language which were important to us from among the many possible categories we could have used. In a different situation in the late 1980s, the teachers in the English Language Institute (ELI) at the University of Hawai'i at Mānoa (UHM) decided to use an essay scoring rubric that had somewhat different categories: content; organization; vocabulary, language use, and mechanics. This rubric was adapted considerably for use at UHM from Jacobs, Zinkgraf, Wormuth, Hartfiel, and Hughey (1981). Thus for pedagogical and political reasons, the teachers at UCLA chose five categories for scoring essays that were quite different from the five categories chosen at UHM. In my view, given that such decisions can differ dramatically in various language courses or programs, these decisions should most often rest with the experts, who most often turn out to be the teachers of the course or program, who will have to use the rubrics, who need to buy into their use, and who can kill a rubric if they do not approve of it.

Step 1.6: *Decide the range of scores you want to use.*

Whether you are designing a holistic or analytic rubric, you will need to decide what score range you want to use. In the case of a holistic scale, you may want to use a 1 to 5 scale, or 0 to 5, or 1 to 10 or whatever else suits your purpose, but remember that for each point on the scale, you may have to write a description of the behavior you will be expecting for a student to receive that rating. For example, you may decide that a 5 is an *advanced writer*, a 4 is a *good writer*, a 3 is an *average writer*, a 2 is a *mediocre writer*, and a 1 is a *very poor writer*. Technically, the possible scores are 1, 2, 3, 4, and 5, and they are described, if ever so vaguely. I would clearly want to add much more detail describing what an advanced writer who would get a score of 5 would be like in terms of whatever criteria are important to me and my colleagues (all combined into one description of the writing of a student at level 5). The same would be true for scores of 4, 3, 2, and 1. In the case of an analytic rubric, you will have to decide what range of scores (1–5; 1–4; 1–3, etc.) you want to use for each category to reflect the categories that are pedagogically relevant in the particular situation as well as the range of abilities found there.

Stage 2: Designing the rubric

Step 2.1: *Put scores on one axis.*

The first, and perhaps simplest, step is to decide which axis of the rubric you want to put the scores on. The holistic rubric in Table 1 has the scores on the vertical axis to the left, while the analytic rubric in Table 2 has them on the horizontal axis along the top. Your reasons for choosing one or the other may at first seem more aesthetic than anything, but since you probably want to make the rubric easy to interpret, simple to use, and accurate, those issues should figure into the design of the rubric's layout as well.

Step 2.2: *Put the categories on the other axis.*

If you are designing an analytic rubric, you will also need to put category labels on the other axis. Notice that Table 1 has no categories at all because it is a holistic rubric. In contrast, Table 2 has the categories on the vertical axis to the left and the possible scores across the top, but of course, they could equally well be on the opposite axes. Again, your reasons for choosing one design or the other will probably depend on what you think will make the rubric easy to interpret, simple to use, and accurate.

Naturally there are advantages and disadvantages to different scoring schemes that have a lot to do with whether you chose to use a holistic or analytic rubric. That takes us to the next step.

Step 2.3: Fill in the rubric descriptors for each score level.

When the band of abilities is wide, as is often the case for holistic rubrics used for proficiency or placement testing, a scale of 1 to 5, or 1 to 9, may do a fine job of putting students into five levels of study, or nine bands of proficiency. In fact, the job of writing descriptors may be fairly easy when you only need to distinguish between widely spread levels of ability. Some schemes simply shift the adjectives and adverbs a bit between levels in these sorts of testing situations. For example, a writing scale designed to spread students from zero level to near native level writing proficiency might look something like the one shown in Table 4.

Table 4.   Draft holistic scale for rating essays written by examinees with a wide range of abilities

score	descriptors
5	well organized; very cohesive; excellent grammar with few errors; wide variety of vocabulary; excellent mechanics (punctuation, capitalization, & spelling)
4	fairly well organized; cohesive to a good degree; reasonably good grammar with some errors; fairly varied vocabulary; good mechanics
3	somewhat organized; some cohesion; adequate grammar with noticeable errors; some variety in vocabulary; problems in mechanics that don't interfere with comprehension
2	not very well organized; not always cohesive; grammar problems with bothersome errors; little variety in vocabulary; poor mechanics interfere with comprehension
1	poorly organized; not cohesive; poor grammar with many errors; very little or no variety in vocabulary; very poor mechanics that strongly interfere with comprehension OR not enough written material to make a judgment

Notice how the five factors that are included in this holistic scale (organization, cohesion, grammar, vocabulary, & mechanics) are in the same order at each score level and that, by-and-large, only the adjectives and adverbs are changing as you read down the list. I just made this scale up in about 15 minutes, but it might serve at least as a draft scale if the abilities of the examinees ranged widely and provision were made to revise it after first trying it out. In fact, this scale is very similar to scales that have and still are used on some of the internationally famous proficiency tests. Notice also that I automatically gave the lowest score of 1 to "OR not enough written material to make a judgment" simply because that sort of thing often arises real-world testing situations. In addition, I have had problems getting raters using this sort of rubric (where adjectives and adverbs are shifted) to agree on difference like those between "Well-organized," "Fairly well organized," and "Somewhat organized." Nonetheless, for assessing wide bands of ability such distinctions seem to be unavoidable. Note also that the rubric in Table 1 above is just a much more elaborate version of the rubric shown in Table 4, with different facets of writing featured and more extensive descriptors.

In contrast, when the band of abilities is fairly narrow, as in a particular course where you want to use an analytic scale, you may decide to use a narrower band of scores, say 1 to 3 simply because you are not likely to be able to make very fine discriminations in multiple categories without taking a great deal of time and effort. One fairly easy way to do this is to label your categories on one dimension and your scores on the other dimension as shown in Table 5, which presents a partly completed rubric for a course-level speaking test with the categories across the top that a group of teachers (including me) decided on (in this case, Fluency, Meaning, Exponents, Register/style, Intonation/stress), and the scores we wanted to give in the column to the left (in this case, 3, 2, & 1). Once the rubric was labeled, we started filling it in by writing a description of what we thought the language behavior(s) would be for an examinee in the top score 3 for the first category. We began with the upper-left descriptor, which in this case, was for the *fluency* performance expected to get a 3 ("Almost completely appropriate flow, pauses, hesitations, fillers, speed, connectedness, and back-channeling" in this case). Next, we wrote the opposite of what we had written for a 3 in the space for a performance of 1 ("Mostly inappropriate flow, pauses, hesitations, fillers, speed, connectedness, and back-channeling" in this case). A score of 2 then became "Not a 3 and not a 1; that is, not *almost completely appropriate* nor *mostly inappropriate*" as shown in Table 5.

Table 5. Labeling and completing an analytic rubric

score	fluency	meaning	exponents	register/style	intonation/stress
3	almost completely appropriate flow, pauses, hesitations, fillers, speed, connectedness, and back-channeling				
2	not a 3 and not a 1, that is, not almost completely appropriate nor mostly inappropriate				
1	mostly inappropriate flow, pauses, hesitations, fillers, speed, connectedness, and back-channeling				

Now that we have done column one, why don't you try to fill in the descriptors for the second column labeled *Meaning* by describing what you might mean by the behaviors of an examinee who is able to get their meaning across. The score of 1 will be just the opposite, and the score of 2 will be in between. And so forth for *Exponents, Register/style,* and *Intonation/stress*. Do you see why I wrote above that this is "One fairly easy way" to make a classroom-appropriate analytic rubric?

Stage 3: Planning the assessment procedures and using the rubric

The goal in designing assessment procedures for productive language skills (speaking and writing) or their interactions with other skills (listening and reading) or knowledges (vocabulary, grammar, pragmatics rules, etc.) is generally to set up situations where the examinees will produce a sufficient quantity of the right kinds of language to serve as the basis for making sound scoring judgments and provide useful information to examinees and other stakeholders as well. To do so well requires a number of steps.

Step 3.1: Decide on the stimulus formats.

Making decisions about the stimulus format involves thinking through what it is that the examinees will encounter while they are doing each item or task in the way of language input or realia. Will they be given written instructions and a prompt to write or speak about? Will they be required to answer questions from an interviewer orally or follow directions from another student? Will they be required to respond to text messages? Describe a series of pictures? Go to the library and find a book? Write an essay? In short, what will they be required to do? Clearly, the range of possible stimulus formats is limited only by the imagination of the teacher/tester creating them. However, choosing among the possibilities should be guided by several factors. For high-stakes proficiency or placement decisions, these stimuli should be clear and directly related to the psychological construct and linguistic theory that motivates the decisions, yet be practical for relatively large-scale assessments. For classroom-level diagnostic, progress, or achievement decisions and feedback, these stimuli should be directly related to the objectives and teaching activities that have happened or will take place in the classroom. In addition, the stimuli should elicit, insofar as possible, the language, functions, and so forth that the rubric is intended to evaluate. Obviously, these decisions are best made by those who are most directly interested and involved in the assessment results. Nonetheless, careful attention to matching stimulus formats to the relevant criteria is very important.

Step 3.2: Decide on the response formats.

Deciding on the format that examinee responses should take is equally important. Will the examinees be required to write, type, speak, follow directions, interact, etc.? And, what effect is this response format likely to have on the performances of the various kinds of examinees involved. Another factor to keep in mind is that the stimulus and response formats should be appropriate in timing for the students to fill the time allotted with their language performance. Thus the required response should be sufficiently narrow to be completed in the allotted time, but also broad enough to fill that time and provide an adequate sample of each examinee's language production for accurate scoring.

Step 3.3: Write clear instructions.

Once the stimulus and response formats are clear, it is essential to provide the examinees with clear instructions about what they are expected to do. This means that the instructions should be so clear that both the examiner and examinee will know exactly what is expected to happen. Thus, it may prove useful to give examinees the instructions in their native tongue to make sure they understand and do not fail to perform as expected because of inadequately understood instructions. If it is not possible to give the directions in their mother tongue because there are multiple nationalities in the class or the teacher does not know their mother tongue, consider giving the directions in the target language and patiently encouraging the examinees to ask questions if they do not understand what they are expected to do. In any case, the goal is to concisely explain the stimulus and response expectations so that students know exactly what is expected of them and will not stray too far from the intended assessment purpose.

Step 3.4: Make sure the instructions and stimulus materials are ready.
The goal in this step is to make sure that all stimulus materials are at hand in sufficient copies (with some extras) so that the assessment procedures will proceed smoothly and efficiently. This is such an important step that the number and quality of the assessment materials should probably be checked a day or two before the assessments are to take place and then again just before the assessments begin.

Step 3.5: Arrange for the mechanics of assessment.
Before actually starting assessment, it is important to make sure that you will have a quiet place to do the actual procedures involved whether it be interviewing students, having them work in pairs, getting them to write essays, or asking them to write emails. This may mean reserving rooms, or otherwise guaranteeing access to space for doing the assessment and the rubrics-based ratings. Make sure that sufficient time is allowed, perhaps with a little extra time to allow for *Murphy's Law*.[1] Once the schedule is set, make sure that all participants (examinees, proctors, raters, etc.) know where they should be and when. It is usually a good idea to do this in writing.

Step 3.6: Actually do the assessment.
Conducting assessment with real students is definitely where the rubric rubber hits the assessment road. To maximize the possibility for success, consider doing the assessment procedures without trying to apply the rubric at the same time. If you audio- or video-record the student output (whether it be in an interview, role play, group work, etc.), you can focus on doing that well and leave the rating process for later, when you can in turn focus on the rating. Having a recording of the students' performances will also allow you to have an additional rater score the performances and permit you to play the performances back to the students while giving them feedback (so they can hear what they did right or wrong as you point things out in their performances).

If any mistakes were made in planning or designing the rubric, or in designing or carrying out the assessment procedures, it is at this point that you will likely realize your mistakes. Such mistakes may lead you to revise your assessment or scoring procedures on the fly, which is okay, but be sure to write down any such changes so you can permanently revise the testing procedures, rubric wording, and so forth later when you have more time.

Step 3.7: Train raters to use the rubric.
Particularly in situations where multiple raters are going to be applying your rubric to rating language samples, consider whether or not you want to do rater training with the goal of calibrating or standardizing the way that different raters apply the rubric. There are a number of issues to consider.

On the one hand, rater training is not always necessary or desirable. In some testing situations, you may actually want naïve raters to use your rubric to react to examinees' language samples in order to determine how ordinary people will judge those samples. For example, if you want to show the students (or do research on) how ordinary people will react to the fluency, intelligibility, etc., of students' speaking samples, you may want to draw on person-on-the-street type raters who are not trained. In other instances, you may simply recognize philosophically that teachers differ in how they judge the language production of students and that is fine, that is, there is no need to strip the teachers of their individual differences and force them to make unnaturally homogeneous judgments. As McNamara

---

[1] For those unfamiliar with *Murphy's Law*, it goes something like this: If it can go wrong, it will.

(1996, p. 127) put it, "A different approach is to accept that the most appropriate aim of rater training is to make raters internally consistent so as to make statistical modeling of their characteristics possible, but beyond this to accept variability in stable rater characteristics as a fact of life, which must be compensated for in some way, either through multiple marking and averaging of scores, or using the more sophisticated techniques of multi-faceted analysis…". McNamara is referring to multifaceted Rasch analysis, and the point he is making is that (when the assumptions of such analyses are met) the logit scores that result statistically compensate for differences among raters in severity. For more on this, see Chapters 4, 5, and 6 below.

On the other hand, you may need raters to all be rating in similar ways so that the resulting decisions are as fair to all students as possible. After all, you do not want those students who happen to get George as a rater to be placed one level lower simply because George tends to rate erratically or rate more severely than the other raters. In the interest of fairness and perhaps measurement reliability (see Chapter 4), you might quite rationally decide that rater training is necessary and important. And, if some raters (e.g., hapless George) do not respond to such training by rating more consistently like the other raters, you may need to put them to tasks other than rating.

If you decide to do rater training, in one way or another, you will probably need to collect or create example language samples at various levels on the scale(s) so you can use them to show raters what types of performances match each of the levels of the descriptors in the rubric. In rater training, it is often a good idea to have raters: (a) study the rubric, (b) practice using it, (c) discuss and negotiate among themselves when their ratings disagree or when they arrive at different meanings from the rubric, (d) practice some more, and so forth. You should also consider providing re-calibration sessions every 2–3 hours, or at least, at the beginning of each day of rating sessions. For an excellent description of a rater training session, see the section headed *Rater Training* in Chapter 5.

Stage 4: Evaluating the reliability/fairness of the rubric

One of the reasons that rater training is important is to enhance the possibility that the rubric will be applied consistently and fairly by all raters. Be sure to consider having more than one rater or more than one rating for each student's language performance if at all feasible. This will usually increase the reliability and credibility of your rating procedures. After all, multiple sources of information applied to any decision making process are generally more reliable than single sources of information. I have done this by swapping tapes with another teacher so that we could get two sets of rubric-based ratings and average them for the students' final scores. While this was considerable work, it was worth it to us because of the increased reliability of our decision making. It may even prove useful to calculate a reliability coefficient for the multiple raters applying the rubric, or for the same rater using the rubric multiple times (for information on calculating reliability coefficients for rubrics-based scores, see Chapter 4). If unreliable raters have been identified, consider the possibility of putting them to some other task in your assessment process (like proctoring, or compiling the score results, or scoring other more objective tests that are being given at the same time, etc.) so they cannot create unreliable and unfair results.

Stage 5: Evaluating the quality of the rubric

At some point after using the rubric to score actual student performances, it is a good idea to evaluate the quality of your rubric and revise it as necessary. (If this is done before reporting score results, it may be necessary to go back and re-rate language samples rated with earlier versions of the rubric.)

Step 5.1: Evaluate the validity of your rubric.
The following questions may prove helpful in evaluating the validity of your rubric (adapted considerably from Mertler, 2001; Tierney & Simon, 2004; and Dornisch & McLoughlin, 2006):

1. Is this type of analytic or holistic rubric appropriate for the assessment purposes?
2. Is the rubric too specific? Too general? Or is it just about the right level of specificity?
3. Are all the descriptors written in the boxes clearly stated and straightforward?
4. Are the performance characteristics clearly stated for each criterion? Are the characteristics clearly stated in the descriptors? Does the rubric address the same characteristics for each examinee's performance at each level? Are the characteristics addressed in each successive level on a progressive scale?
5. Are the categories of language being assessed in the rubric important? Are the categories and descriptors assessing what they were intended to assess?
6. Does the rubric unintentionally require anything in the examinees' performances that is not included in the rubric descriptors? Is there anything important showing up in their performances that is not currently included in the descriptors, but should be?
7. Does this rubric assess the knowledge and skills that make up the purpose(s) of the assessment (i.e., the construct, domain, unit objectives, instructional activities, etc.)?

Step 5.2: Evaluate the usability of your rubric.
The following questions may prove helpful in evaluating the usability of your rubric (adapted from the same sources as the questions in Step 5.1):

1. Is the number of criteria appropriate? Are they easy to understand and use? Is the number of levels used in the rubric appropriate for these language criteria? Are they easy to use?
2. Does the language in the descriptors clearly differentiate between the levels of performance for each criterion? Is the wording of the descriptors appropriate for the ages, educational level, reading level, cultural background, etc. of the examinees?
3. Is the overall layout of the rubric clear, friendly, efficient, useful, and so forth? Is adequate space provided for rater comments?

Stage 6: Planning feedback and revising for pedagogically useful ratings

The aim in planning feedback and revising for pedagogically useful ratings is to maximize the usefulness of the scores that result from the rubric-based assessment process. The point is to incorporate feedback into the assessment process and revise the rubric and assessment procedures so they will be pedagogically useful for the examinees, teachers, and other stakeholders involved. To do so well requires at least two steps.

Step 6.1: Plan for student and teacher feedback.
Language teachers and assessment specialists often restrict the type of information they provide by only reporting a numerical score to students. Telling a student that they earned a score of 80 on the rubric scale of 100 shown in Table 2 does have some meaning. That is, the student will know that they scored better than students who scored 79 or below

and worse than those who scored 81 or higher, but that only shows the student how they scored relative to other students, which is a very norm-referenced approach to interpreting assessment results. Wise teachers in classroom situations know instinctively that it is better to give feedback in the form of verbal descriptions of what the students know or can do. Thus, instead of reporting a score of 80 to the student, it would be better to give them the verbal description of the performances that led to that score, like those shown in Table 6. Notice that the descriptors (and the scores) come from the second, third, and fourth columns of Table 2. Notice also how these verbal descriptors provide much more information than does the score of 80, or even the separate sub-scores of 16, 17, 14, 18, and 15.

Table 6. Score report for a student scoring 80 including only the descriptors that apply from the analytic scale for rating composition tasks (adapted from Brown & Bailey 1984, pp. 39–41)

language categories	descriptors	scores
organization: introduction, body & conclusion	adequate title, introduction, & conclusion; body of essay is acceptable but some evidence may be lacking, some ideas aren't fully developed sequence is logical but transitional expressions may be absent or misused	16
logical development of ideas: content	essay addresses the issues but misses some points ideas could be more fully developed some extraneous material is present	17
grammar	ideas getting through to the reader, but grammar problems are apparent and have a negative effect on communication run-on sentences or fragments present	14
punctuation, spelling, & mechanics	correct use of English writing conventions left & right margins, all needed capitals, paragraphs indented, punctuation & spelling; very neat	18
style & quality of expression	attempts variety; good vocabulary; not wordy register ok style fairly concise	15
	total score	80

Such verbal feedback will be even more effective if the teacher can sit down with the student and talk about what the descriptions mean. Naturally, a teacher who was the rater (and took careful notes while doing the ratings) can sit down with the students, show them the language performance (the tape, essay, etc.), and go over the rating descriptions in even more detail, showing which of the individual characteristics within the language categories were low, medium, or high within that category.

Step 6.2: Set up a cycle of revision and improvement.
With only modest rewording, the stages and steps described above can be adapted to an ongoing revision process, one that will provide for constant and continuous revision and improvement of your rubric and assessment procedures. This step will help avoid using a rubric that is becoming out-of-date and increasingly irrelevant to your course or program. The reworded list of stages and steps that may prove useful in such a revision process is shown in Table 7.

Table 7. Suggested stages and steps in rubric revision process (reworded from Table 3 stages and steps)

stage		step
1: evaluating the plan	1.1	Refine your goal.
	1.2	Go back to the source material.
	1.3	Brainstorm ways to improve the rubric and assessment procedures.
	1.4	Are you happy with the analytic or holistic nature of your rubric?
	1.5	Review and revise the categories if necessary.
	1.6	Review and revise the range of scores you are using if necessary.
2: evaluating the design of the rubric	2.1	Are the scores on the one axis appropriate? Useful?
	2.2	Are the categories on the other axis appropriate? Useful?
	2.3	Are the rubric descriptors for each score level appropriate? Useful?
3: critiquing the assessment procedures and rubric	3.1	Are the stimulus formats appropriate? Useful?
	3.2	Are the response formats appropriate? Useful?
	3.3	Are the instructions written clearly?
	3.4	Are the instructions and stimulus materials ready for use?
	3.5	Are the mechanics of assessment adequate? Ready?
	3.6	Are the assessment procedures appropriate? Useful?
	3.7	Are the raters adequately trained to use your rubric?
4: evaluating the rubric's reliability and fairness		
5: evaluating the quality of the rubric	5.1	Is the rubric valid?
	5.2	Is the rubric useful?
6: planning feedback and revision for pedagogically useful ratings	6.1	Is the student and teacher feedback appropriate? Useful?
	6.2	Continue the cycle of revision and improvement by returning to Stage 1.

What resources can help in creating rubrics?

Language teachers need to realize that rubrics are neither new nor novel, but they can be very useful for assessing and giving systematic, useful feedback on students' language performances (be they oral, written, or an interaction of two or more skills). To those ends, it is useful to know that there are resources out there on the internet that can help in designing rubrics.

For example, the *Teachnology* website at (http://www.teach-nology.com/web_tools/rubrics/languagearts/) provides free-of-charge links to example rubrics and rubric makers available elsewhere on the internet. Teachers can also join the *Teachnology* website at a platinum level (currently $29.99) for more resources at http://www.teach-nology.com/platinum/rubrics/.

Another helpful website that is completely free is *Rubistar*, which can be found at http://rbistar.4teachers.org. The menus for creating rubrics for (a) Oral Projects and (b) Research and Writing are particularly useful for language teachers. After I registered (free) and explored the website for a few minutes, I was able to create the rubric shown in Table 8 using their templates in less than four minutes (based on selecting available descriptors). Naturally, tailoring descriptors or creating new ones in the *Rubistar* website will take longer than the four minutes I spent creating the rubric shown in Table 8.

While I am a bit concerned about putting websites in this book because they are so prone to disappearing or changing, I nonetheless did include them because I want to encourage you to explore websites like these and try some of the tools that they make available.

Table 8.   Oral presentation rubric created on the *Rubistar* website in four minutes

teacher name: _____
student name: _____

category	4	3	2	1
enthusiasm	facial expressions and body language generate a strong interest and enthusiasm about the topic in others	facial expressions and body language sometimes generate a strong interest and enthusiasm about the topic in others	facial expressions and body language are used to try to generate enthusiasm, but seem somewhat faked	very little use of facial expressions or body language; did not generate much interest in topic being presented.
preparedness	student is completely prepared and has obviously rehearsed	student seems pretty prepared but might have needed a couple more rehearsals	the student is somewhat prepared, but it is clear that rehearsal was lacking	student does not seem at all prepared to present
speaks clearly	speaks clearly and distinctly all (100–95%) the time, and mispronounces no words	speaks clearly and distinctly all (100–95%) the time, but mispronounces one word	speaks clearly and distinctly most (94–85%) of the time	mispronounces no more than one word; often mumbles or can not be understood or mispronounces more than one word
vocabulary	uses vocabulary appropriate for the audience; extends audience vocabulary by defining words that might be new to most of the audience	uses vocabulary appropriate for the audience. includes 1–2 words that might be new to most of the audience, but does not define them	uses vocabulary appropriate for the audience; does not include any vocabulary that might be new to the audience	uses several (5 or more) words or phrases that are not understood by the audience
posture and eye contact	stands up straight, looks relaxed and confident; establishes eye contact with everyone in the room during the presentation	stands up straight and establishes eye contact with everyone in the room during the presentation	sometimes stands up straight and establishes eye contact	slouches and/or does not look at people during the presentation

Conclusion

I strongly encourage you to try using rubrics in your teaching and assessment whether at the classroom or institutional levels. I have found them to be useful for providing information on productive language skills or interactions of skills in ways that cannot be accomplished in any other way. An added feature of rubrics is that the types of verbal/descriptive feedback teachers can provide with rubrics-based assessments are so much more useful than simply and curtly presenting students with a numerical score. For example, which would be more useful as feedback to me from you on the quality and usefulness of this chapter: A verbal description of the strengths and weaknesses you felt the chapter has? Or a score ranging on a scale from 1 to 10 (1=*a really pointless chapter* to a 10=*a really useful chapter*)? Yes, I think your students feel that way too.

References

Alderson, J. C. (1991). Bands and scores. In J. C. Alderson & B. North (Eds.), *Language testing in the 1990s*. London: Modern English Publications and the British Council.

Brown, J. D., & Bailey, K. M. (1984). A categorical instrument for scoring second language writing skills. *Language Learning, 34*(4), 21–42.

Dornish, M. M., & McLoughlin, A. S. (2006). Limitations of web-based rubric resources: Addressing challenges. *Practical Assessment, Research, & Evaluation, 11*(3), 1–8.

Fulcher, G. (1996). Does thick description lead to smart tests? A data-based approach to rating scale construction. *Language Testing, 13*(2), 208–238.

Jacobs, H. L., Zinkgraf, S. A., Wormuth, D. R., Hartfiel, V. F., & Hughey, J. B. (1981). *Testing ESL composition: A practical approach*. Rowley, MA: Newbury House.

McNamara, T. (1996). *Measuring second language performance*. London: Longman.

Mertler, C. A. (2001). Designing scoring rubrics for your classroom. *Practical Assessment, Research & Evaluation, 7*(25). Retrieved October 26, 2010 from http://PAREonline.net/getvn.asp?v=7&n=25.

Tierney, R., & Simon, M. (2004). What's still wrong with rubrics: focusing on the consistency of performance criteria across scale levels. *Practical Assessment, Research & Evaluation, 9*(2). Retrieved January 9, 2011 from http://PAREonline.net/getvn.asp?v=9&n=2.

Assessing Student Language Performance: Types and Uses of Rubrics

Larry Davis
Kimi Kondo-Brown
University of Hawai'i, Mānoa

Introduction

Rubrics take a variety of forms and may be used for numerous purposes. To be useful, the type and content of a rubric must reflect both the purposes of assessment and the educational context in which it is used. This chapter will discuss the types of rubrics used for language performance assessment as well as the uses of rubrics in language instruction, and will end with three case studies of rubrics used in Japanese language teaching contexts.

An essential goal of education is that students gain the knowledge and abilities required to carry out the various tasks of life, effectively using their knowledge and skills when the need arises. But, how are we to judge whether such knowledge and skills, and the ability to make use of them, have been acquired? Language performance assessments address this issue directly by requiring students to use what they know to complete some type of language-related task. As Brown, Hudson, Norris, and Bonk (2002, p. 6) put it:

> Language performance assessment of all sorts therefore utilizes test instruments and procedures which (a) consistently elicit meaningful communication in the second language based on task performance; (b) elicit sufficient amounts of second language communication so that trustworthy interpretations can be made about students' abilities; and (c) provide for the systematic and meaningful, if subjective, evaluation of the communicative performances of students.

A key element of part (c) is that the judgment of performance is subjective; unlike a multiple-choice test with a single correct answer, performance assessments require variable and potentially complex responses where quality is a matter of opinion. Rubrics provide an

---

Davis, L., & Kondo-Brown, K. (2012). Assessing student language performance: Types and uses of rubrics. In J. D. Brown, (Ed.), *Developing, using, and analyzing rubrics in language assessment with case studies in Asian and Pacific languages* (pp. 33–55). Honolulu: University of Hawai'i, National Foreign Language Resource Center.

important tool for making such judgments, for communicating what the judgments mean, and for guiding the educational efforts of students and teachers.

As a first step, we would like to be clear about what is meant by the terms used in this chapter. *Assessment* refers to "the systematic gathering of information about student learning in support of teaching and learning" (Norris, 2006, p. 579) and language performance assessments include tests as well as other kinds of classroom assignments, such as homework and projects, that are evaluated in a systematic way. As used here, a *rubric* refers to a set of criteria for grading which: (a) lists the dimensions by which a performance will be judged, (b) lists the grades or scores that may be awarded (e.g., A-F, 1–5), and (c) describes the characteristics of performance at different grade/score levels (Arter & McTighe, 2001). Although this definition is commonly used within classroom assessment, the term *rating scale* is also used to describe this type of instrument, particularly within the language assessment literature. (In language testing, the word rubric is sometimes associated with the technical term *test rubric*, which refers to an extended description of a test; Bachman & Palmer, 1996).

Types of rubrics

Rubrics may differ in a variety of ways. As mentioned in Chapter 2, one common difference is whether a single score is awarded for each performance (*holistic rubrics*), or whether several scores addressing different aspects of performance are given (*analytic rubrics*). Rubrics may also differ in the extent to which they are tailored to evaluate the performance of a specific task (*task-dependent rubrics*) or whether they are designed to evaluate language ability more generally (*task independent rubrics*; Brown et al., 2002). These dichotomies are discussed below, along with a few other examples that do not fit the full definition of a rubric given above, yet share some of the same characteristics.

Holistic and analytic rubrics

Holistic rubrics

As the name suggests, a holistic rubric is designed to evaluate performance as a whole; a single score is awarded, although several descriptors may be used to describe ability at each score level (e.g., see Table 1). Within writing assessment, holistic scoring usually entails reading the text once and then assigning a score, as compared to analytical scoring where a text may be read multiple times, each time assigning a score for a different feature. Early proponents of holistic scoring within the domain of English L1 composition argued that holistic scoring better captures the full complexity of good writing and also reflects the full involvement of the reader with the text; attempting to separate performance into different dimensions was seen as failing to capture this complexity (White, 1985; Hamp-Lyons, 1991). Holistic rubrics are also relatively fast to use since only a single scoring decision must be made, and are attractive for situations such as placement or standardized testing, where there is a premium on producing scores quickly and efficiently.

A major shortcoming of the holistic rubric is that it does not take into account the possibility that different aspects of the performance may vary in quality. This shortcoming is particularly important for language learners, where separate aspects of language ability may develop at different rates (Hamp-Lyons, 1991; Weigle, 2002). Because some students may not fit neatly into a single category, it can be difficult to know how to interpret a particular score. For example, an essay might receive a grade of *good* (rather than *poor* or *excellent*) because it had excellent overall organization but weak sentence structure, while a second paper might receive the same score but for opposite reasons. A single score also means the feedback provided to learners is less detailed and may therefore be less helpful for supporting improvement. On the other hand, feedback made using a holistic rubric can be made more detailed by checking or circling individual descriptors, across different score levels if necessary, to give an indication of the specific qualities of the performance (Stevens & Levi, 2005)

Table 1. A holistic rubric for singing in Japanese

mastery/achieved		developing/non-mastery		
5 advanced	4 proficient	3 developing	2 novice	1 non-ratable
can sing a Japanese song with ease and accuracy	can sing a Japanese song with minimal difficulty and no significant errors	can sing a Japanese song, but with difficulty and a few significant and/or many minor errors	can only sing a Japanese song with great difficulty and many significant errors	no response, unable to attempt a song

note: This rubric was created for use with children learning a Japanese song. The task and score descriptors are based on the standards for world languages at the kindergarten level published by the Hawai'i Department of Education.

Analytic rubrics

In an analytic rubric, the performance is broken down (or analyzed) into dimensions and a separate score awarded for each (e.g., see Table 2). Awarding separate scores for different components has several advantages (Cohen, 1994; Hamp-Lyons, 1991; Weigle, 2002):

- It provides more detailed feedback. (But, this advantage is lost if scores are aggregated and only a single overall score is reported.)
- It better accounts for uneven performance or uneven development of skills.
- It may be easier for inexperienced raters to use. In an empirical study of verbal reports made by raters using both analytic and holistic rubrics, Barkaoui (2010) observed that the analytic rubric seemed to make scoring easier by breaking down the decision making process into a series of more manageable steps, and by providing a basis for a more focused and organized application of the scoring criteria.
- It may be more reliable, in that awarding multiple scores is similar, in theory, to increasing the number of items in a test. But, empirical studies of the relative reliability of holistic and analytic scoring have produced conflicting results (Barkaoui, 2007).
- Different dimensions can be assigned larger or smaller score values to indicate the relative importance of different aspects of performance.

A disadvantage of analytical rubrics is the possibility that scoring takes longer due to the additional time needed to make a series of scoring decisions rather than just one. In addition, scorers may continue to score holistically despite the use of an analytic rubric. Examples of such behavior include giving a similar score across all categories (*halo effect*; McNamara, 1996) or selecting an overall score first and then adjusting the sub-scores to fit.

Table 2. A generic analytic rubric for Japanese writing tasks

	4 excellent	3 good	2 passing	1 fail
content	addresses all aspects of prompt	omits one aspect of the prompt	omits more than one aspect of the prompt	does not respond to the prompt
organization	logical and flows smoothly throughout	logical and flows smoothly most of the time	somewhat illogical and disorganized	not enough to evaluate
structure: range and accuracy	a good range of patterns and expressions; very accurate: no or almost no grammatical errors	a good range of patterns and expressions; more or less accurate: several grammatical errors	a limited range of patterns and expressions; frequent or very frequent grammatical errors	not enough to evaluate
vocabulary: range and accuracy	a good range of vocabulary; appropriate and accurate vocabulary choices	a moderate range of vocabulary; a few inaccurate vocabulary choices	a limited range of vocabulary; several inaccurate vocabulary choices	not enough to evaluate
Kana spelling	use of effective *Kana* throughout	use of effective kana most of the time; occasional misspelling	ineffective use of *Kana*; frequent misspelling	not enough to evaluate

note: This rubric was used in a beginning-level Japanese language class for a variety of writing tasks. Adapted from Kondo-Brown (2012) Material 2–7A. Used with permission.

Because they provide relatively detailed feedback, analytic rubrics are well-suited to many of the purposes of classroom assessment. However, the use of analytic rubrics requires adequate time to explicitly evaluate performance on a variety of different features, and such rubrics will likely be easiest to use when the performance can be reviewed several times. This is no problem for homework or written assignments, and analytic rubrics may even save considerable grading time in these situations by eliminating the need to write the same comment over and over. On the other hand, when decisions must be made quickly on the basis of a single viewing (as when grading an oral presentation), it can be a challenge to keep track of several different aspects of performance and then score these independently. For such situations, it might be wise to keep an analytic rubric as simple as possible. Alternately, raters should take care to become familiar with the rubric and typical student performances, so that the scoring criteria can be applied quickly and consistently.

Task-dependent and task-independent rubrics[1]

Task-dependent rubrics "use real-world criteria to estimate the degree to which a student's performance on a single task will be replicable in the real world" (Brown et al., 2002). Task-dependent rubrics focus on successful task-completion, and the performance may potentially be judged on both the language used as well as the practical result (Ellis, 2003; e.g., see Table 3a). For example, one might grade the performance of ordering a pizza on both the linguistic

---

[1] Task-dependent and task-independent rubrics have also been referred to as *task-specific* and *generic* rubrics in the general educational assessment literature (Wiggins, 1998; Khattri, Reeve, & Kane, 1998).

content (e.g., Were the toppings pronounced in an understandable way?) as well as the practical result (e.g., Was the correct pizza obtained?).

In contrast, task-independent rubrics focus on more general linguistic abilities that are thought to play a role in performance across a domain of tasks, or form a part of language ability generally (e.g., see Table 3b). In terms of interpretation, scores from task-dependent rubrics often describe relatively concrete behaviors and are therefore easy to understand, but the scores (and any inferences based on the scores) only apply to the task for which the rubric was written. Task-independent scores provide a general indication of ability, but may be less predictive of how a student will do in a specific situation and may be harder to interpret in that they are defined in terms of more abstract constructs.

Table 3a. Task-dependent rubric

1 inadequate	3 able	5 adept
Examinee chooses the wrong hotel, OR examinee writes the fax in a manner that would cause serious confusion on the part of the boss concerning which hotel to use, OR examinee writes the fax in a pragmatically inappropriate manner which would result in future difficulties for examinee's relationship with boss.	Examinee produces a fax message recommending the Plaza Inn and provides some form of correct rationale for the choice (based on the parameters set by the boss, i.e., distance, pool availability, and price). An able performance will not necessarily list the exact hotel specifications, from the hotel brochure for the Plaza Inn (that is, examinee need not give exact distance and price).	Examinee's fax message recommends the Plaza Inn and provides appropriate rationale (but does not necessarily list exact hotel specifications). Examinee produces a pragmatically and stylistically appropriate fax message (demonstrating understanding of relationship relative to that set by boss on the answering machine message).

Table 3b. Task-independent rubric

1 inadequate	3 able	5 adept
The content does not satisfy the purpose of the task. The organization of the message is likely to cause confusion for the reader. Grammar and usage problems are likely to cause confusion for the reader. The message does not meet the format or style conventions of the task genre, or is socially or otherwise inappropriate for the context.	The content satisfies the purpose of the task, but may be lacking in detail or elaboration. The organization is clear and appropriate to the task. Grammar and usage problems may occasionally cause minor confusion for the reader. The message format and style is generally appropriate for the task genre and the social context, although there may be some faults.	The content fully satisfies the purpose of the task, and contains an appropriate amount of detail or elaboration. The organization is clear and appropriate. Minor grammar and usage problems may be present, but do not cause confusion. The message uses appropriate format and style for the task and follows appropriate social conventions.

note: The first example is a task-dependent rubric adapted from Brown et al. (2002) that was constructed for use with college-aged English language learners (the original version awarded intermediate scores of 2 and 4 for performances that contained features from two adjacent score bands). The task was to listen to a voice mail from your boss requesting a recommendation for a hotel, and then write a fax supplying the requested information. The second example is a task-independent rubric that might be used with a variety of such informational writing tasks, constructed for this chapter.

One of the best known types of task-dependent rubrics is the *primary trait rubric*, which focuses on a dimension of performance that has been identified as most important for achieving the purpose of a particular task (Hamp-Lyons, 1991, Lloyd-Jones, 1977; e.g., see Table 4). Primary trait rubrics have been associated with writing assessment, and in particular, the National Assessment for Academic Progress (NAEP), a major standardized testing program for K–12 students in the United States[2]. A major issue in the use of primary trait rubrics is that they can be challenging to construct: identifying the key feature to be used as a basis for scoring, as well as describing how this feature changes with increasing ability, requires a detailed understanding of what students do when carrying out the task. Moreover, such an understanding must be repeatedly developed for each task to be assessed. Although primary trait rubrics can provide specific feedback to students, their use in foreign language assessment has been limited (Weigle, 2002), likely due to the time and sophistication required to construct them along with the limited domain of use for the final product.

Regarding task-dependent rubrics more generally, Wiggins (1998) has pointed out that while such rubrics provide specific feedback, the need to construct a new rubric for each task makes them expensive to develop in terms of energy and time. He also argues that the instructional target in most situations usually extends beyond the performance of a single task and suggests that generic rubrics are therefore more useful for classroom assessment. We would also point out that while task-dependent rubrics provide specific feedback, a more generic rubric may be used repeatedly across a domain of tasks, making it possible to document improvement over time (or persistent problems). On the other hand, task-dependent rubrics can provide detailed and practical feedback for improving the performance of a particular task, which can be useful when successful task completion is the focus of instruction, as in learning survival language for example. Task-dependent rubrics might also be easier for non-specialist stakeholders (e.g., parents) to understand in that they provide relatively specific and concrete descriptions of what the test-taker did (or did not) do.

Table 4. NAEP primary-trait rubric for narrative writing

1 **event description**	Paper is a list of sentences minimally related or a list of sentences that all describe a single event; or a description of a setting or character.
2 **undeveloped story**	Paper is a listing of related events. More than one event is described, but with few details about setting, characters, or the events. (Usually there is no more than one sentence telling about each event.)
3 **basic story**	Paper describes a series of events, giving details (in at least two or three sentences) about some aspect of the story (the events, the characters' goals, or problems to be solved). But the story may be undeveloped or lack cohesion because of problems with syntax, sequencing, events missing.
4 **extended story**	Paper describes a sequence of episodes, including details about most story elements (i.e., setting, episodes, characters' goals, problems to be solved). But the stories are confusing or incomplete (i.e., at the end of the story the characters goals are ignored or problems inadequately resolved; the beginning does not match the rest of the story; the plot is weak; the internal logic or plausibility of characters' actions is not maintained).

---

[2] NAEP writing assessments now use a holistic rubric (Arter & McTighe, 2001).

5 developed story	Paper describes a sequence of episodes in which most of the story elements are clearly developed (i.e., setting, episodes, characters' goals, or problems to be solved) with a simple resolution of these goals or problems at the end. May have one or two problems, include too much detail, or the end may be inconsistent with the rest of the story. Or the story may contain one highly developed episode with subplots.	
6 elaborated story	Paper describes a sequence of episodes in which almost all story elements are well developed (i.e., setting, episodes, characters' goals, or problems to be solved). The resolution of the goals or problems at the end are elaborated. The events are presented and elaborated in a cohesive way.	

note: This rubric was designed for use with narrative writing by English-speaking children at the 4th and 8th grades (4th graders would be expected to have lower scores than 8th graders). The rubric was used as part of research study examining classroom writing, tied to the 1992 NAEP writing assessment (Gentile, Martin-Rehrmann, & Kennedy, 1995).

Rubric-like instruments

A variety of other instruments have been used to organize scoring criteria, but they lack one or more of the elements that make up a true rubric. These rubric-like scoring aids include checklists and numerical rating scales (Linn & Gronlund, 1995; Luoma, 2004). A *checklist* is a detailed list of features with a place to mark the presence or absence of each feature or to roughly indicate the quality of the feature (e.g., *great, okay, improve* in Table 5). Checklists often target very specific details of a performance and are well-suited to providing focused feedback on behavior. On the other hand, beyond listing a set of desired behaviors (e.g., *greets the audience at the start of the presentation*), there is often little description of what constitutes good or poor performance; in particular, it can be quite difficult to interpret what a check mark (√) means for a complex phenomenon like pronunciation. In addition, no indication is given of the relative importance of the various items, and the simple sum of behaviors does not necessarily equal the overall quality of performance. Checklists are "essentially diagnostic and descriptive" (Luoma, 2004, p. 79) and are useful for giving feedback, but less helpful for assigning scores or grades.

Table 5. A checklist used for peer review of an oral presentation

		great	okay	improve
content and delivery	Did he/she clearly say the topic of the presentation?			
	Do you think this is a good topic for a presentation in our class?			
	Did the body of the talk support the main topic?			
	Were the points of the body logically organized?			
	Was there a clear conclusion?			
	Did he/she manage time well? (not too much or too little time spent on one thing)			

continued...

Table 5. A checklist used for peer review of an oral presentation (cont.)

	great	okay	improve
Did he/she face the audience and make eye contact?			
Did he/she show enthusiasm in the presentation?			
Did he/she speak without having to look at their notes too much?			
Was voice volume loud enough to easily hear?			
Was the speaking speed appropriate (not too fast and not too slow)?			
Was he/she able to speak fluently and without too much pausing?			
Did he/she have good posture when standing?			
Was his/her pronunciation clear and easy to understand?			

note: This is a checklist for a university-level ESL academic listening and speaking class, used as one part of a peer-review form for an academic presentation. Students delivered presentations on a topic of their choice (8–10 minutes) that were videotaped for later review. In the next class session, several students viewed the video of each presentation, filled out this checklist, and wrote additional comments for the presenter. A more extensive version of the checklist was given to students before the presentation to guide their preparation.

A *numerical scale* includes a list of features (usually a relatively small number) and provides a scale with several levels, but the characteristics of performance at each level are not described (Table 6). This arrangement requires little reading and can be quick to use, but only works when there is a consistent understanding of what the numbers mean across scorers and/or through time (Luoma, 2004). Unfortunately, research in writing and speaking assessment suggests that such consistency is doubtful; on the contrary, raters may give similar scores for quite different reasons (Douglas, 1994; Orr, 2002; Sakyi, 2000; Vaughan, 1991). Moreover, no explanation of the scores is given, severely limiting the interpretability of results and the usefulness of the assessment for feedback. Nonetheless, numerical scales are relatively easy to construct, and when combined with additional specific comments they may be useful in low-stakes situations for briefly summarizing the overall strengths and weaknesses of a performance.

Table 6. A numerical scale used for a Japanese classroom unit test

scoring criteria	very good		good			minimum passing			non-passing		
task completion (amount of information)	18	17	16	15	14	13	12	11	10	5	0
easiness to read (accuracy, organization, spelling)	14	13	12	11	10	9	8	7	6	3	0
proper beginning/ending	8	7	6		5	4		3	2		0

note: This was a checklist used in a university beginning-level Japanese language class. Students were asked to write a letter to a prospective pen pal in Japan including appropriate opening and ending remarks, name, university, major, hobbies, and hometown/country. Adapted from Kondo-Brown (2012) Material 2–5. Used with permission.

Pedagogical uses for rubrics

Are rubrics necessary? Intuitive (or impressionistic) grading, where decisions are based on the unspoken sum of the instructor's experience, values, and professional judgment, has a long history in writing assessment (Charney, 1984; Hamp-Lyons, 1991) and undoubtedly remains a presence in the day-to-day grading that occurs in many classrooms. Where the focus is on making specific comments regarding strengths and weaknesses of a performance, it is entirely reasonable for teachers to rely on their own intuitions and judgment. But, where a grade is to be awarded, and where the grade will count for something, then transparency and consistency in the grading decision is likely to be appreciated by students as well as anyone else who needs to understand what the grades actually mean. Rubrics are useful tools for increasing the transparency and consistency of grading, as well as the efficiency of the feedback process. Other pedagogical uses for rubrics have also been suggested (Fiderer, 1999; Stevens & Levi, 2005), and the general uses of rubrics are summarized below in terms of:

- Improving the consistency and efficiency of grading
- Providing feedback and supporting student learning
- Guiding instruction
- Generating a record of student achievement
- Communicating with others outside the classroom

Improving the consistency and efficiency of grading

An often-cited use for rubrics is to increase the consistency of scoring, either across individual graders, or across time with a single rater (Bachman & Palmer, 1996; McNamara, 1996; Weigle, 2002). Rubrics can help focus the rater's attention on the relevant dimensions of performance, and rating scale descriptors become points of reference that can be used to locate specific performances on the scale. Overall, the effect is to increase the likelihood that different performances are judged to the same standard and that this standard reflects the skills, knowledge, or other constructs targeted by the assessment.

Well-written rubrics can also simplify feedback in that for a certain grade, the rubric descriptors essentially provide a set of comments about the strengths and weaknesses of the work. Targeted feedback can be provided by circling relevant descriptors, even circling descriptors across different score bands, if needed. This strategy in particular can save considerable time in grading by eliminating the need to write the same comment over and over again. To maximize this benefit, however, it is important to incorporate the typical comments made on an assessment (i.e., common student problems or strengths) when writing or modifying a rubric.

Supporting student learning and providing feedback

A rubric provided prior to an assessment provides students with a description of what constitutes good performance, and creates a basis for students to focus their efforts and be productively critical of their own work. Following the assessment, feedback tied to a rubric can help students to understand what they are doing well and what can be improved. In particular, rubrics can be useful for pointing out the general strengths and weaknesses of a student's work, where such trends might be less obvious from specific comments made on an assignment. In addition, where a rubric is used across a variety of assignments, trends in improvement (or lack thereof) also become clearer.

Guiding instruction

Consistent information about student achievement has obvious value for evaluating and modifying instruction. In particular, scores produced using rubrics can support teacher impressions regarding student performance and make it easier to build an accurate picture of the specific strengths and weaknesses of a class. In addition, rubrics provide a consistent standard for evaluating performance of students in multiple classes or across multiple sections of the same class, which can be used to guide coordination of curriculum and instruction.

Also, rubrics can promote a certain discipline on the part of the teacher regarding the goals and expectations for learning. First, constructing a rubric requires describing the criteria by which a performance will be judged; this in turn requires careful thought regarding the nature of what constitutes good performance, the educational goals in play, and the developmental paths of students. Second, a rubric provides a detailed description of the educational target, which can be used for directing instructional efforts. Finally, rubrics can be used to align assignments and grading with established learning standards or outcomes (if such outcomes are used as a basis for building the rubric).

Keeping records of student achievement

Rubric-based grades or scores can provide an organized, and potentially detailed, record of student achievement. As mentioned above, such records can be used for evaluating the progress of students and guiding instruction. They also provide a more transparent basis for assigning course grades, and if aligned with learning standards, have the potential to serve as evidence of the achievement of student learning outcomes. Such information may be useful for institutional accountability purposes or for demonstrating individual teaching effectiveness in support of promotion or other personnel decisions.

Communicating with others

As mentioned above, rubrics may help increase scoring consistency by communicating a standard grading scheme to those involved in marking. Rubrics can also be used to communicate what grades or scores mean to stakeholders such as parents and can communicate expectations to tutors, teaching assistants, or others who may be engaged in helping students and therefore need to understand the target of an assignment or other assessment.

Examples of different types of rubrics in use

In this section, we will describe a few cases in which various types of rubrics were used in different Japanese instructional contexts. In addition to the rubrics themselves, we will provide descriptions of the context and reasons for employing the particular rubric(s), and comment on issues related to use of the rubric(s). Our goal here is to provide a few brief examples of how rubrics actually fit into their contexts of use and raise a few issues that might be considered when using rubrics to judge language performance.

Case study 1: The use of holistic and analytic rubrics for oral performance tests in a beginning-level college Japanese language course

Context

Lower-division Japanese language courses at the University of Hawai'i at Mānoa (UHM) employ an oral role-play task as part of the midterm and final examinations. For this role-play, Japanese language teachers have the choice of using prompts and rubrics provided to all sections of a given course, or to develop their own. One of the authors (Kimi) developed prompts and two types of rubrics (holistic and analytic) for her own first-semester Japanese language courses at UHM to investigate which would be easier to use and which would be more useful for communicating to students their strengths and weaknesses. The role-play prompts consisted of three contextualized tasks that formed a sequence of events, with each task written on a separate card (Figure 1). Using the cards, the students were led to engage in face-to-face conversations and transactions in the target language domains. During the test, a card was given to the student, who read the prompt on the card aloud and then performed the task. The procedure was then repeated with the second and third cards. The test took approximately 15 minutes per student and was audio-recorded. Student performances were rated immediately, and the audio recordings were later reviewed to confirm the accuracy and consistency of the ratings. In order to enhance transparency in the grading method and clarify teacher expectations, a handout that explained the testing procedure and a copy of the scoring rubric were given to the students prior to the test administration.

	Task 1	Task 2	Task 3
situation	You are visiting Tokyo as an exchange student. One late morning, while you are attending a campus event featuring Hawaiian Culture, a Japanese student starts talking to you in Japanese.	You are now at a post office on campus.	After the post office, you decide to go to a Ramen shop.
task	Engage in a conversation with the student and try to get to know each other better (for example, ask and answer questions about schooling, hometown, and hobbies. Then, ask her if she has been to Hawai'i. If the answer is yes, ask her a question about Hawai'i.	Tell the clerk that you want to mail a letter to Hawai'i by express mail. Also, say you need 110-yen stamps. Ask how much in total and make a payment with a 5000-yen bill.	You are now at the entrance of the Ramen shop by yourself. After being seated, look at the menu in Japanese and order something to eat and drink. While you are eating, ask for more water.

Figure 1. Sample prompts for a Japanese midterm oral test for a beginning-level college Japanese language class. Adapted from Kondo-Brown (2012) Material 2–10. Used with permission.

Rubric

The holistic and analytic rubrics for this oral achievement test are shown in Tables 7 and 8. In order to ensure the content validity of the test, the match between the test instruments and the student learning outcomes (SLOs) was carefully considered. Accordingly, the drafting of the rubrics was informed by the relevant SLOs, by performance samples collected from previous students who had performed at different levels, and by various published books on classroom assessment (e.g., Brown, 1998; Popham, 2008). The draft scale descriptors then went through multiple revisions as they were actually used.

The holistic scale was designed to assess the students' overall performance on a single scale with four different levels of achievement (*excellent*, *good*, *satisfactory*, and *unsatisfactory*) with ranges that correspond roughly with grades of A, B, C, and D (i.e., 90–100, 80–89, 70–79, & 60–69). For example, those who scored 90 or above were viewed as having done an excellent job of displaying the expected learning outcomes and would be deserving of a grade of A. When the characteristics of a student did not neatly fit into a single achievement level, the level that included the most features was used to assign a score. The analytic scale, on the other hand, was designed to assess how well the students performed on six scoring criteria (i.e., *task completion*, *comprehension*, *language knowledge and control*, *interactional skill*, *fluency*, and *comprehensibility*). The scale was weighted, with task completion and comprehension being given slightly more weight (18 points) than the other scoring criteria (16 points). For each of the criteria, the student performances were rated along a continuum from *mastery* (the student demonstrated the expected outcomes with excellence) to *non-mastery* (the student did not demonstrate the expected outcomes). The analytic rubric had some characteristics of a numerical scale in the sense that the descriptions were not provided for all the score levels; instead, only the two ends of the continuum were described.

Table 7. Sample holistic speaking rubric for beginning-level college Japanese students. Adapted from Kondo-Brown (2012) Material 2–11A. Used with permission.

score (grade)	descriptors
100–90 (excellent) ☺☺	transactional and interpersonal communication skills are excellent; a variety of information about self (school, hometown, hobbies) is exchanged appropriately use highly formalized language (e.g., *hajime mashite, doozo yoroshiku onegai shimasu*); use of learned patterns, expressions, and vocabulary is extensive and creative in performing familiar transactional and interpersonal tasks (e.g., mailing something at the post office, ordering food at a restaurant, making a payment); demonstrates appropriate listening manner by showing interest in the interlocutor's speech (e.g., timely use of *aa, soo desu ka, Ii desu nee*); language use and pronunciation are highly accurate, smooth, and clear; comprehension level is excellent, and it is very easy to communicate; demonstrates ability to ask for help at appropriate times without using English
80–89 (good) ☺	transactional and interpersonal communication skills are generally good; a sufficient variety of information about self is appropriately presented and exchanged; the use of learned patterns, expressions, and vocabulary is mostly effective in performing familiar transactional and interpersonal tasks; occasional minor errors occur but do not interfere with communication; demonstrates a more or less appropriate listening manner by showing interest in the interlocutor's speech; comprehension level is generally good, although there are occasional misunderstandings which require occasional repetition or rephrasing of questions; language use and pronunciation are mostly accurate, smooth, and clear.; demonstrates ability to ask for help at appropriate times without using English
70–79 (satisfactory) 😐	transactional and interpersonal communication skills are acceptable; a limited amount of information about self is presented and exchanged; the use of learned patterns, expressions, and vocabulary in performing familiar transactional and interpersonal tasks is limited and often inaccurate and/or inappropriate; there is frequent difficulty in understanding speech which requires a considerable amount of repetition and rephrasing; speech is often halting or uneven with long pauses; apparent difficulty in pronouncing words
60–69 (unsatisfactory) ☹	ineffective and inappropriate presentation of self; the use of learned patterns, expressions, and vocabulary to perform familiar transactional and interpersonal tasks is very limited and/or mostly inaccurate or inappropriate; student difficulty in understanding even slow and simple speech as well as serious errors in language use make it impossible to complete the task or engage in any real meaningful communication

Table 8. Sample analytic speaking rubric for beginning-level college Japanese students. Adapted from Kondo-Brown (2012) Material 2–12A. Used with permission.

non-mastery	criteria and score range	mastery
task completion		
responses are poorly developed and do not complete the tasks; unable to ask for assistance in Japanese to complete the task	10 12 14 16 18	responses are fully developed and complete the task; can use appropriate communication strategies in Japanese to complete the task (e.g., ask to repeat the question)
comprehension		
frequent misunderstanding of questions, needs to repeat and/or paraphrase the questions frequently	10 12 14 16 18	easily understands the questions
language knowledge & control		
does not show control of basic vocabulary and structures (e.g., frequent grammatical or vocabulary errors, little variation in vocabulary or structure)	8 10 12 14 16	demonstrates the ability to speak at a basic sentence-level with variety and accuracy in vocabulary and structure
interactional skill		
inappropriate and ineffective attitude as a conversation partner (e.g., no *aizuchi*)	8 10 12 14 16	demonstrates excellent interactional skills as a conversation partner (e.g., effective use of *aizuchi*)
fluency		
production is fragmentary. responses are slow and often halting and disrupted by unnaturally long pauses	8 10 12 14 16	responses are prompt and even with little or no unnatural pausing, occasional self-corrections
comprehensibility/intelligibility		
some problems with pronunciation and intonation that may impede intelligibility	8 10 12 14 16	few problems with pronunciation and intonation, completely intelligible

Results and implications

The analytic rubric, which provided ratings for six criteria, turned out to be a useful and effective tool for providing feedback on student performance, especially for those students who did not perform equally well across different criteria (e.g., scoring at the mastery level, 16 or 18 points, on *task completion* but scoring at the non-mastery level, 8 or 10 points, on *language knowledge and control*, or *fluency*). The analytic rubric allowed the instructor (Kimi) to inform her students about which elements of their performances reached the mastery level and which needed more practice.

However, this does not mean that the holistic rubric did not provide adequate feedback. When using the holistic rubric, students were informed of the strengths and weaknesses in their performances by simply circling or underlying certain descriptors and adding brief comments. In addition, although some studies have suggested that holistic scales may generate less reliable results compared to analytic scales (e.g., Hamp-Lyons, 1991), when a Pearson product-moment correlation coefficient was performed on ratings from two trained practicum student raters using the holistic scale to judge the same group of students ($n=14$), the inter-rater correlation coefficient was high ($r=.967$, $p<.001$; Kondo-Brown, 2012). In terms of communicating with students about teacher expectations, both types of rubric were helpful but in different ways: the analytic rubric was more useful in explaining the dimensions of what was considered good oral performance, while the holistic scale was more useful for describing the key features of oral performance that were expected at different achievement levels.

Case study 2: The use of task-independent and task-dependent rubrics for oral performance tests in an elementary-school Japanese language program

Context

The rubrics in this case were used as part of a longitudinal oral assessment study developed for evaluating a two-year Japanese language program at a local elementary school (Kondo-Brown, 2002a). The purpose of the project was to periodically assess the degree to which the students had achieved the expected learning outcomes, for use in judging and improving program effectiveness. The oral test, which took approximately 15 minutes per student, was designed to assess students' abilities to comprehend and produce vocabulary, routines, and patterns which would have been learned during the two-year program (through the fourth and fifth grades). In order to ensure the content validity of the test prompts and rubrics, the instruments were developed by carefully considering the program curriculum, which was based on the Hawai'i Department of Education World Languages Standards (available as a pdf file at http://www.hcps.k12.hi.us/). Classroom observations also informed development of the instruments, and feedback on the assessment materials was obtained from a Japanese language teacher who taught in the program.

The test materials included prompts on ten daily topics (e.g., greeting and self-introduction, weather, date/time, foods; Kondo-Brown, 2002a). As an example, one of the ten tasks (greeting and self-introduction) is shown in Table 9. Note that the students could be prompted at two levels: the *mastery* and *beyond-mastery* levels. All students were prompted at the mastery-level; most of the mastery-level prompts were simple questions that would require short answers. The beyond-mastery level prompts were primarily used as additional questions for heritage language (HL) students. The test was administered at three different times: at the end of the third grade (before entry into the program), the fourth grade, and the fifth grade (upon exiting the program). Each student was interviewed and audio recorded by one of three trained testers. The recorded performances were rated by two raters (one of whom was a tester). An average of the two ratings was used as the student's final score.

Table 9.   Task 1 Prompts (greeting and self-introduction) for young learners of Japanese. Adapted from Kondo-Brown (2002a, p. 178). Used with permission.

mastery level tasks	beyond mastery level tasks
Greet the student, *Ohayoo go zaimasu!* [Good morning!]. Ask questions about student's name, age, and grade: *O-namae wan an desu ka?* [What's your name?], *Nan-sai desu ka?* [how old are you?], *Nan-nensei desu ka?* [What grade are you in?]. Urge the student to ask "What is your name?" in Japanese.	Ask whether the student speaks Japanese at home: *Uchi de kazoku to nihongo o hanashi masu ka?* [Do you speak Japanese at home?]. Ask the student to describe who she/he speaks with in Japanese: *Dare to hanashi masu ka?* [Whom do you speak with?].

Rubrics

During the first year of the project, only a task-independent rubric, which was a general rating scale used across all tasks, was used (Table 10). During the second year, task-dependent rubrics (scales specific to individual tasks) were experimentally developed in order to examine how the difference in rubric type (independent/general vs. dependent/specific) might influence the test results (see Table 11 for a sample task-dependent scale used for Task 1: greeting and self-introduction). A task-dependent rubric was written for each task by randomly selecting four examples of task performance at each score level and then describing the common features present in the four examples. With either rubric, the testers/raters scored student performances using a 7–point scale: non-mastery was worth 1, 2, or 3 points; mastery was worth 4, 5, or 6 points; and beyond-mastery earned 7 points. Also, note that with either rubric, the descriptors included not only the characteristics of student performance at the given level, but also the degree of interviewer support required for the test taker to complete the task. Inclusion of the degree of interviewer support in the scoring descriptors is recommended for discriminating between oral performance levels, especially for young learners (Kondo-Brown, 2004a).

Table 10.   Task-independent rubric for young learners of Japanese. Adapted from Kondo-Brown (2002a, p. 194). Used with permission.

non-mastery (unsatisfactory performance on the task) 1–3 points	mastery (satisfactory performance of the task) 4–6 points	beyond mastery (more than satisfactory performance of the topic) 7 points
cannot respond to most or all of the prompts accurately even with support; shows difficulty in participating in simple, meaningful exchanges; apparent lack of vocabulary and expressions to complete the task	*can* respond to all or most of the mastery level prompts accurately with or without support; participates in simple, meaningful exchanges; uses sufficiently broad learned vocabulary and expressions to complete the task; pronunciation and intonation are good	*can* respond to all of the mastery level prompts accurately without support; can respond to additional beyond-mastery level prompts; participates in simple, meaningful exchanges with ease; no problem with pronunciation and intonation

Table 11. Sample task-dependent rubric for young learners of Japanese. Adapted from Kondo-Brown (2002a, p. 195). Used with permission.

	non-mastery			mastery			beyond mastery
1	2	3	4	5	6		7
cannot talk about self at all	can greet appropriately	can greet appropriately	can greet appropriately	can greet appropriately	can greet appropriately		same as rating 6 except can respond to questions about the use of Japanese language at home
	can respond to one question about self	can respond to two questions about self	can respond to two questions about self	can respond to two questions about self	can respond to three questions about self		
	cannot ask someone's name	cannot ask someone's name	can ask someone's name	can ask someone's name	can ask someone's name		
	utterances have long pauses, and have minor errors	utterances have long pauses, and have minor errors	utterances are somewhat hesitant but accurate	utterances are accurate and prompt	utterances are accurate and prompt		
	frequent support may be necessary	frequent support may be necessary	infrequent support may be necessary	infrequent support may be necessary	no support is necessary		

Results and implications

To compare the scores produced using the task-dependent and task-independent rubrics, 20 audio-recorded performances for each of the ten tasks were scored using both types of rubrics, with the same tester used to produce both scores. The means and standard deviations for scores from each type of rubric (n=20) as well as the correlations between the two sets of scores were calculated (Table 12). As shown in the table, for any given task, not only were the means more or less equivalent, but also the two sets of scores were highly correlated (ranging from $r=.87$ to $r=.98$). Drawing on the classical testing theory definition of equivalent test forms, the overall mean scores (combined from all tasks), variances, and covariances produced using the two different rubrics were compared (for details, see Kondo-Brown, 2002a, p. 179). It turned out that the type of rubric did not influence the test results: both types of rubrics produced approximately equal ratings. Thus, given the fact that the results obtained by two different rubrics were equivalent, the task-independent rubric might be preferred because it was easier and faster to create. However, the raters reported that the task-dependent scales were easier to use than the task-independent scale. Also, the teacher thought the task-dependent rubric was more useful because it provided more information for the teacher and students.

Table 12. Comparison of ratings using task-independent (TI) and task-dependent (TD) scales for young learners of Japanese. Adapted from Kondo-Brown (2002a, p. 178). Used with permission.

task number		1	2	3	4	5	6	7	8	9	10
results using task-dependent rubrics	Mean	4.70	3.75	4.40	5.15	3.45	3.65	3.70	3.70	1.40	3.70
	SD	1.05	1.58	1.39	1.06	0.92	1.31	1.52	1.55	1.07	1.35
results using task-independent rubrics	Mean	4.60	3.94	4.55	5.05	3.25	3.50	3.90	3.85	1.25	3.75
	SD	1.11	1.70	1.32	1.07	0.77	1.32	1.45	1.46	0.77	1.34
correlation coefficients		.92	.94	.94	.92	.90	.87	.90	.97	.98	.96

Case study 3: The use of an analytic rubric for scoring a Japanese composition placement test

Context

Although the rubrics discussed in case studies 1 and 2 were developed for criterion-referenced purposes (that is, the rubrics were tailored for the specific learning outcomes of a course/program), rubrics may also be developed for norm-referenced purposes. Placement testing is one such norm-referenced context, where the purpose is to detect differences between students so that they can be placed into a class with other students of similar proficiency. At UHM, the Japanese placement test consists of three multiple-choice sections: grammar, listening, and reading. A composition task was also included on an experimental basis. One objective for including this task was to determine whether a short composition test could be an effective placement tool for discriminating writing proficiency within two groups of incoming Japanese students at UHM: heritage and non-heritage students (Kondo-Brown, 2004b). Other objectives associated with use of the composition task were to (a) examine the internal consistency of the scores obtained using the Japanese composition scoring rubric, (b) apply multifaceted Rasch analysis to investigate the scoring consistency and possible biases of trained teacher raters when using the rubric (Kondo-Brown, 2002b), and (c) apply generalizability theory analysis to investigate the relative effects on dependability of scores of the numbers of raters and categories (see Chapter 7 of this volume). The students were instructed to write on a topic of their choice (describe your vacation, yourself, or Hawai'i) in a space with 20 lines. Three teachers, who were trained to use the rubric, independently rated the short compositions written by 234 incoming students of Japanese. Average scores of the three ratings were used as the final scores.

Rubric

A rubric for scoring the Japanese compositions (see Table 13) was created by modifying the *ESL Composition Profile* of Jacobs, Zinkgraf, Wormuth, Hartfiel, and Hughey (1981). Jacobs et al.'s composition profile consists of five components (*content, organization, vocabulary, language use,* and *mechanics*) and has been used widely as an assessment tool for scoring second language (L2) writing in norm-referenced settings. Jacobs et al.'s original composition profile was a weighted scale with content having the most weight (30%) and mechanics the least (5%); in the Japanese composition rubric each of the five categories was weighted equally with a possible score range of 7 to 20 points (see Table 13). Second, there were minor changes to the language features addressed under mechanics. For example, the Japanese composition rubric excluded capitalization as a descriptor because there is no capitalization in Japanese. Instead, it included descriptors addressing the use of basic Japanese scripts (Kana—the Japanese basic syllabary and Kanji—Chinese characters), which are common criteria included in Japanese L2 writing rubrics (e.g., Morita, 1981; Tanaka, Tsubone, & Hajikano, 1998). Third, for the language use dimension, grammar-related descriptors irrelevant to Japanese (e.g., articles and prepositions) were replaced by grammar-related descriptors relevant to Japanese (e.g., particles and inflections/conjugations). Finally, in the organization section, the consistency of writing style was included based on Tanaka et al.'s (1998) study.[3]

Table 13. Rubric for scoring Japanese L2 compositions in a college placement test. Adapted from Kondo-Brown (2002b, pp. 30–31). Used with permission.

	score	level	criteria
content	20–18	excellent to very good	knowledgeable; substantive; thorough development of thesis; relevant to assigned topic
	17–14	good to average	some knowledge of subject; adequate range; limited development of thesis; mostly relevant to topic, but lacks detail
	13–10	fair to poor	limited knowledge of subject; little substance; inadequate development of topic
	9–7	very poor	does not show knowledge of subject; non-substantive; not pertinent; OR not enough to evaluate
organization	20–18	excellent to very good	fluent expression; ideas clearly stated/supported; succinct; well-organized; logical sequencing; cohesive; consistent style
	17–14	good to average	somewhat choppy; loosely organized but main ideas stand out; limited support; logical but incomplete sequencing; inconsistent style
	13–10	fair to poor	non-fluent; ideas confused or disconnected; lacks logical sequencing and development
	9–7	very poor	does not communicate; no organization; OR not enough to evaluate
vocabulary	20–18	excellent to very good	sophisticated range; effective word/idiom choice and usage; word form mastery; appropriate register
	17–14	good to average	adequate range; occasional errors of word/idiom form, choice, usage but meaning not obscured
	13–10	fair to poor	limited range; frequent errors of word/idiom form, choice, usage; meaning confused or obscured
	9–7	very poor	essentially translation; little knowledge of Japanese vocabulary, idioms, word form; OR not enough to evaluate

---

[3] There are two formal Japanese writing styles: the *desu/masu* style and the *dearu* style. While the *desu/masu* style is a *soft* type of writing used for personal letters or narratives, the *dearu* style is a formal, *hard* type of writing generally used in newspaper articles, formal documents, theses, etc.

language use	20–18	excellent to very good	effective complex constructions; few errors of agreement, tense, number, word order, pronouns, inflections, particles, etc.
	17–14	good to average	effective but simple constructions; minor problems in complex constructions; several errors of agreement, tense, number, word order, pronouns, inflections, particles, etc.
	13–10	fair to poor	major problems in simple/complex constructions; frequent errors of negation, agreement, tense, number, word order, pronouns, inflections, particles, etc.; meaning confused or obscured
	9–7	very poor	virtually no mastery of sentence construction rules; dominated by errors; does not communicate; OR not enough to evaluate
mechanics	20–18	excellent to very good	*Kana* and *Kanji* are well-formed and used appropriately; few errors of spelling, punctuation, paragraphing
	17–14	good to average	occasional errors in the use of *Kana* and *Kanji*; occasional errors of spelling, punctuation, paragraphing but meaning not obscured; occasional use of English
	13–10	fair to poor	infrequent or no use of *Kanji*; frequent errors of spelling, punctuation, paragraphing; poor handwriting; meaning confused or obscured; frequent use of English
	9–7	very poor	no mastery of *Kana*; dominated by errors of spelling, punctuation, paragraphing; handwriting illegible; Or not enough to evaluate

Results and implications

The ratings for the heritage and non-heritage groups were both more-or-less evenly distributed over the range of possible scores (Kondo-Brown, 2004b; see Figure 2). This information was interesting and useful because multiple-choice test scores for the heritage language group were clustered at the upper end of the scale (i.e., the test was relatively easy for them) and the multiple-choice scores therefore did a poor job of discriminating between individual heritage language students (Kondo-Brown, 2004b). In contrast, the composition test appeared to be more of a challenge and was able to discriminate between different heritage language students, potentially allowing for more accurate placement of these individuals.

Furthermore, the three trained teacher raters were found to be self-consistent in assessing Japanese L2 compositions (Kondo-Brown, 2002b). However, at the same time, significant differences in overall rater severity were observed among the raters and each of the raters showed a unique bias pattern (e.g., one rater was harsher on vocabulary and more lenient on content; for details, see Kondo-Brown, 2002b). While the Japanese composition rubric could be used to produce reliable ratings, in order to obtain the best possible results multiple ratings are still recommended. Furthermore, there is an issue of practicality. Although the composition test could effectively place all kinds of incoming students into different proficiency levels, including more proficient heritage language students, it may not be a practical placement procedure especially when there is large group of students to be tested and scores must be produced quickly. Not surprisingly, a national survey has suggested that productive skills are in fact much less commonly assessed for placement purposes than are receptive skills (Brown, Hudson, & Clark, 2004). However, even if administrations of multiple-choice tests are more practical for most placement situations, in this case a composition test might still be administered to more proficient students to improve the quality of placement decisions.

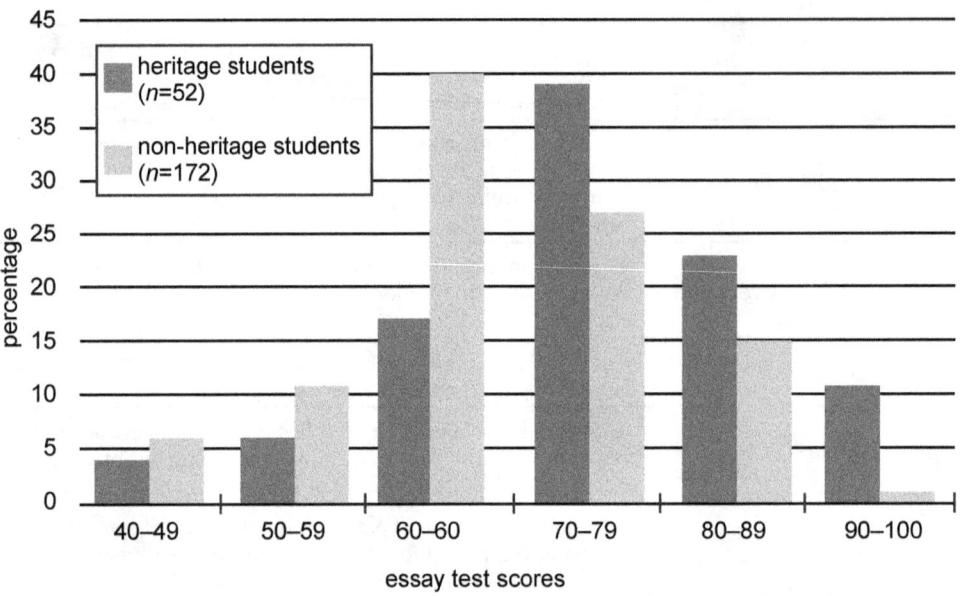

Figure 2. Score distribution of the Japanese composition by group (heritage vs. non-heritage students). Adapted from Kondo-Brown (2004b, p. 15).

Some final points regarding the use of rubrics

To conclude the discussion, a few issues regarding the use of rubrics are worth mentioning. First, for assignments and assessments that are tied to instruction, it is crucial that the rubric address the instructional goals, standards, or learning outcomes that underlie the assignment/assessment. When constructing rubrics, it is necessary to cover the full scope of the educational target being assessed; it is usually not enough to simply settle for narrow behaviors that can be easily counted or evaluated. In addition, when adopting an existing rubric it is necessary to carefully evaluate its usefulness for the specific situation in which it will be used. A rubric developed for one purpose is not automatically useful for a different purpose.

Also, when the focus is on producing scores, especially for summative purposes, it is obviously important that interpretation of the rubric be consistent. Fairness dictates that different raters score performances in a similar way (if multiple raters are used) and that the first paper in a pile be judged to the same standard as the last. While using a rubric may, in itself, improve consistency in scoring, consistency also depends on a uniform application of the rating scale which can be increased by using actual examples of performance to help establish what different levels of ability look like. The descriptors used in rubrics are necessarily brief and may be fairly abstract; a few well-chosen exemplars can therefore supplement a rubric by providing additional definitions of ability that better capture the full complexity of performance. For classroom teachers, it may be well worth the trouble to save photocopies of a few key papers, or audio or video copies of representative oral performances.

Moreover, where multiple raters or graders are used, some form of rater training will likely be needed to establish consistent use of the rubric (Fulcher, 2004; Weigle, 2002). Training helps raters to be more consistent in their own judgments, which is a necessary condition for inter-rater reliability (McNamara, 1996; Weigle, 1994, 1998; for more on inter-rater reliability, see Chapter 4 of this book). Training may also help to reduce differences in severity among raters, especially for particularly hard or easy raters (Lim, 2009) or raters who show bias towards a particular prompt or scoring category (Wigglesworth, 1993).[4] Training may involve activities such as discussion of how to apply the rubric, discussion of how to score specific examples, and practice scoring of samples for which scores have been established. A full discussion of rater training is beyond the scope of this chapter, but it is enough to say here that it is unlikely that different people will produce consistent scores without some degree of coordination and/or training. [For a detailed example of rater training, see Chapter 5.]

To conclude, in this chapter, we have discussed the types and uses of rubrics in pedagogical situations and provided a few examples of rubrics in action. Our hope is that this chapter provides some idea of the options available when using rubrics to evaluate language performance. Although we have described some common types of rubrics, the case studies demonstrate that there are no absolute rules as to the form a rubric should take, or how it should be used. Rather, the design (or selection) of a rubric and its use should be guided by the needs of the situation. For example, the fact that a rubric is well-known or seen as authoritative is typically a poor reason, by itself, to select a rubric for a particular context. There may be good reasons for choosing to use a well-known rating scale (it facilitates communication with other professionals or stakeholders, for one) but it is critical to ensure that (a) the abilities measured by the rubric match the abilities targeted by the assessment (which in turn reflect the educational goals of the learning context) and (b) the format of the rubric is appropriate for the uses to be made of it. We believe rubrics are highly useful tools for guiding decision making when scoring, but they should serve, not dominate, the larger purposes of assessment.

References

Arter, J., & McTighe, J. (2001). *Scoring rubrics in the classroom: Using performance criteria for assessing and improving student performance*. Thousand Oaks, CA: Corwin.

Bachman, L. F., & Palmer, A. S. (1996). *Language testing in practice*. Oxford, UK: Oxford University.

Barkaoui, K. (2007). Participants, texts, and processes in ESL/EFL essay tests: A narrative review of the literature. *Canadian Modern Language Review, 64*, 99–134.

Barkaoui, K. (2010). Variability in ESL essay rating processes: The role of the rating scale and rater experience. *Language Assessment Quarterly, 7*, 54–74.

Brown, J. D. (Ed.). (1998). *New ways of classroom assessment*. Alexandria, VA: Teachers of English to Speakers of Other Languages.

Brown, J. D., Hudson, T., & Clark, M. (2004). *Issues in placement survey* (Networks #40). Honolulu: University of Hawai'i, National Foreign Language Resource Center. Retrieved December 2008 from: http://nflrc.hawaii.edu/NetWorks/NW40/SurveyResults.html

Brown, J. D., Hudson, T., Norris, J. M., & Bonk, W. J. (2002). *An investigation of second language task-based performance assessments* (Technical Report #24). Honolulu, HI: University of Hawai i, Second Language Teaching & Curriculum Center.

---

[4] Rater training is unlikely to completely eliminate differences in rater severity, however (Weigle, 1994; McNamara, 1996, case 3 above). When using multiple raters, checking rater agreement is a must.

Charney, D. (1984). The validity of using holistic scoring to evaluate writing: A critical overview. *Research in the Teaching of English, 18*, 65–81.

Cohen, A. D. (1994). *Assessing language ability in the classroom* (2nd ed.). Boston, MA: Heinle & Heinle.

Douglas, D. (1994). Quantity and quality in speaking test performance. *Language Testing, 11*, 125–144.

Ellis, R. (2003). *Task-based language learning and teaching.* Oxford, UK: Oxford University.

Fiderer, A. (1999). *40 rubrics and checklists to assess reading and writing.* Jefferson City, MO: Scholastic Professional.

Fulcher, G. (2003). *Testing second language speaking.* Harlow, UK: Longman.

Gentile, C. A., Martin-Rehrmann, J., & Kennedy, J. H. (1995). *Windows into the classroom: NAEP's 1992 writing portfolio study* (Report No. NAEP–23–FR–06). Washington, DC: National Center for Educational Statistics. Retrieved from the ERIC website: http://www.eric.ed.gov/PDFS/ED378584.pdf

Hamp-Lyons, L. (1991). Scoring procedures for ESL contexts. In Hamp-Lyons, L. (Ed.), *Assessing second language writing in academic contests* (pp. 241–276). Norwood, NJ: Ablex.

Jacobs, H. L., Zinkgraf, S. A., Wormuth, D. R., Hartfiel, V. F., & Hughey, J. B. (1981). *Testing ESL composition: A practical approach.* Rowley, MA: Newbury House.

Khattri, N., Reeve, A. L. & Kane, M. B. (1998). *Principles and practices of performance assessment.* Mahwah, NJ: Lawrence Earlbaum.

Kondo-Brown, K. (2012). *Nihongo kyooshi no tame no hyooka nyuumon* [Introduction to assessment for Japanese language teachers]. Tokyo, Japan: Kuroshio Shuppan.

Kondo-Brown, K. (2004a). Investigating interviewer-candidate interactions during oral interviews for child L2 learners. *Foreign Language Annals, 37*, 602–615.

Kondo-Brown, K. (2004b). Do background variables predict students' scores on a Japanese placement test? Implications for placing heritage language learners. *Journal of the National Council of Less Commonly Taught Languages, 1*, 1–19.

Kondo-Brown, K. (2002a). A longitudinal evaluation study on child JFL learners' oral performances. *Japanese Language and Literature, 36*, 171–199.

Kondo-Brown, K. (2002b). An analysis of rater bias with FACETS in measuring Japanese L2 writing performance. *Language Testing, 19*, 1–29.

Lim, G. S. (2009). *Prompt and rater effects in second language writing performance assessment.* (Unpublished doctoral dissertation). Retrieved from ProQuest Dissertations and Theses. (UMI No. 3392954)

Linn, R. L., & Gronlund, N. E. (1995). *Measurement and assessment in teaching* (7th ed.). Englewood Cliffs, NJ: Prentice Hall.

Lloyd-Jones, R. (1977). Primary trait scoring. In C. R. Cooper & L. Odell (Eds.), *Evaluating writing: Describing, measuring, judging* (pp. 33–69). New York: National Council of Teachers of English.

Luoma, S. (2004). *Assessing speaking.* Cambridge, UK: Cambridge University.

McNamara, T. F. (1996). *Measuring second language performance.* London: Longman.

Morita, F. (1981). *Sakubun no hyooka* [Evaluating compositions]. *Nihongo Kyooiku, 43*, 17–33.

Norris, J. M. (2006). The why (and how) of assessing student learning outcomes in college foreign language programs. *The Modern Language Journal, 90*, 576–583.

Orr, M. (2002). The FCE Speaking test: Using rater reports to help interpret test scores. *System, 30,* 143–154.

Popham, W. J. (2008). *Classroom assessment: What teachers need to know* (5th ed.). Boston: Allyn & Bacon.

Sakyi, A. A. (2000). Validation of holistic scoring for ESL writing assessment: How raters evaluate compositions. In A. J. Kunnan (Ed.), *Fairness and validation in language assessment: Selected papers from the 19th Language Testing Research Colloquium, Orlando, Florida* (pp. 129–152). Cambridge, UK: Cambridge University.

Stevens, D., & Levi, A.J. (2005). *Introduction to rubrics: An assessment tool to save grading time, convey effective feedback, and promote student learning.* Sterling, VA: Stylus.

Tanaka, M., Tsubone, Y., & Hajikano, A. (1998) *Dainigengo to shite no nihongo ni okeru sakubun hyooka kijun: Nihongo kyooshi to ippan nihonjin no hikaku* [Evaluation criteria for writing by non-native speakers: A comparison of survey results for Japanese teachers and non-teachers]. *Nihongo Kyooiku, 96,* 17–33.

Vaughan, C. (1991). Holistic assessment: What goes on in the rater's mind? In L. Hamp-Lyons (Ed.), *Assessing second language writing in academic contexts* (pp. 111–125). Norwood, NJ: Ablex.

Weigle, S. C. (1994). Effects of training on raters of ESL compositions. *Language Testing, 11,* 197–223.

Weigle, S. C. (1998). Using FACETS to model rater training effects. *Language Testing, 15,* 263–287.

Weigle, S. C. (2002). *Assessing writing.* Cambridge, UK: Cambridge University.

White, E. (1985). *Teaching and assessing writing.* San Francisco, CA: Jossey-Bass.

Wiggins, G. (1998). *Educative assessment: Designing assessments to inform and improve student performance.* San Francisco, CA: Jossey-Bass.

Wigglesworth, G. (1993). Exploring bias analysis as a tool for improving rater consistency in assessing oral interaction. *Language Testing, 10,* 305–319.

4

Issues in Analyzing Rubric-Based Results

James Dean Brown
University of Hawai'i at Mānoa

Catherine (Katarina) Anne Edmonds
University of Hawai'i at Hilo

Introduction

This chapter addresses many of the issues that arise in doing basic statistical analyses of rubric-based scores as well as in understanding more advanced statistical procedures that can help teachers, assessment specialists, and administrators develop, revise, analyze, and understand rubric-based assessments.

In the main section on doing basic statistical analyses for rubric-based scores, we will examine the different kinds of scales that rubrics create and address whether those scales are nominal, ordinal, interval, or ratio in nature. We will also show the basics of describing the scores that result from rubric-based assessment, investigating the degree of relationship between sets of scores, and estimating the interrater/intrarater reliability and standard error of measurement of those same scores. This section will end by listing the sorts of questions that basic statistical analyses can address.

The second main section is designed to help with understanding statistically more advanced analyses often used with rubric-based scores (especially those reported in Chapters 5–7). This section will begin with a subsection that explains the basics necessary to understand (a) what generalizability theory (G-theory) is, (b) how both the generalizability study and decision study stages work in such research, and (c) what types of questions G-theory can address. The second subsection will explain the basics needed to understand some of the useful extensions of G-theory including D-studies for absolute decisions, phi(lambda), signal-to-noise ratios, along with the sorts of questions these extensions of G-theory can address. The final subsection will explain the basics necessary to understand multifaceted Rasch measurement, fit statistics, vertical rulers, probability curves, bias analysis, and the types of questions Rasch analysis can address.

Brown, J. D. & Edmonds, C. A. (2012). Issues in analyzing rubric-based results. In J. D. Brown, (Ed.), *Developing, using, and analyzing rubrics in language assessment with case studies in Asian and Pacific languages* (pp. 57–84). Honolulu: University of Hawai'i, National Foreign Language Resource Center.

The conclusion section attempts to pull all of this information together into a chart that readers can use to decide what sorts of analyses they need to use to answer many of the different sorts of questions that arise in statistically analyzing and reporting on the results of rubric-based assessments. Let's turn now to the basics.

Doing basic statistical analyses for rubric-based scores

What kind of scales do rubrics create? Nominal, ordinal, interval, or ratio?

In language research, there are several ways to measure things numerically in what are called *scales of measurement*, which are of four kinds:

Nominal scales
Nominal scales (aka *categorical scales* or *dichotomous scales*, when there are two categories) classify or categorize into natural categories like gender (male or female groups) or artificial categories like language level (elementary, intermediate, or advanced groups).

Ordinal scales
Ordinal scales (aka *ranked scales*) order things using ordinal numbers (e.g., the relative usefulness of language classroom activities as rated by students: 1st, 2nd, 3rd, and so forth) and thereby show the order of the objects on the scale, but not the distances between those ordered points on the scale.

Interval scales
Interval scales also show the order of things, but with equal intervals between the values on the scale (e.g., the distances between language test scores of 1, 2, 3, 4, etc. along a scale are assumed to be the same).

Ratio scales
Ratio scales are similar to interval scales, but they are even more precise in that a zero value makes sense as do ratios among the values on the scale (e.g., a scale like age can be zero, and it makes sense to say that 60 years is twice as many as 30, that is, they are in a ratio of 2 to 1).

Sometimes interval and ratio scales are grouped together into one category called *continuous scales*. Each of these scale types is useful for quantifying different characteristics of language learning and teaching for purposes of language assessment and research.

With respect to rubric-based ratings, testers and researchers sometimes make the mistake of thinking that the resulting ratings are only ordinal scales. That would be true if a score of 1 was interpreted as meaning the student was first, and 2 as second, and so forth. But we don't typically do that, so it is generally most useful to interpret rubric based ratings as measures on interval scales, or continuous scales, if you prefer.

How should the results from rubrics be described?

A good deal of information can be gleaned from simple descriptive statistics like the mean, standard deviation (*SD*), minimum score, maximum score, and range. To illustrate one way these statistics can easily be calculated, we provide Figure 1, which shows a small example set of data in an *Excel*™ spreadsheet (here adapted from the study presented in Chapter 7). Notice that each of the possible rater/category combinations are listed across the top (e.g., R1C labels the scores for Rater 1 Content; R2O is for Rater 2 Organization scores; R3V is for Rater 3 Vocabulary scores; R1L is for Rater 1 Language scores; R2M is for Rater 2 Mechanics scores, etc.), and that the total scores (based on the 100 point rubric scale, which is the average of the three raters' totals for each examinee) are shown to the right. Notice also that all the scores for each writing sample (with its associated ID# in the left most column) are contained in a single row. In the bottom right portion of Figure 1, the calculations are shown for the total-score mean, *SD*, minimum score, maximum score, and range as they were calculated in *Excel*™.

The mean can be viewed for classroom assessment purposes as the arithmetic average. Notice that we have typed the label *Mean* in the lower right part of Figure 1 in what is called cell Q23 (for column Q, row 23; for these letters and numbers, see the edges of the spreadsheet). We then calculated the mean by typing the=AVERAGE(RANGE) function as=AVERAGE(R2:R21) (since the range in this case includes the cells in the column from R2 to R21) in cell R23, and the spreadsheet program calculated the mean for those data (74.20 in this case). To help the reader see what we did, we also typed the function we used in cell S23 (Note that we wouldn't ordinarily do this when simply doing the analysis ourselves).

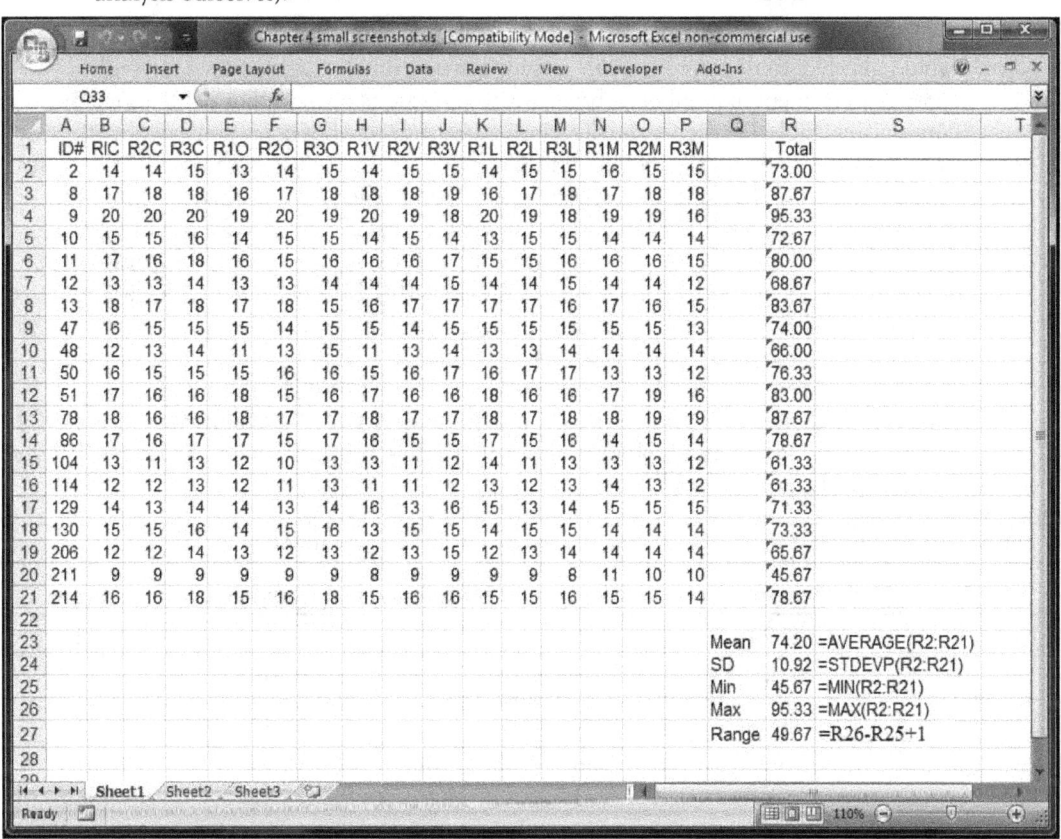

Figure 1. Screen shot of example *Excel*™ spreadsheet of data for three raters and five categories and total scores as well as descriptive statistics.

The standard deviation is a "sort of average of the distances of all scores from the mean" (Brown, 2005, p. 102), which can be calculated in *Excel*™ using the=STDEVP(RANGE) function [where the range is in the column from R2 to R21, it would be=STDEVP(R2:R21) as shown in Figure 1, which in this case turned out to be 10.92]. The minimum score is the lowest score, which can be calculated in *Excel*™ using the=MIN(RANGE) function [where range is from R2 to R21, it would be=MIN(R2:R21) as shown in Figure 1, which in this case turned out to be 45.67]. The maximum score is the highest score, which can be calculated in *Excel*™ using the=MAX(RANGE) function [where range is the cells in the row from say R2 to R21, it would be=MAX(R2:R21) as shown in Figure 1, which in this case turned out to be 95.33]. And the range is simply the maximum minus the minimum plus one [i.e., the value in cell R26 minus the value in cell R25 plus 1 [or=R26–R25+1 as shown in Figure 1]. [Note that the range is sometimes calculated without adding one.] These basic descriptive statistics can thus be calculated by any language teacher with access *Excel*™. Indeed, if you want to see how easy this is, open your *Excel*™ spreadsheet (it's probably there somewhere on your computer), type in the data, and then try doing the calculations with the functions that we described above.

In many cases, these statistics will be all that is necessary to help teachers describe and think about their rubric-based test results. For much more on these statistics and how to calculate them by hand or using *Excel*™, see Brown, 2005, pp. 98–107.]

I would also like to illustrate ways to present the descriptive statistics in a research report or assessment manual on rubric-based score results in ways that will be clear and illuminating. Table 1 presents the descriptive statistics for the scores achieved by the students in the study that is presented in Chapter 5 (Table 4 of that chapter). The results are shown for 40 individual students (see the IDs on the left) averaged across 10 raters who each rated five language categories (language traits). Table 1 focuses on individual examinee's performances. So you can clearly see that examinee 16 scored highest with a score of 15.90, while examinee 36 scored lowest with 7.70. The standard deviation for examinee 17 of 5.12 indicates that the raters varied most from each other for that examinee, and the standard deviation for examinee 36 of 2.55 indicates that the raters varied least from each other for that examinee. It is also possible to easily see that a number of students had a minimum rating of 5, but only two had a maximum rating of 20. In addition, the lowest and highest ranges were for IDs 32 and 20, who had ranges of 3 and 13, respectively.

Table 1. Descriptive statistics of scoring for students (from Table 4 in Chapter 5)

ID	Mean	SD	Minimum	Maximum	Range
1	7.90	2.61	5	10	5
2	12.40	4.04	9	16	7
3	11.00	3.59	7	15	8
4	10.30	3.38	8	15	7
5	10.10	3.33	6	15	9
6	14.70	4.70	11	17	6
7	12.80	4.10	10	16	6
8	11.40	3.69	7	15	8
9	13.00	4.18	10	15	5
10	9.30	3.05	6	12	6
11	11.20	3.76	7	18	11
12	14.40	4.62	11	17	6
13	12.40	3.98	9	15	6

14	15.10	4.83	12	19	7
15	12.80	4.09	10	16	6
16	15.90	5.09	12	20	8
17	15.70	5.12	10	20	10
18	15.40	4.90	12	19	7
19	9.90	3.21	7	13	6
20	11.60	4.10	6	19	13
21	8.80	2.91	5	12	7
22	11.60	3.89	7	16	9
23	11.40	3.76	7	16	9
24	15.00	4.88	10	19	9
25	12.80	4.25	7	17	10
26	13.10	4.23	10	16	6
27	11.70	3.90	8	17	9
28	9.60	3.29	5	14	9
29	11.80	3.89	8	15	7
30	13.50	4.35	9	16	7
31	11.70	3.74	10	15	5
32	8.70	2.79	7	10	3
33	11.70	3.94	7	15	8
34	12.70	4.06	10	15	5
35	11.70	3.76	9	14	5
36	7.70	2.55	5	10	5
37	10.20	3.26	8	13	5
38	10.50	3.48	6	15	9
39	14.10	4.65	9	18	9
40	15.60	4.97	12	19	7

Table 2 presents the descriptive statistics for the same study, but with a focus on the 10 raters in that study (Table 2 is taken from Table 5 in Chapter 5) averaged across 40 examinees and five language categories. So you can clearly see that Rater 7 gave the highest average scores with a mean of 13.80 and Rater 4 gave the lowest with 10.40. Rater 6 had the scores that varied the most with a standard deviation of 3.47, while Rater 5 had the scores that varied the least with a standard deviation of 2.10. And, so forth.

Table 2. Descriptive statistics of scoring for raters (from Table 5 in Chapter 5)

	rater									
	1	2	3	4	5	6	7	8	9	10
Mean	12.30	13.45	12.58	10.40	10.93	11.25	13.80	10.58	13.65	11.38
SD	3.38	2.54	2.64	2.38	2.10	3.47	3.12	3.31	2.86	3.38
Minimum	7.00	8.00	7.00	6.00	6.00	5.00	8.00	5.00	9.00	5.00
Maximum	20.00	20.00	19.00	17.00	15.00	20.00	19.00	16.00	18.00	17.00
Range	14.00	13.00	14.00	12.00	10.00	16.00	12.00	12.00	10.00	13.00

Table 3 presents the descriptive statistics for the same study, from yet another perspective. This time the focus is on the five language categories in the rubric (this table is taken from Table 6 in Chapter 5) averaged across 40 examinees and 10 raters. So you can clearly see that the category labeled Punctuation, Spelling and Mechanics (PSM) was scored most severely with a mean of 91.20, while Organization and Ideas (O&I) was the most leniently scored with a mean of 100.60. Grammar and Accuracy (G&A) had the largest range with a minimum of 76.00 and a maximum of 118, and a range of 43 although there is only a 1 point difference from Punctuation, Spelling, and Mechanics (PSM) which has a minimum of 70 and a maximum of 111, and a range of 42. And so forth.

Table 3. Descriptive statistics of scoring for items overall (from Table 6 in Chapter 5)

	O&I	G&A	PSM	SQE	MDI
Mean	100.60	96.78	91.20	92.70	100.30
SD	11.79	14.12	15.04	10.49	10.50
Minimum	84.00	76.00	70.00	78.00	84.00
Maximum	117.00	118.00	111.00	107.00	115.00
Range	34.00	43.00	42.00	30.00	32.00

How can the degrees of relationship between sets of rubric scores be investigated?

In dealing with sets of rubric-based scores, the statistic of choice for investigating the degree to which two sets of scores are related (or go together) is the imposingly labeled Pearson product-moment correlation coefficient. These correlation coefficients can be calculated in an *Excel*™ spreadsheet using the =CORREL(RANGE1,RANGE2) function. For example, to calculate the correlation coefficient for two sets of data in the ranges B2:B50 and C2:C50, it is only necessary to find an empty cell, then type =CORREL(B2:B50,C2:C50), and hit enter. The correlation coefficient should then appear in that cell (for further directions on how to do this in *Excel*™, see Brown, 2005, pp. 139–145). Correlation coefficients typically range from .00 to 1.00 if the relationship between the two sets of numbers is positive (i.e., if the two sets of numbers go up in the same direction), but can range from .00 to –1.00 if the relationship between the two sets of numbers is negative (i.e., if one set of numbers goes up while the other set goes down). Zero correlation means that there is no relationship between the two sets of numbers, +1.00 means the relationship is perfect with the two sets of numbers going up in the same direction, and –1.00 means the relationship is perfect with the two sets of numbers going up in opposite directions. Naturally, everything in between .00 and positive or negative 1.00 is also possible and must be interpreted as lesser or greater degrees of relationship, depending on the value obtained. For example, a correlation coefficient of .95 (negative or positive) shows a high degree of relationship, while other values indicate moderate (e.g., .80) or low (e.g., .15) degrees of relationship.

Among other things, correlation coefficients can be useful for looking at the degree to which the scores on individual items or scoring categories are related to subset scores or total scores for purposes of item analysis. For example, the second column of numbers in Table 4 shows the correlation (r) between the scores for each category in the Introduction interview and the total scores for the Introduction interview. Notice in this case that the scores for Communication Skill, Vocabulary, Grammar, and Fluency correlate moderately (i.e., .76, .77, .79, & .79, respectively) with the total scores on this interview. In short, whatever they are doing is moderately correlated with the total scores. The other three categories (Pronunciation, Language Steadfastness, & Cultural Authenticity) correlate a bit lower at .53, .49, and .59. It might be worthwhile in revising the rubric to consider the fact that some categories are not as highly related to the total scores as others. If the goal is to make the categories as homogeneous as possible, the rubric might be revised to eliminate those three low-correlating scales, or just the lowest one. If the goal is to have meaningful and different categories, more tolerance would be appropriate for such low correlations. The correlation coefficients are just numbers. What they mean is the responsibility of the test developers to interpret. [For more on this topic, see Tables 6 and 7 and the associated text in Chapter 6.]

Table 4. Item statistics for the original versions of the introduction (a portion of Table 6 in Chapter 6)

introduction: subtest description	Mean	r	SD	SD^2
communicative skill	2.01	.76	.79	.62
vocabulary	1.84	.77	.63	.39
grammar	1.69	.79	.60	.36
pronunciation	2.27	.53	.53	.28
fluency	1.77	.79	.56	.32
language steadfastness	2.41	.49	.67	.45
cultural authenticity	1.27	.59	.54	.29
total (rubric scores)	13.25	.43	2.93	8.59
average of rubric scores	1.89		.42	.18

Correlation coefficients can also be useful for investigating the degree to which the scores on categories, subtests, tests, and so forth are related to each other. Chapter 6 contains examples of this application of correlation coefficients (see Tables 8 & 9 and the associated text in Chapter 6). As we will show next, correlation coefficients also play a role in estimating and interpreting the reliability of rubric-based scores.

What is the interrater/intrarater reliability of the scores based on a given rubric?

Typically the steps we take in developing rubrics and the procedures for using them will provide the basis for investigating and demonstrating the reliability of the test scores. The reliability of the test scores depends largely on the careful specification of the measurement procedures to be used and adherence to these specifications in the design and implementation of the assessment. Reliability also depends on the quantification of the observation, because the estimation of reliability statistically will partly depend on the level of measurement applied to the test scores (Bachman, 2004). The reliability of a set of scores can only be estimated. Brown explains that:

> [t]he degree to which a test is consistent, or reliable, can be estimated by calculating a reliability coefficient...Reliable coefficients, or reliability estimates as they are called, can be interpreted as the percent of systematic, or consistent, or reliable variance in the scores on a test" (2005, p. 175).

Thus, reliability is an important characteristic of any measurement. After all, we would like any of the scales at our post office to come up with the same weight for our package, wouldn't we? Indeed, we would like a particular scale to indicate the same weight for a package if it were weighed repeatedly. These are issues of reliability that are no less important when we are measuring the language abilities of our students. Indeed, reliability may be more important when making decisions about the lives and futures of human beings. The reliability of a set of test scores can be calculated in many ways, but regardless of how it is calculated, the interpretation of the resulting reliability estimate is about the same.

The central concern is with how consistent the test is in terms of the percent of variance in the scores that is reliable and the percent that is attributable to error. If reliability=.75, then 75% of the variance in the scores can be said to be reliable or consistent, and the remaining .25, or 25% is considered measurement error that is not accounted for. Hence, a reliability estimate of .75 shows that the scores are only moderately reliable for the particular group of students who were being assessed. If a decision is likely to be based entirely on this assessment and the decision is an important one, it will probably be worth revising and improving the rubric and assessment procedures to make them even more consistent. If on the other hand, the assessment is one of many involved in the decision making and stakes are low, perhaps reliability of .75 for the scores would be considered high enough.

Thus interpretation of reliability estimates is a matter of thinking about the importance of the decision, the number of other measures available, the type of measurement, and so forth. We would all like our assessment procedures to be 99% reliable all the time, but that may not be reasonable. The cost necessary to achieve .99 reliability in terms of the students' time, the assessment development costs, the raters' time and effort, and so forth may simply not be worth it given the stakes involved, the number of other measures available, the type of measurement, and so forth.

Remember that reliability estimates described here are derived from the performances of a specific group of students. As a result, the estimate is closely connected to that group of students. Thus any claims about the reliability of the scores resulting from this assessment procedure can only be made with reference to the specific group of students involved. However, testers sometimes very cautiously claim that similar reliability is likely to occur if this assessment procedure is applied to a group of *very similar* students with a very similar range of abilities.

In using rubrics, we are concerned with reliability because we want to be sure that the scores we produce based on the rubric and the resulting decisions are consistent and fair. When we estimate the reliability of rubric-based scores, we are typically concerned with *internal consistency reliability*. Internal-consistency reliability utilizes strategies that estimate the consistency of a test based only on information internal to the test that is available in one administration of a single test (Brown, 2005). One commonly used approach to estimate the reliability of rubric-based scores is Cronbach alpha. Procedures for calculating one type of Cronbach alpha are explained for the simplest two rater version in Brown (2005, pp. 178–179). If more than two raters are employed, other procedures need to be used. The only reasonably easy way to calculate Cronbach alpha for three or more raters is to use a statistical program like *SPSS*™, where Cronbach alpha can be calculated (in version 19) by selecting *Analyze*, then selecting *Scale*, and then *Reliability analysis*...[For more on these statistics and how to calculate them, see Bachman, 2004, pp. 153–191; Brown, 2005, pp. 169–198.]

In assessments that produce rubric-based ratings for compositions, interviews, role-plays, etc., one common source of error may be inconsistency among the raters. Thus one concern in any study or testing project involving rubric scoring will typically be the degree to which raters, or more accurately their ratings, are reliable. If there are several different raters, the concern is typically for consistency across raters, or *inter-rater reliability*. If there is only one rater, who did independent ratings on several different occasions, the concern is usually for consistency across occasions, or *intra-rater reliability*. Since intra-rater reliability is actually quite rarely reported, let's focus on inter-rater reliability here.

Inter-rater reliabilty is calculated by lining up the scores of two raters and calculating the correlation coefficient for the two sets of numbers. This can be done in an *Excel*™ spreadsheet or a statistical analysis program like *SPSS*™ (for directions on how to do this in *Excel*™, see Brown, 2005, pp. 139–145). For purposes of reliability analysis, correlation coefficients typically range from .00 to 1.00 (if you happen to get a negative value that should be rounded to .00 for purpose of reliability analysis). Under these conditions, a correlation coefficient for the scores of two raters can be interpreted as the proportion or percentage (by moving the decimal two places to the right) of reliable score variation for either of the two raters. A correlation coefficient of .70 would indicate that 70% of variation in the first rater's scores was reliable, and by the same token, 70% of the variation in the second rater's scores can also be said to be reliable.

When averaging the two raters' scores (or adding them) before making a decision based on them, the reliability of the two sets of ratings taken together becomes pertinent. To estimate that assessment specialists typically use the Spearman-Brown prophecy formula:

$$r_{xx'} = \frac{n \times r}{(n-1)r + 1}$$

where: $r_{xx'}$=two-rater reliability

r=correlation between the two sets of ratings

n=number of raters

For example, given the single-rater reliability of .70, the Spearman-Brown prophecy formula would estimate the two-rater reliability as follows:

$$r_{xx'} = \frac{n \times r}{(n-1)r+1} = \frac{2 \times .70}{(2-1).70+1} = \frac{1.40}{(1).70+1} = \frac{1.40}{1.70} = .8235294 \approx .82$$

So the estimated reliability for two raters taken together would be about .82. Thus 82% of the variation in combined ratings can be said to be reliable, and of course, by extension, 18% must be said to be unreliable.

Using the interrater correlations approach to reliability with three or more raters is explained in Brown (2005, pp. 186–188). It should be noted that these procedures can also be used to investigate what the potential bang-for-the-buck would be if you were to increase the number of raters to 3, 4, 5, or even 10 raters. However, doing so only tells you the relative benefits of adding various numbers on one dimension, raters in this case. What if you also wanted to estimate the effects of increasing (or decreasing) the numbers on two dimensions, like the numbers of raters *and* the numbers of rating categories? That is an area where generalizability theory is necessary and useful (see the section below on Generalizability theory).

Table 5 shows the inter-rater correlation coefficients for rater pairs, as well as two-rater to five-rater reliability estimates (calculated with the Spearman-Brown prophecy formula discussed above). Notice that separate reliability estimates are presented for the scores in each of the five categories (content, organization, vocabulary, language use, and mechanics) as well as for the total scores. These six estimates are presented for each possible pairing of raters (1 & 2, 2 & 3, and 1 & 3), as well as to illustrate what is likely to happen (again using the Spearman-Brown prophecy formula) if there is only one rater, two raters, three raters, four raters, or five raters (even though there were in fact three raters). On the basis of these sorts of estimates, decisions can be made about what would likely happen if different numbers of raters were used in future applications of this writing assessment rubric. Looked at another way, if reliability of .85 is sufficient for the purpose of a particular institution, these figures could be used to justify using only one rater (which would probably result in reliability of about .881). If in contrast, reliability of .98 is absolutely essential, then it appears that four raters should be used.

Table 5. Classical test theory inter-rater correlation coefficients for rater pairs, as well as two-rater to five-rater reliability estimates (adapted from Table 3 in Chapter 7)

type of reliability	content	organization	vocabulary	lang use	mechanics	total
raters 1 & 2	.831	.814	.859	.826	.875	.904
raters 2 & 3	.886	.836	.861	.820	.848	.902
raters 1 & 3	.811	.770	.859	.794	.859	.881
1–rater reliability	.811	.770	.859	.794	.848	.881
2–rater reliability	.896	.870	.924	.885	.918	.937
3–rater reliability	.928	.909	.948	.920	.944	.957
4–rater reliability	.972	.964	.980	.969	.978	.983
5–rater reliability	.985	.980	.989	.983	.988	.991
Cronbach alpha	.937	.923	.947	.927	.948	.984

One additional statistic that is not provided in the study in Chapter 7 is the standard error of measurement (SEM). The focus of that study was on dependability and redesigning the rubric and rating procedures to improve the dependability of the resulting scores. Hence, it was not necessary to present the SEM. However, when the cut-point and decision making are important issues, the SEM provides a useful additional way to think about the reliability of scores.

Calculating the SEM is very easy once the descriptive statistics and reliability estimate are available. For example, for the study reported in Chapter 7, the reliability shown in Table 3 was .957 for three-rater reliability and the standard deviation for the 100 point scale (shown in Table 1 of Chapter 7) was 11.04. The equation for the SEM is as follows:

$$SEM = SD\sqrt{1 - r_{xx}}$$

where: SD = standard deviation

$r_{xx'}$ = reliability

So in the example, where reliability is .957 and the standard deviation is 11.04, the SEM would be as follows:

$$SEM = SD\sqrt{1 - r_{xx'}} = 11.04\sqrt{1 - .957} = 11.04\sqrt{.043} = 11.04(.2073644) = 2.2893029 \approx 2.29$$

For decision making purposes, it would be wise to consider people who have a score within plus or minus one SEM of the cut-point as being too close to the line for a reliable decision. For example, if the cut-point for passing the writing test in our example were set at 70 out of 100, any student who scored between 67.71 and 72.29 would be within one standard error of the cut-point and might be expected to score within that range 68% of the time, sometimes on the other side of the decision line. More precisely, a student who scored 69 points would be within one SEM of the cut-score and so might be on the other side of the line by chance alone if he/she were to take the test again. The responsible thing for decision makers to do if a student is within one SEM of the cut-point is to gather additional information about that student. This could take the form of talking to the student's writing teacher, looking at the student's other writing samples, or testing the student again. In any case, the SEM provides an indication of students for whom decisions at the exact cut-point might not be reliable, so in the interest of fairness, they should be dealt with a bit differently from those other students who are further away from the cut-point for whom the decisions are likely to be much more reliable.

Questions that basic statistical analyses can address

Basic statistical analyses (i.e., descriptive statistics, reliability estimates, Spearman-Brown prophecy formula, standard error of measurement) provide useful tools that can help in describing the results of rubric-based assessments and making decisions about how best to revise such rubrics and the assessment procedures in which they were used. Descriptive statistics are particularly useful for answering questions like the following:

1. How easy or difficult is this set of assessment procedures for the particular group of examinees involved?
2. How able are the examinees relative to this particular set of assessment procedures?
3. How difficult are the different rating categories relative to each other?
4. How relatively severe or lenient are the raters relative to each other?
5. How well are the students' scores dispersed?
6. How well are the scores in each category dispersed?
7. How highly related are the scores for rating categories with the total scores?
8. How highly related are the scores for each rating category with the scores for other categories?
9. How highly related are the scores assigned by one rater with the scores for other raters?
10. How reliable are the ratings?
11. How reliable are the scores when 1, 2, 3, 4, etc. raters are used?

12. How many raters do we need to achieve the level of reliability we want?
13. How much can we expect examinees' scores to vary by chance alone (particularly important near cut-points)?

For Examples of these basic statistical analyses, see the following tables and associated text: Chapter 5 (Tables 3–5), Chapter 6 (Tables 1–9), and Chapter 7 (1–3).

Understanding advanced analyses for rubric-based scores

Generalizability of rubric-based scores

The Spearman-Brown prophecy formula is sometimes used to estimate *what if* predictions for additional (or fewer) numbers of raters on one dimension. However, sometimes it is desirable to estimate what-if predictions for numbers of raters, numbers of categories, numbers of subtests, and so forth on multiple dimensions simultaneously. That is where generalizability theory comes in.

What-if predictions like these on multiple dimensions are particularly important and informative with regard to re-designing rubrics and assessment procedures in order to maximize the generalizability (analogous to the CTT concept of reliability) of the scores under the conditions that pertain at a particular institution. So let's consider generalizability theory in a bit more depth.

Generalizability studies

G-theory investigations are performed in two stages. The first is called the generalizability study (or G-study), where planning and calculating basic statistics (called variance components) takes place. In this stage, analysis of variance (ANOVA) procedures are used to isolate and estimate *variance components* (VCs) for each facet in the study and for all possible interactions of those facets. For example, Brown and Bailey (1984) presented a study of rubrics-based ratings for writing samples. That study was made up of three facets: persons (p), categories (c), and raters (r). The design was what is called a fully crossed design. The relationships between pairs of facets are either crossed or nested.

Crossed facets are those that are the same under all other facets. For example, if two raters rated the same essays using the *same* five categories (say organization, content, vocabulary, grammar, and mechanics), the categories would be *crossed* with raters (symbolized as $c \times r$, or cr). Categories are crossed with raters because the members of the subordinate categories are the *same* for each rater as follows:

rater	1					2				
categories	1	2	3	4	5	1	2	3	4	5

If the categories had been systematically different for each rater, categories would be labeled as *nested* within raters (or simply $c:r$). The fact that categories are nested within raters describes the relationship between categories and raters, which is nested because the members of the subordinate categories are *different* for each of the raters as follows:

rater	1					2				
categories	1	2	3	4	5	6	7	8	9	10

Examinees (or participants, or students) are typically called *persons* in G studies. In the Brown and Bailey (1984) rubric-based writing study, persons were said to be crossed with the other facets because all persons were assessed under the same conditions, that is, all persons wrote their essays under the same conditions and were rated for the same five categories (in this case, organization, logical development of ideas, grammar, mechanics, and quality of expression using the rubric shown in Table 2 of Chapter 2) by the same two raters. Thus, the G-study design in that paper is a persons crossed with categories crossed with raters ($p \times c \times r$, or pcr) design.

Once the G-study is clearly planned, most researchers use GENOVA (a suite of generalizability theory analysis programs available for free download from http://www.education.uiowa.edu/casma/GenovaPrograms.htm) to calculate analysis of variance (ANOVA) results and derive variance components from the means squares and degrees of freedom in the ANOVA (for more on the nuts and bolts of deriving the variance components from the ANOVA results, see Brennan, 1983, 2001).

Brown and Bailey (1984) report the variance components that they derived in this manner using GENOVA in its early mainframe computer version as shown in Table 6.

Table 6. Variance components and percentages of variance for p, r, c, pc, pr, cr, prc,e (adapted from Table 1 in Brown & Bailey, 1984)

variance sources	VC	% of variance
persons	1.95	29.02
categories	0.80	11.90
raters	0.16	2.38
pc	0.70	10.42
pr	1.17	17.41
cr	0.13	1.93
prc,e	1.81	26.93
total	6.72	99.99

Notice in Table 6 that the VC for persons is relatively large in real (1.95) and percentage (29.02%) terms compared with the other variance components and their interactions. Notice also the 11.90% of the variance is accounted for by differences among the categories and that variation among raters is actually fairly small at 2.38%. The pc, pr, and prc,e[1] interactions are interesting because they show that inconsistencies across categories among persons are creating 10.42% of the variance, while inconsistencies across raters among persons are accounting for more at 17.41%, and inconsistencies across both categories and raters among persons are even more influential accounting for 26.93% of the variance (plus error). These three interactions involving persons are all considered sources of error variance in relative (i.e., norm-referenced) decisions as opposed to dependable variance. Thus, through G-theory, it is possible to study and understand the relative contributions of different sources of error (pc, pr, and prc,e in this case) to the unreliability of a set of scores (and as we will show next, by extension, we can come to understand their relative impact on generalizability itself).

---

[1] The highest order interaction (or the most complex one), in this case prc, also contains undifferentiated error, thus the e in prc, e.

Decision studies

The VCs are the most important part of the G-study because they provide the basis for all calculations in the second stage Decision study (or D-study). In this part, the variance components are used to calculate generalizability coefficients for various combinations of numbers of each facet. Generalizability coefficients are analogous to reliability coefficients in classical test theory. In the Brown and Bailey (1984) *prc* study, the two facets of interest are categories and raters, so the authors calculated generalizability coefficients for various numbers of raters and categories. The goal of such a D-study is to understand the effects of numbers of categories and raters on generalizability so as to help in deciding on the best combination of numbers of categories and raters for a future, revised version of the assessment procedures and rubric in light of all the practical conditions and constraints (including other issues like the amount of time involved in administering, scoring, reporting the results, etc.).

Such generalizability estimates for norm-referenced tests are calculated using the general equation that follows:

$$E\rho^2(\delta) = \frac{\hat{\sigma}_p^2}{\hat{\sigma}_p^2 + \hat{\sigma}_e^2(\delta)}$$

Thus, the generalizability estimate is the ratio of estimated persons variance ($\hat{\sigma}_p^2$) to the estimated persons variance plus error variance ($\hat{\sigma}_p^2 + \hat{\sigma}_e^2(\delta)$). In the Brown and Bailey (1984) study, there were three facets [persons (*p*), categories (*c*), and raters (*r*)] and four possible interactions [*pc*, *pr*, *cr*, & *prc,e*]. Since only interactions that include *p* are used in calculating relative error (i.e., the type of error in norm-referenced tests), only the *pc*, *pr*, and *prc* interactions are used to calculate the error component in the generalizability estimates for norm-referenced purposes as follows:

$$\hat{\sigma}_e^2(\delta) = \frac{\hat{\sigma}_{pr}^2}{n_r} + \frac{\hat{\sigma}_{pc}^2}{n_c} + \frac{\hat{\sigma}_{prc,e}^2}{n_r n_c}$$

Notice that the *n* values in each of the denominators are included to adjust for varying numbers of raters and categories in this example. Substituting $\frac{\hat{\sigma}_{pr}^2}{n_r} + \frac{\hat{\sigma}_{pc}^2}{n_c} + \frac{\hat{\sigma}_{prc,e}^2}{n_r n_c}$ for the $\hat{\sigma}_e^2(\delta)$ in the generalizability estimate equation above, the formula for the generalizability coefficient becomes:

$$E\rho^2(\delta) = \frac{\hat{\sigma}_p^2}{\hat{\sigma}_p^2 + \frac{\hat{\sigma}_{pr}^2}{n_r} + \frac{\hat{\sigma}_{pc}^2}{n_c} + \frac{\hat{\sigma}_{prc,e}^2}{n_r n_c}}$$

Using the VCs from Brown and Bailey (1984) to calculate a generalizability coefficient for five categories (n_c=5) and two raters (n_r=2) involves substituting VC values for $\hat{\sigma}_p^2$, $\hat{\sigma}_{pc}^2$, $\hat{\sigma}_{pr}^2$, and $\hat{\sigma}_{prc,e}^2$ (1.95, .70, 1.17, and 1.81, respectively) into the equation and replace n_c with 5 and n_r with 2. The generalizability coefficient turns out to be about .68 as follows:

$$E\rho^2(\delta) = \frac{1.95}{1.95 + \frac{.70}{5} + \frac{1.17}{2} + \frac{1.81}{5(2)}} = .6827731 \approx .68$$

Table 7 shows the results using this equation for various numbers of categories and raters (or values of n_c and n_r). Notice in Table 7 that the generalizability for five categories and two raters is shown as .68, the result just calculated above. The other values in Table 7 were simply calculated by adjusting the values of n_c and n_r. With the variance components in hand, the whole process took about 30 minutes using the *Excel*™ spreadsheet program.

Table 7. Generalizability coefficients for different numbers of categories and raters (norm-referenced) (adapted from Brown & Bailey, 1984)

		\multicolumn{8}{c}{number of categories}

		1	2	3	4	5	10	15	20
number of raters	1	.35	.45	.49	.52	.54	.58	.59	.62
	2	.47	.58	.64	.66	.68	.70	.74	.75
	3	.54	.65	.70	.73	.76	.79	.80	.81
	4	.57	.69	.74	.77	.79	.83	.84	.85
	5	.60	.72	.77	.80	.81	.85	.87	.87
	10	.66	.78	.83	.85	.87	.90	.92	.92
	15	.68	.80	.85	.87	.89	.92	.94	.94
	20	.70	.81	.86	.88	.90	.93	.95	.95

Tables like that shown in Table 7 can be very useful for considering potential changes in assessment and rubric design because such tables show what is likely to occur if the numbers of raters and categories are varied in specific ways. For example, if we want to achieve generalizability of .75 at a minimum, we can see that we could do that with five categories and three raters or four categories and four raters, or three categories and five raters, and so forth. The final decision will depend on the conditions and priorities of the particular people and institution involved. However, G-theory does allow for making such decisions on a rational basis while simultaneously considering other issues like available resources, amount of time, stakes involved, number of other pieces of information, etc.

Questions G-theory can address

G-theory provides a useful set of tools that can help make decisions about revisions in rubrics and assessment procedures. In short, G-theory is particularly useful for answering questions like the following:

1. What is the relative importance of persons, raters, categories, and their interactions in producing variance?
2. How many raters should we use to generate generalizable norm-referenced scores?
3. How many rating categories should we use to produce generalizable norm-referenced scores?
4. What is the best trade-off between raters, rating categories, and practicality for producing generalizable norm-referenced scores?

For Examples of these G-theory analyses, see Chapter 7 (Tables 4–6) and associated text. For further examples of G-theory analyses of rubrics-based scores, see Bachman, Lynch, and Mason (1995); Brown (2008); Brown and Ahn (2011); Brown and Bailey (1984); Lee, (2005, 2006); Lee and Kantor (2005); Lynch and McNamara (1998), and Schoonen (2005).

Useful extensions of G-theory

In Chapter 7, Brown and Kondo-Brown report their variance components and percentages of variance in a manner similar to Table 6 above (see Tables 4 & 5 of Chapter 7) and provide their interpretation of those variance components in the prose associated with the two tables. In the D-study that follows their G-study, using the same general formula for the

G-coefficient that is shown above, they provide example calculations for the case of three raters and five categories as follows:

$$E\rho^2(\delta) = \frac{\hat{\sigma}_p^2}{\hat{\sigma}_p^2 + \frac{\hat{\sigma}_{pr}^2}{n_r} + \frac{\hat{\sigma}_{pc}^2}{n_c} + \frac{\hat{\sigma}_{prc,e}^2}{n_r n_c}}$$

$$E\rho^2(\delta) = \frac{4.6380782}{4.6380782 + \frac{.4692167}{3} + \frac{.3217313}{5} + \frac{.5456360}{3(5)}} = .947473595 \approx .947$$

Brown and Kondo-Brown also report generalizability estimates (for relative decisions) for different numbers of raters and categories (see Table 6 in Chapter 7). A full explanation for all of these initial D-study results is provided in Chapter 7.

We are summarizing the Chapter 7 results here because we want to illustrate how the D-study can be extended even further to provide useful analyses and results for rubrics-based assessments. For example, G-theory provides similar D-study procedures (with different VCs used to calculate error) for calculating dependability estimates for absolute decisions (i.e., criterion-referenced testing purposes).[2] G-theory also allows for calculating the dependability of assessment procedures at different cut-points for decision-making by using a statistic called phi(lambda), as well as a different way of interpreting dependability called signal-to-noise ratios.

D-studies for absolute decisions

For absolute decisions (i.e., for criterion-referenced decisions like diagnosis or achievement), the dependability estimate $[E\rho^2(\Delta)]$ with the error labeled upper-case delta error as follows:

$$E\rho^2(\Delta) = \frac{\hat{\sigma}_p^2}{\hat{\sigma}_p^2 + \hat{\sigma}_e^2(\Delta)}$$

Again, in this study, the facets are persons (p), categories (c), and raters (r), and their interactions are pc, pr, rc, and prc. Since all facets except the persons facet and all interactions contribute to error in absolute decisions, all except the persons facet are used in the calculating the error term as follows (recall that the n values in the denominators are used to adjust for varying numbers of raters and categories in this example):

$$\hat{\sigma}_e^2(\Delta) = \frac{\hat{\sigma}_r^2}{n_r} + \frac{\hat{\sigma}_c^2}{n_c} + \frac{\hat{\sigma}_{pr}^2}{n_r} + \frac{\hat{\sigma}_{pc}^2}{n_c} + \frac{\hat{\sigma}_{rc}^2}{n_r n_c} + \frac{\hat{\sigma}_{prc,e}^2}{n_r n_c}$$

Substituting $\frac{\hat{\sigma}_r^2}{n_r} + \frac{\hat{\sigma}_c^2}{n_c} + \frac{\hat{\sigma}_{pr}^2}{n_r} + \frac{\hat{\sigma}_{pc}^2}{n_c} + \frac{\hat{\sigma}_{rc}^2}{n_r n_c} + \frac{\hat{\sigma}_{prc,e}^2}{n_r n_c}$ for the $\hat{\sigma}_e^2(\Delta)$ in the dependability coefficient for relative decisions equation above:

$$E\rho^2(\Delta) = \frac{\hat{\sigma}_p^2}{\hat{\sigma}_p^2 + \frac{\hat{\sigma}_r^2}{n_r} + \frac{\hat{\sigma}_c^2}{n_c} + \frac{\hat{\sigma}_{pr}^2}{n_r} + \frac{\hat{\sigma}_{pc}^2}{n_c} + \frac{\hat{\sigma}_{rc}^2}{n_r n_c} + \frac{\hat{\sigma}_{prc,e}^2}{n_r n_c}}$$

---

[2] Note that the terminology has changed here a bit: these estimates are usually termed *dependability* estimates when they are applied to criterion-referenced tests for absolute decisions, but they are labeled *generalizability* coefficients when they are applied to norm-referenced tests for relative decisions.

For example, to calculate the dependability coefficient for three raters and five categories, we insert the VC values (from Table 5 in Chapter 7) for $\hat{\sigma}_p^2, \hat{\sigma}_r^2, \hat{\sigma}_c^2, \hat{\sigma}_{pr}^2, \hat{\sigma}_{pc}^2, \hat{\sigma}_{rc}^2$, and $\hat{\sigma}_{prc}^2$ (4.6380782, .0754414, .0028414, .4692167, .3217313, .0498768, and .5456360, respectively) into the equation and place the numbers 5 where n_c is found and 3 where n_r is found. The result is .942 as follows:

$$E\rho^2(\delta) = \frac{4.6380782}{4.6380782 + \frac{.0754414}{3} + \frac{.0028414}{5} + \frac{.4692167}{3} + \frac{.3217313}{5} + \frac{.0498768}{3(5)} + \frac{.5456360}{3(5)}}$$

$= .94188591 \approx .942$

The values in Table 8 were calculated using that same equation with various combinations of values for n_c and n_r. Looking across the top for the number of categories and down the left side for the number of raters, consider again the present assessment conditions, where five rubric categories and three raters were used and notice that the resulting dependability estimate (for absolute decisions) is .942 (in bold italics). Table 8 also indicates that the dependability (absolute) for five categories and two raters would be .921, but with five categories and one rater, it would be .864, and so forth. Thus this table can be used to consider various changes in the design and what their effects would likely be on the dependability of absolute (criterion-referenced) decisions. Again, the ultimate decision must be made depending on the conditions in the particular institution involved.

Table 8. Dependability coefficients (for absolute decisions, CRT) with different numbers of categories and raters

		category														
		1	2	3	4	5	6	7	8	9	10	11	12	13	14	15
rater	1	.760	.822	.845	.857	.864	.869	.873	.875	.878	.879	.881	.882	.883	.884	.884
	2	.838	.888	.906	.916	.921	.925	.928	.930	.931	.933	.934	.935	.935	.936	.937
	3	.868	.913	.929	.937	*.942*	.945	.948	.949	.951	.952	.953	.954	.954	.955	.955
	4	.884	.926	.940	.948	.953	.956	.958	.960	.961	.962	.963	.964	.964	.965	.965
	5	.894	.933	.948	.955	.959	.962	.964	.966	.967	.968	.969	.970	.970	.971	.971
	6	.900	.939	.952	.959	.964	.966	.968	.970	.971	.972	.973	.974	.974	.975	.975
	7	.905	.943	.956	.963	.967	.969	.971	.973	.974	.975	.976	.976	.977	.977	.978
	8	.909	.945	.958	.965	.969	.972	.974	.975	.976	.977	.978	.979	.979	.980	.980
	9	.911	.948	.960	.967	.971	.974	.976	.977	.978	.979	.980	.980	.981	.981	.982
	10	.914	.950	.962	.969	.972	.975	.977	.978	.979	.980	.981	.982	.982	.983	.983
	11	.915	.951	.963	.970	.974	.976	.978	.980	.981	.982	.982	.983	.983	.984	.984
	12	.917	.952	.965	.971	.975	.977	.979	.981	.982	.982	.983	.984	.984	.985	.985
	13	.918	.953	.966	.972	.976	.978	.980	.981	.982	.983	.984	.985	.985	.985	.986
	14	.920	.954	.966	.973	.976	.979	.981	.982	.983	.984	.985	.985	.986	.986	.987
	15	.920	.955	.967	.973	.977	.980	.981	.983	.984	.985	.985	.986	.986	.987	.987

Phi(lambda)

Measurement theory tells us that the dependability of decisions based on scores can vary considerably depending on where the decision cut-points are put on the scoring scale. Fortunately, a statistic exists for estimating the dependability of scores at various cut-points on any scale, which can be very useful for decision makers. The statistic is called the phi(lambda) dependability index, or $\Phi(\lambda)$, where lambda is the cut-point expressed as a proportion. Phi(lambda) is similar to a reliability coefficient in that it gives an estimate of the degree to which classifications into clear-cut categories (e.g., pass-fail, admit-deny, etc.) are consistent for making decisions at a particular cut-point.

One way to use $\Phi(\lambda)$ is to calculate it for different possible cut-points in order to decide where the cut-point might make the most sense. Table 9 presents the $\Phi(\lambda)$ estimates for different possible cut scores (when five categories and three raters are used in scoring). If the cut-score for a placement decision were at the mean of 70, the table indicates that the dependability would only be .836, that is, the lowest $\Phi(\lambda)$ shown in the table. We know that $\Phi(\lambda)$ is always lowest at the mean on the test (Brennan 1980, 1984). Since, the mean of the scores in this study was shown to be 70.06 in Table 9, it stands to reason that $\Phi(.70)$ (rounded from .7006) will be the lowest value of $\Phi(\lambda)$, or .836 in this case.

Table 9. Phi(lambda) dependability estimates for various cut-points

cut-point score	Phi(lambda)
95	$\Phi(.95)=$ .973
90	$\Phi(.90)=$ .962
85	$\Phi(.85)=$ .942
80	$\Phi(.80)=$ .910
75	$\Phi(.75)=$ .864
70	$\Phi(.70)=$ .836
65	$\Phi(.65)=$ .865
60	$\Phi(.60)=$ .911
55	$\Phi(.55)=$ .943
50	$\Phi(.50)=$ .962
45	$\Phi(.45)=$ .973
40	$\Phi(.40)=$ .981
35	$\Phi(.35)=$ .985
30	$\Phi(.30)=$ .988
25	$\Phi(.25)=$ .991
20	$\Phi(.20)=$ .992
15	$\Phi(.15)=$ .994
10	$\Phi(.10)=$ .995

Clearly then, putting at cut-point right at the mean score on any assessment is probably not a good idea. However a cut-point of 80 or above for placing students into the upper level would yield dependability of at least .910, and a cut-point of 60 or below for placement of students into the lower level would yield .911. Again, depending on the needs and distributions of abilities in a particular institution, this sort of information can help language professionals make rational decisions about the placement of cut-points so that ultimately the decisions they make based on the scores will be more dependable in practice. [For more on phi(lambda) and another example of its use, see Brown (2007).]

Signal-to-noise ratios

Brennan (1984, p. 306) suggests using *signal-to-noise ratios* as a "useful alternative coefficient for norm-referenced interpretations" (p. 306) and defines signal-to-noise ratios as follows: "The signal is intended to characterize the magnitude of the desired discriminations. Noise characterizes the effect of extraneous variables in blurring these discriminations. If the signal is large compared to the noise, the intended discriminations are easily made. If the signal is weak compared to the noise, the intended discriminations may be completely lost" (p. 306).

Table 10 shows the signal-to-noise ratios for various combinations of numbers of raters and categories for the data analyzed in Table 8. For example, the signal-to-noise ratio for five categories and three raters is 18.04, which means that there is about 18 times as much signal as there is noise. Think of it as a radio signal, would you be happy if the signal you were getting from your favorite FM program was 18 times as strong as the noise (or static)? We would. What about a five to one ratio (like the 5.14 for two categories and one rater), that's not so good, right? Aside from the fact that the signal-to-noise ratio is interpreted differently from the generalizability statistics discussed above, the reading of table is very similar to reading Tables 8.

Table 10. Signal-to-noise ratios (for relative decisions) with different numbers of categories and raters

		\multicolumn{15}{c}{category}
		1	2	3	4	5	6	7	8	9	10	11	12	13	14	15
rater	1	3.47	5.14	6.12	6.76	7.22	7.56	7.82	8.03	8.20	8.34	8.46	8.57	8.65	8.73	8.80
	2	5.59	8.72	10.72	12.10	13.12	13.90	14.51	15.01	15.43	15.77	16.07	16.32	16.54	16.74	16.91
	3	7.03	11.36	14.30	16.43	18.04	19.30	20.31	21.14	21.84	22.43	22.94	23.38	23.77	24.11	24.41
	4	8.06	13.39	17.18	20.01	22.20	23.95	25.38	26.57	27.57	28.43	29.18	29.83	30.40	30.91	31.37
	5	8.84	15.00	19.53	23.01	25.76	28.00	29.85	31.40	32.73	33.87	34.87	35.75	36.52	37.22	37.84
	6	9.45	16.30	21.50	25.57	28.86	31.56	33.82	35.74	37.39	38.82	40.08	41.19	42.18	43.07	43.87
	7	9.94	17.38	23.16	27.78	31.56	34.70	37.37	39.64	41.62	43.35	44.87	46.22	47.44	48.53	49.51
	8	10.34	18.29	24.59	29.71	33.94	37.51	40.56	43.19	45.48	47.50	49.29	50.89	52.32	53.62	54.79
	9	10.67	19.06	25.83	31.40	36.06	40.03	43.44	46.41	49.02	51.32	53.38	55.22	56.88	58.38	59.75
	10	10.96	19.73	26.91	32.90	37.96	42.30	46.07	49.36	52.27	54.86	57.17	59.25	61.13	62.85	64.41
	11	11.20	20.31	27.87	34.23	39.67	44.36	48.46	52.07	55.27	58.13	60.70	63.02	65.12	67.04	68.80
	12	11.42	20.83	28.72	35.43	41.21	46.24	50.66	54.56	58.05	61.17	63.99	66.54	68.87	70.99	72.95
	13	11.60	21.28	29.48	36.51	42.62	47.96	52.67	56.87	60.62	64.01	67.07	69.85	72.39	74.72	76.87
	14	11.77	21.69	30.17	37.50	43.90	49.53	54.54	59.01	63.02	66.65	69.95	72.96	75.71	78.24	80.57
	15	11.91	22.05	30.79	38.39	45.07	50.99	56.26	60.99	65.26	69.13	72.66	75.88	78.84	81.57	84.09

Questions that extensions of G-theory can address

Extensions of G-theory provide additional useful tools that can help in making decisions about revisions in rubrics, assessment procedures, and cut-points, and may prove useful for answering questions like the following:

1. How many raters should we use to generate dependable criterion-referenced scores?
2. How many rating categories should we use to produce dependable criterion-referenced scores?
3. What is the best trade-off between raters, rating categories, and practicality for producing dependable criterion-referenced scores?
4. What is the relative dependability of decisions made at different possible cut-points?
5. How much clear, informative variance (signal) is being produced by the assessment procedures compared to random, meaningless variance (noise)?

Examples of these extensions of G-theory are provided above, but you can also find examples and further explanations in Brown (2007).

Multifaceted Rasch analysis

McNamara (1996) proposes that consideration be given to the effect of the presence of the rater in the performance assessment process. He also advocates examining other possible sources of influence on patterns of test scores in addition to the candidate and rater characteristics, and he conceptualizes such influences in performance assessment as *facets*, or aspects of the assessment setting. The interactions of these facets, McNamara claims, may determine the likelihood of particular test scores. Making a clear distinction between *raw scores* on the one hand and what they are thought to indicate of the latent, or underlying, abilities of the candidates, known technically as *measures*. Analyses called *multifaceted Rasch measurement* can be performed using a computer program known as FACETS (Linacre, 2008) to compensate for aspects of the test situation which vary from candidate to candidate.

In performance-based assessment, the instrument elicits a performance or behavior which is then judged or rated, by means of a rubric, requiring that raters interact with the rubric, and this interaction can affect the scoring of the examinee's performance. The multifaceted Rasch approach accepts that the most appropriate aim of rater training is to make raters internally consistent. Internal consistency among raters will make statistical modeling of their characteristics possible. This approach also accepts variability in stable rater characteristics as a fact of life. In order for scores to be stable and fair, assessment designers should account for any such variability in some way, either through multiple marking and averaging of scores, or by using the more sophisticated techniques of multifaceted Rasch measurement, which can simultaneously examine how the variables like the examinees, raters, and categories affect the scores individually and relative to each other.

The FACETS computer program is available for download at http://www.winsteps.com/facets.htm (for $149.00 at the moment) and is designed, according to the website, "to handle really tough applications of unidimensional Rasch measurement. It constructs measures from complex data involving heterogeneous combinations of examinees, items, tasks, judges along with further measurement and structural facets."

Rasch multifaceted measurement defined

In multifaceted Rasch analysis (hereafter referred to as Rasch analysis), item difficulties and candidate or person abilities (often collectively referred to as locations) are generated and reported on a logit[3] scale. The scale expresses probabilities of response as a logarithm of the naturally occurring constant e. It is an interval which allows locations (of items and persons) to be determined individually and/or in relation to other items, persons, or locations. Therefore, all the items, student abilities, and rater performances can be located on a common scale.

The mean of item difficulties (i.e., the difficulty of the test) is arbitrarily set at zero. Items that are more difficult than the mean are positive in sign and those easier than the mean are negative. In practice, the more difficult items have values of around +2 or higher and the much easier items have values of –2 or lower. Person abilities are mapped on the same scale as item difficulty. A person of ability zero (the mean) has a 50% chance of getting correct an item of zero difficulty, and a higher chance of getting an item incorrect if the item difficulty is less than zero. The probability of getting the item correct increases as the item difficulty decreases, and the probability of getting the item correct decreases as the item difficulty increases.

Rasch analysis is used to examine the degree to which variables and levels of those variables produce different scores relative to each other—all on the same logit scale. Thus, these analyses can simultaneously examine the degree to which different raters are severe or lenient and rating categories are difficult or easy.

In the explanation that follows, we will use examples from the Housman, Dameg, Kobashigawa, and Brown study in Chapter 6. That study describes the development of a rubric for scoring an oral storytelling task for 270 elementary school learners of Hawaiian. Each student was rated by one of five raters. The rubric had seven categories with three points possible in each of the categories. There were four parts to the assessment procedure: Introduction, Lei Series, Slipper Series, and Short Oral Response items. Each student went through the Introduction interview (which was rated using the rubric) and either the Lei Series of pictures, or the Slipper Series. Then they were presented with the Oral Response items. We will focus on the analysis of the Introduction interview results (where n=270) as an example of the sorts of things that can be learned from Rasch analysis of rubrics-based data.

Fit statistics

Because Rasch analysis of item difficulties and person abilities can only be appropriately interpreted if the data fit the Rasch model, we must begin by considering the information provided by FACETS for *examinee fit, rater fit,* and *category fit. Examinee fit* describes how well individuals' responses to all items in a test corresponded to the pattern of responses exhibited by all other participants in the same test. Rater fit describes how well individual raters' scores adhered to an expected pattern of responses for all raters. Category fit describes how well individual categories adhered to an expected pattern of responses for all categories. Examinees, raters, or categories not fitting the predicted pattern of responses are termed *misfitting* and this often indicates (a) examinees with abilities outside the possible range of scores or other examinee issues (like fatigue, inattention, etc.), (b) raters with insufficient training or attention to the task, or (c) categories with poorly written descriptors.

Table 11. Fit analyses for introduction for examinee, rater, & category facets (adapted from Table 10 in Chapter 6)

introduction facet	# misfit	RMSE	separation	reliability	Chi-square (fixed)
examinees	7	.89	2.50	.82	$p=.00$
raters	0	.12	.25	.06	$p=.36$
categories	0	.14	13.59	.99	$p=.00$

[3] The term *logit* is derived from *log odds* of a response, i.e., log odds units.

Table 11 gives the misfit results for the Introduction interview scores including five statistics: # Misfit, RMSE, Separation, Reliability, and Chi-square (fixed). The # *Misfit* shows the number of examinees, raters, or categories that "did not fit the general pattern of responses in the matrix, and can thus be classified as relatively misfitting..." (McNamara, 1996, p. 171). Notice that there were seven misfitting examinees. In this case, this result tells us that these seven examinees did not fit the measurement model because their response patterns were not as expected. RMSE stands for *root mean square standard error*, which is used to calculate the separation index discussed in the next paragraph and is used to estimate the standard error. The lower the RMSE the better the data fit the measurement model. The RMSE values in Table 11 range from .12 to .89 so they are relatively high indicating that none of these facets are fitting the model as well as might be desired. The *separation* index indicates the degree to which the examinees, raters, and categories spread out relative to their degree of precision (Linacre, 2008, p. 149). The higher the separation index value, the more effectively each facet is spreading its elements out. In this case, the separation index for categories is much higher than the other values and indeed the value for raters is very low (indicating that the raters are clustering together in their scoring). The *reliability* estimates would be more accurately labeled *separation reliabilities*. For instance, the moderately high reliability for examinees (.82) indicates that the examinees consistently differ from each other, which is what we are generally trying to achieve in a norm-referenced testing situation like the one described in Chapter 6. In contrast, the low reliability for raters (.06) can be viewed as a positive indicator showing that the raters are not consistently different from each other in terms of the severity or leniency of their ratings. The reliability for categories (.99) indicates that the categories consistently differ from each other in difficulty to a very high degree, which probably means that they are consistently doing different things (not a bad characteristic at all). In the *chi-square (fixed)* analyses, the examinees and categories facets chi-square statistics for the Introduction scores were significant ($p<.01$), while the chi-square for raters was not. All of this simply means that the examinees probably differed from each other in ability for reasons other than chance; that the categories did the same; and, that the raters probably differed from each for reasons that can only be attributed to chance.

Vertical rulers

In Chapter 6, three facets were included: examinees, raters, and categories. The Rasch analysis puts all three facets on a common logit scale called a vertical ruler. This vertical ruler makes it easy to compare the elements of the three facets. Thus in the vertical ruler shown in Figure 2 for the Introduction interviews, we can see how examinees abilities varied, how severe or lenient raters were, and how difficult or easy the different categories were. On the logit scale a higher score equals a positive logit, that is, a higher measure. Similarly, a lower score equals a negative logit, that is, a lower measure. In more detail, notice that the first column in the vertical ruler contains the measure scores. This scale is shown in logit scores where the mean is 0 and the range is –/+ 5 (in this case). Column 2 indicates where examinees fell on the scale. There is one asterisk for every 3 examinees (as labeled at the bottom of the column) and one dot for individual examinees. Columns 3 and 4 show where the five raters (R1, R2, R3, R4, & R5) and seven categories [Communicative Skill (Com), Vocabulary (Voc), Grammar (Gra), Pronunciation (Pro), Fluency (Flu), Steadfastness (Ste), and Cultural Authenticity (Cul)] fit on the scale. Column 5 describes where the raw scores fit along the logit scale.

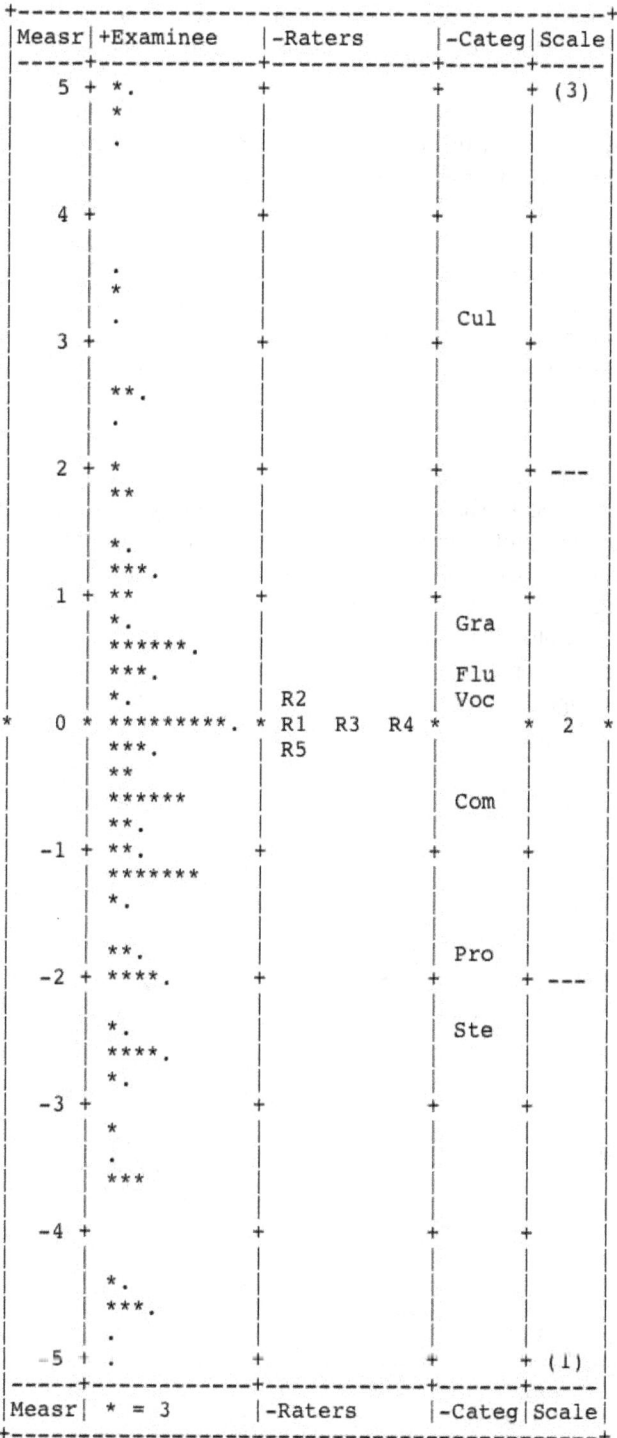

Figure 2. Vertical ruler for the introduction (Figure 1a from chapter 6).

Notice on the Introduction interview vertical ruler that examinee scores ranged reasonably well from +5 to –5 indicating that their ability levels were widely dispersed. In the column for raters, note that R2 was the most severe, R5 was the most lenient, and R1, R3, and R4 fell in between. More importantly, the differences among raters were clearly very small. As for categories, they clearly ranged quite a bit in difficulty. Cul was at about the same level as examinees with scores a bit above +3 logits so this category was difficult in the sense that the ratings tended to be low. In contrast, the Ste ratings were at the same level as examinees who scored between –2 and –3 logits so the ratings in this category were high. The other five categories in descending order of difficulty were: Gra, Flu, Voc, Com, and Pro. Column 5 tells us how raw ratings 1, 2, and 3 matched up to the true interval logit scores on the far left for the Introduction interview ratings overall. The fact that all three score ranges are about the same indicates that the entire range of 1–3 was being used in approximately equal intervals by the raters.

Probability curves

Rasch analysis also provides what are called *probability curves*. These curves are useful because they graphically show the degree to which the points on the rating scale are discrete or overlapping. The probability curves for the Introduction interviews are shown in Figure 3. The ideal for scales that have discrete points would be no overlap at all. However, we have never seen that in practice. The best that we can hope for would be probability curves that have a distinct hill-like appearance with some, but not too much, overlap between hills. The curves for Introduction interview in Figure 3 appear to be reasonably separate and hill-like with some overlap.

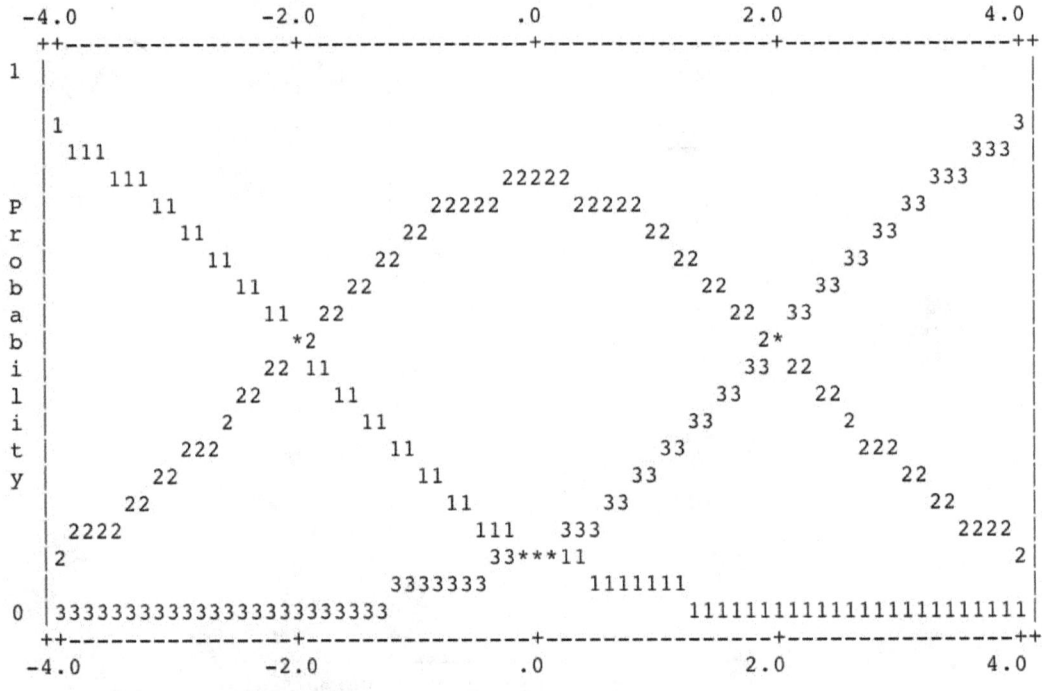

Figure 3. Introduction probability curves (Figure 3a in Chapter 6).

Bias analysis
One extension of Rasch analysis that can usefully be applied to rubric-based assessment results is called bias analysis. *Bias analysis* is applied using the FACETS program to carefully examine the interactions of the facets under analysis. For instance, the interactions of persons and raters, persons and categories, and raters and categories could usefully have been used to examine the rubric-based results in Chapters 5 and 6. For an actual example of a bias analysis of rubrics-based data, see Kondo-Brown (2002).

Questions that Rasch analysis can address
Clearly then, Rasch analysis can be very useful for analyzing the results of rubrics-based assessments and for answering questions like the following:

1. How are the performances of examinees, raters, and categories related when they are put on the same logit scale?
2. How able are the examinees relative to the rubric categories, and vice versa?
3. To what degree are the different raters scoring in the same ways?
4. How severe or lenient are the raters relative to each other?
5. To what degree are the different categories producing similar scores?
6. How difficult or easy are the categories relative to each other?
7. How well are the different scores on the scale differentiated from each other?
8. To what degree are the raters and rating categories biased (i.e., interacting)?

For examples of Rasch analyses of rubrics based scales, see the following tables and associated text: Chapter 5 (Figures 4–7 and Tables 6–9) and Chapter 6 (Tables 10 and Figures 1a–2c). For further examples of Rasch analyses of rubrics-based scores, see Brown (2011), Brown, Hudson, Norris, & Bonk (2002, pp. 54–60), and Kondo-Brown (2002).

Conclusion

In each of the sections above, we have suggested the types of research questions that each form of analysis can address. Table 12 summarizes those questions by listing them and identifying which type of analysis and exact statistic or analysis will generally be most appropriate for answering each question. Explanations for each are provided above as well as references to other chapters and resources that may help in applying them.

Consider a question like the fifth one: "How well are the students' scores dispersed?" Table 11 recommends that you use the classical test theory examinee standard deviation to address this question. Since, by definition, the standard deviation does indeed indicate the degree to which the scores are dispersed, or spread out, that recommendation seems reasonable. Conversely, the table can be used the other way around to figure out what type of question a statistic or analysis in the right hand column is suited for asking. For example, according to Table 11, the signal-to-noise ratio in the ninth row from the bottom on the right can be used to answer the following question: How much clear, informative variance (signal) is being produced by the assessment procedures compared to random, meaningless variance (noise)?

We hope that this chapter will help readers understand the studies presented in Chapters 5, 6, and 7. We also hope that this chapter will help readers think through not only minimum ways to statistically analyze their rubric-based assessment results, but also new ways of doing such analyses and new sorts of questions that can be addressed. If so, we will have succeeded.

Table 12. Guide for selecting the type of analysis and exact statistic or analysis needed for answering key questions in rubric-based assessment

research question	type of analysis	exact statistic or analysis
How easy or difficult is this set of assessment procedures for the particular group of examinees involved?	CTT	score mean
How able are the examinees relative to this particular set of assessment procedures?	CTT	examinee mean
How difficult are the different rating categories relative to each other?	CTT	category mean
How relatively severe or lenient are the raters relative to each other?	CTT	rater means
How well are the students' scores dispersed?	CTT	examinee standard deviation
How well are the scores in each category dispersed?	CTT	category standard deviations
How highly related are the scores for rating categories with the total scores?	CTT	correlation coefficients
How highly related are the scores for each rating category with the scores for other categories?	CTT	correlation coefficients
How highly related are the scores assigned by one rater with the scores for other raters?	CTT	correlation coefficients
How reliable are the ratings?	CTT	interrater reliability or Chronbach alpha
How reliable are the scores when 1, 2, 3, 4, etc. raters are used?	CTT	Spearman-Brown prophecy formula
How many raters do we need to achieve the level of reliability we want?	CTT	Spearman-Brown prophecy formula
How much can we expect examinees' scores to vary by chance alone (particularly important near cut-points)?	CTT	standard error of measurement
What is the relative importance of persons, raters, categories & their interactions in producing variance?	G-theory	generalizability study variance components
How many raters should we use to generate dependable norm-referenced scores?	G-theory	G coefficients (for relative error) in a D-study
How many rating categories should we use to produce dependable norm-referenced scores?	G-theory	G coefficients (for relative error) in a D-study
What is the best trade-off between raters, rating categories, & practicality for producing dependable norm-referenced scores?	G-theory	G coefficients (for relative error) in a D-study

How many raters should we use to generate dependable criterion-referenced scores?	G-theory	G coefficients (for absolute error) in a D-study
How many rating categories should we use to produce dependable criterion-referenced scores?	G-theory	G coefficients (for absolute error) in a D-study
What is the best trade-off between raters, rating categories, & practicality for producing dependable criterion-referenced scores?	G-theory	G coefficients (for absolute error) in a D-study
What is the relative dependability of decisions made at different possible cut-points?	G-theory	Phi(lambda) for different possible cut-points
How much clear, informative variance (signal) is being produced by the assessment procedures compared to random, meaningless variance (noise)?	G-theory	signal-to-noise ratio
How are the performances of examinees, raters, & categories related when they are put on the same logit scale?	Rasch facets	vertical ruler & associated statistics
How able are the examinees relative to the rubric categories, & vice versa?	Rasch facets	vertical ruler & associated statistics
To what degree are the different raters scoring in the same ways?	Rasch facets	vertical ruler & associated statistics
How severe or lenient are the raters relative to each other?	Rasch facets	vertical ruler & associated statistics
To what degree are the different categories producing similar scores?	Rasch facets	vertical ruler & associated statistics
How difficult or easy are the categories relative to each other?	Rasch facets	vertical ruler & associated statistics
How well are the different scores on the scale differentiated from each other?	Rasch facets	probability curves
To what degree are the raters & rating categories biased (i.e., interacting)?	Rasch facets	bias analysis

References

Bachman, L. F. (2004). *Statistical analyses for language assessment*. Cambridge, UK: Cambridge University.

Bachman, L. F., Lynch, B. K., & Mason, M. (1995). Investigating variability in tasks and rater judgments in a performance test of foreign language speaking. *Language Testing, 12*(2), 239–257.

Brennan, R. L. (1980). Applications of generalizability theory. In R. A. Berk (Ed.), *Criterion-referenced measurement: The state of the art* (pp. 186–232). Baltimore: Johns Hopkins.

Brennan, R. L. (1983). *Elements of generalizability theory*. Iowa City: ACT Publications.

Brennan, R. L. (1984). Estimating the dependability of scores. In R. L. Brennan (Ed.), *A guide to criterion-referenced test construction* (pp. 231–266). Baltimore: Johns Hopkins.

Brennan, R. L. (2001). *Generalizability theory*. New York: Springer.

Brown, J. D. (2005). *Testing in language programs: A comprehensive guide to English language assessment* (New edition). New York: McGraw-Hill.

Brown, J. D. (2007). Multiple views of L1 writing score reliability. *Second Language Studies, 25*(2), 1–31. Also retrieved from the World Wide Web at http://www.hawaii.edu/sls/uhwpesl/25(2)/BrownWritingGstudy.pdf

Brown, J. D. (2008). Raters, functions, item types, and the dependability of L2 pragmatic tests. In E. Alcón Soler & A. Martínez-Flor (Eds.), *Investigating pragmatics in foreign language learning, teaching and testing* (pp. 224–248). Clevedon, UK: Multilingual Matters.

Brown, J. D., & Ahn, R. C. (2011). Variables that affect the dependability of L2 pragmatics tests. *Journal of Pragmatics, 43*(1), 198–217.

Brown, J. D., & Bailey, K. M. (1984). A categorical instrument for scoring second language writing skills. *Language Learning, 34*, 21–42.

Brown, J. D., Hudson, T., Norris, J. M., & Bonk, W. (2002). *An investigation of second language task-based performance assessments*. Honolulu: Second Language Teaching & Curriculum Center, University of Hawai'i.

Kondo-Brown, K. (2002). An analysis of rater bias with FACETS in measuring Japanese L2 writing performance. *Language Testing, 19*, 1–29.

Lee, Y.-W, & Kantor, R. (2005). *Dependability of ESL writing test scores: Evaluating prototype tasks and alternative rating schemes*. TOEFL Monograph MS-31. Princeton, NJ: ETS.

Lee, Y.-W. (2005). *Dependability of scores for a new ESL speaking test: Evaluating prototype tasks*. TOEFL Monograph MS-28. Princeton, NJ: ETS.

Lee, Y.-W. (2006). Dependability of scores for a new ESL speaking assessment consisting of integrated and independent tasks. *Language Testing, 23*(2), 131–166.

Linacre, J. M. (2008). *User's guide to FACETS: Rasch-model computer programs*. Chicago: Author.

Lynch, B. K., & McNamara, T. F. (1998). Using G-theory and many-facet Rasch measurement in the development of performance assessments of the ESL speaking skills of immigrants. *Language Testing 15*, 158–180.

McNamara, T. F. (1996). *Measuring second language performance*. New York: Longman.

Schoonen, R. (2005). Generalizability of writing scores: An application of structural equation modeling. *Language Testing, 22*(1), 1–30.

Section III:
Case studies in Asian and Pacific languages

Māori Language Proficiency in Writing: The Kaiaka Reo Year Eight Writing Test

Catherine (Katarina) Anne Edmonds
University of Hawai'i at Hilo

Introduction

Kaiaka Reo Year Eight Writing refers specifically to the test at the core of this chapter, which was part of a larger test development process that resulted from Aotearoa-New Zealand government recognition that there was a need for a Māori language proficiency tool that could be used in Māori medium settings. It was developed within a kaupapa Māori paradigm that takes into account the historical impact of colonisation and education that led to the decline and loss of the Māori language from the 1840s to the present day (for a list of teacher education programmes for Māori medium education, see Edmonds, 2008 Appendix A or Ministry of Education, 2008; for a thorough chronicaling of the historical events involved, as well as for interesting discussions of Māori medium assessment and the genesis of thinking about Māori language proficiency and developing tools to measure such proficiency, see Edmonds, 2008).

Attention in this chapter will focus on the rubric-based writing test itself including its developmental process as well as investigation of its reliability and validity. Two distinct phases are discussed in detail. Kaiaka Reo Phase One, a process that began in 1999 and continued into 2001. This process involved the conceptualisation, development, pilot, trial, and initial analysis of the Kaiaka Reo Year Eight writing test. Kaiaka Reo Phase Two is concerned with the process of determining the reliability and validity of the Kaiaka Reo Year Eight Writing Test 2006–2008.

In 1999–2001, the New Zealand Ministry of Education under its assessment strategy commissioned the University of Waikato to develop a Māori language proficiency assessment tool in the form of proficiency tests for Year Five and Year Eight Māori immersion students. This programme of work became known as Kaiaka Reo. The task of developing the tests was to be undertaken by a development team from *Te Pua Wānanga ki te Ao* (The School of

Māori and Pacific Development). These comprised a battery of six test sets for Year Five and one test set for Year Eight. Each test set had four components: listening, speaking, reading, and writing.

Kaiaka Reo Year Eight writing

The Kaiaka Reo Year Eight writing test was built on the assumption that the first administration generated information and data that accurately reflected the language competency of the students. The communicative language abilities represented by a sample of forty Year Eight Māori medium students (from the original test population of approximately 200 students) contributed to the scoring rubric of an analytical rating scale which a group of Māori educators used to rate the communicative language performance of the students.

A priority for Māori stakeholders is "*Ko te tū tangata o te ākonga i te ao Māori, i te ao whānui anō hoki*" (Ministry of Education, 2000, p. 7). This means that it is incumbent on any education initiative in Māori to ensure that the pedagogies and practices that their children engage in will enable them to stand tall in the Māori world, as well as in the wider society nationally and internationally. Kaiaka Reo is no exception. It too must demonstrate that it is reliable and valid in Māori society, New Zealand society, and the global context.

The purpose of this chapter, therefore, is to describe the developmental process as well as investigate the reliability and validity of the Kaiaka Reo Year Eight test in writing as a tool to establish the Māori language writing proficiencies of Year Eight students in primary school Māori medium settings in New Zealand. The knowledge gained about the language proficiency (in writing) of students from Māori medium settings will have important implications for Māori curriculum development in New Zealand. This initial effort to establish the reliability and validity of Māori language proficiency testing will inform future proficiency testing of the Māori language and provide support and a precedent for other indigenous groups, who like Māori, are developing epistemologies and processes about themselves, for themselves, in their own native languages.

Under the Ministry of Education directive, the test developers of Te Pua Wānanga ki te Ao determined that the main purpose of the proficiency tests was to reflect the underlying Māori language competence of the students. The test items were to take cognisance of theory related to second language testing and methodology (including grammatical competence, discourse competence, and phonological competence) as well as Māori culture. It was also necessary to be sensitive to the cognitive abilities and skills that could be expected of young students in taking tests. The writer of this chapter managed the 2000–2001 Kaiaka Reo programme.

Te Pua Wānanga ki te Ao commenced the testing process by hiring experts external to the University of Waikato in the areas of cognitive theory and language testing, and in curriculum development in countries involved in language revitalisation, in order to critique and advance the 1999 process. This review informed the development of the new tests and confirmed that the process should be underpinned by Māori philosophy. In addition to that initial critique, the team was fully informed and kept on track by non-Māori experts in areas where we lacked expertise, such as the area of testing. The non-Māori experts, teachers in Māori medium settings, academics in education institutes, and all stakeholders were represented on our Advisory Committee.

Māori medium test materials were developed for the 2001 Year Five and Year Eight students in Level 1 total immersion Māori medium schools. Particular language competencies in listening and reading were assessed indirectly using multiple-choice items. When it came to the productive components of speaking and writing, the students were presented with a picture sequence that required the production of spoken language or written language as appropriate to describe the sequence of events.

The written test required the students to write about the life cycle of the tuatara, a lizard-like reptile of ancient lineage that is native to New Zealand. These tasks were purported to be based on the abilities of students according to their years of schooling, as indicated in the national Māori language curriculum statement (Ministry of Education, 1996).

Although the Kaiaka Reo test development programme was conducted in 2000–2001, the analyses of the reliability and validity of the productive modes of speaking and writing were not carried out at that time because the Kaiaka Reo Team did not have the testing background. The intention was that the New Zealand Council of Education Research (NZCER) would conduct the analyses for reliability and validity. However, at the time that the analysis was due to be carried out, NZCER acknowledged that they did not have the Māori language capacity to analyse the students' written responses to determine authentic Māori language proficiency. Thus the assessment of the student performance on the tests remained a score that had been converted to a band score, based on the overall scores of the total population that participated and was not further analysed. What was needed therefore was an a posteriori process to determine the reliability and validity of the proficiency test Kaiaka Reo Year Eight Writing. This process would affirm that it is possible to develop a reliable and valid test for Māori, or indeed any indigenous language being revitalised in total immersion schools, using tests in that language which were linguistically and culturally appropriate.

This study is concerned with, and restricted to, the investigation of the reliability and validity of the Kaiaka Reo Year Eight Māori language test for assessing Māori language proficiency in writing. The study is carried out against a backdrop of *kaupapa Māori* principles and worldwide indigenous language and culture revitalisation movement.

Statement of purpose Kaiaka Reo Year Eight

The purpose of this chapter is to assess the degree to which the Kaiaka Reo Year Eight test in writing, that was developed *by Māori for Māori in te reo Māori* in 2000–2001, is a reliable and valid tool to determine the Māori language proficiency (in writing) of Year Eight students in Māori medium primary school settings in New Zealand.

At a statistical level, the research is concerned with the ability of an analytical rubric-based scale to verify the reliability of rater performance in terms of their internal consistency and performance across all sub-components of Māori language proficiency using a multifaceted Rasch model of measurement. The model will demonstrate how the raters performed according to the model's expectations as shown through fit statistics. Although the analysis will show that some of the categories are easier, and some more difficult, these will be consistent with what is expected of Rasch analysis.

The descriptors of proficiency adapted from Brown (2005, p. 56) include the following: Organisation and Ideas; Grammar and Accuracy; Punctuation, Spelling and Mechanics; Style and Quality of Expression; and Māori Discourse Intelligibility. The descriptor Māori Discourse Intelligibility is an addition to the scale. These descriptors are agreeable with Māori perceptions of what constitutes proficiency. Level descriptors from one to four are provided that expand on the categories stated above. Together, these provide a basis for rating decisions of student writing by Māori medium educators.

This chapter is based on the premise that *kaupapa Māori* (Māori philosophical principles) is integral to any proficiency testing for the Māori language. To not use kaupapa Māori, would be to render the testing invalid.

In order to achieve the purposes of this project, the following three research questions were posed:

1. To what degree is the Kaiaka Reo Year Eight writing test a reliable assessment tool for assessing the Māori language proficiency of year eight students in Māori medium settings?

2. To what degree is the Kaiaka Reo Year Eight writing test a valid assessment tool for assessing the Māori language proficiency of year eight students in Māori medium settings?

3. How will the study improve the Kaiaka Reo Year Eight writing test?

None of the discussion above exists in a vacuum; therefore an overarching concern for this chapter is the appropriateness of the conceptualisations of reliability and validity for determining Māori language proficiency. In particular, the Māori language proficiency of 11–13 year old students at Year Eight learning through the medium of Māori in a society where English is dominant in the community and visually (such as most media) in the home as well. Many issues of language background, for example, years of attendance at Kōhanga Reo, and the quality of teaching in kura kaupapa Māori, and the influence of English, the dominant language, in Māori and mainstream contexts in New Zealand society are known to impact the second language student of Māori. These issues are an integral part, however, of interpreting student performance and arguing for the validity of Kaiaka Reo Year Eight Writing.

Furthermore, a posteriori analysis for reliability and validity is justifiable in the evolution and explication of Māori language proficiency for the present situation where the Māori community wishes to measure its progress in developing the proficiency of their young Māori language learners in their traditional ancestral language.

Kaiaka Reo Phase One

Background to Kaiaka Reo Phase One

Kaiaka Reo was born out of policy from the New Zealand government's Ministry of Māori Development and Ministry of Education, namely the Māori language and Māori education strategic plan in the year 1999. Policy at that time saw a need for assessment materials for the Māori language, and the Ministry of Education therefore contracted Te Pua Wānanga ki te Ao of the University of Waikato to develop an initial set of proficiency tests for Year Five (9–10 year old pupils) in Māori-medium schooling. Within a three-month period, a small team from Te Pua Wānanga ki te Ao managed to conduct a scoping study that surveyed the linguistic background of pupils in Māori-medium, and then created a proficiency test that could be used diagnostically. They also created a "pedagogically motivated description of the test language" that would help in curriculum development (Bishop, 1996, p. 11). In the year 2000, the Ministry decided to move that work along and commissioned SMPD to further develop the tool. This chapter analyses the Kaiaka Reo Year Eight 2001 writing test that was developed and administered to students, whose numbers were nearly equivalent to 70% of the Level One Māori medium students in primary schools in 2001. The program of work originally had a life span of 13 months, which was extended to 18 months.

The Kaiaka Reo Team were driven by a philosophy not unlike that stated by Durie (1998, p. 79):

> While there is a role for the state, it is essentially a facilitatory one....Māori leaders have insisted that Māori knowledge, and Māori heritage generally belong to Māori and must form the seed from which positive Māori development can grow.

Children may attend 'kura' (school) upon their fifth birthday, this being Year 1. Table 1 sets out the comparative ages and levels for New Zealand primary education and the United States elementary levels.

Table 1. Age and level grades of New zealand primary schools and United States elementary schools

age	NZ year level	US grade level
5–6	1	K
6–7	2	1
7–8	3	2
8–9	4	3
9–10	5	4
10–11	6	5
11–12	7	6
12–13	8	7

The Year Five and Year Eight schools who participated in the 2001 testing programme were self-selected in that the Kaiaka Reo Team had decided to include every Māori immersion school that indicated a wish to participate. Despite the financial constraints, the Advisory Committee felt that *He whakataurekareka i te iwi*, that is, it would be culturally demeaning, more culturally insensitive, and culturally demoralising to invite the schools to participate only to turn around and advise some that they were surplus to the requirements of sampling. Furthermore, the Māori immersion population is not large: only 65 schools qualified as such in the year 2001. Forty-four schools elected to participate, 65–70% of the targeted population.

Background of Kaiaka Reo participants

The information presented here relates to a total of 202 Year Eight Māori students from 44 Level 1 immersion schools, comprising 65% of the Māori immersion schools that participated in the overall testing process conducted nationwide in New Zealand in the year 2001.

Table 2 indicates that these students were mostly in the 11 to 13 year age range, with almost equal numbers of girls (49.5%) and boys (50.5%) (Littler, 2001, p. 5).

Table 2. Background information on year eight students Kaiaka Reo 2001

number of students (%)	years in Kohanga Reo	total
0–1	7 (4%)	
1–2	16 (9%)	
2–3	43 (25%)	
3–4	73 (42%)	
4–5	35 (20%)	174 (100%)
	years learning Māori	
0–1	3 (3%)	
1–2	7 (4%)	
2–3	11 (6%)	
3–4	16 (8%)	
4+	159 (81%)	196 (100%)
	gender	
female	100 (49.5%)	
male	102 (50.5%)	202 (100%)

Almost all the students had attended Kōhanga Reo, 62% having three or more years there. Of these students 81%, had spent four or more years learning in the medium of Māori (Littler, 2001, p. 4). Only 165 students were used in the sample for final analysis because of cases of missing data. The results of their performance were ranked into four quartiles, A, B, C, and D. The top 25%, being the first quartile, were classified as A, the next 25% B, and so on. The student performances analysed in this report number 40, ten from each of the bands, their scores being the nearest to the midpoints of the four quartiles. Therefore, the descriptions that follow relate only to those forty participants. This procedure was used to obtain a sample representative of all levels and for no other purpose.

The forty participants come from the 165 students, from 20 of the 44 schools that participated in the overall testing process with a good regional spread from Kaikohe in the far north of the North Island to Christchurch in the South Island. All the schools were Level One, that is, 80–100% immersion in the Māori language. The schools within the sample range from small rural country schools with class numbers of six students, to larger town schools with class numbers of 28 students. The students in the study were represented only as a number, from 1–40.

Background of the Kaiaka Reo materials development

The Project Director of the Kaiaka Reo project, the then Dean of Te Pua Wānanga ki te Ao, who had been at the fore of the establishment of Kōhanga Reo in the early 1980s, was determined that the assessment tool was unquestionably going to be for students in Māori immersion settings. His experience told him that Māori were to drive the programme and that Māori and non Māori development members had to be committed to the survival of Māori language and culture, true believers of education in the medium of Māori. The Kaiaka

Reo Team was firmly of the view that proficiency tests developed by Māori were crucial to the education and wellbeing of students learning in the medium of Māori.

Time was of the essence and therefore the development team took the approach that it was in the project's interests and a more efficient use of time and resources, to contract external experts to guide them in the areas where the team lacked expertise such as test construction and test analyses. They accepted and trusted that the advice provided by the external experts contracted to the project was sound and based on theory and experience. The intention of the project was to demonstrate how a team of native speaking Māori educators could develop Māori language proficiency tests in a self-determined and autonomous way. In the creation of the proficiency tests for Kaiaka Reo, they were mindful of the precautions pointed out by Hollings, Jeffries, and McArdell (1992), which said there was a need to ensure that the language and socio-cultural factors of tests should not only be Māori, but also be relevant to the modern world that children lived in. They went on to say that it was incumbent on the test developers to combine traditional cultural factors with the world children know today and to decide the standards against which language proficiency was to be measured, not to mention the appropriate assessment procedures to be used in the measurement.

In an attempt to assess language proficiency, the team also had to contend with the problem of defining *proficiency* and the criteria and standards by which learners were to be measured. There were no models of proficiency tests available (that the team was aware of) for indigenous languages for the age groups of Year Five (aged 8–10 years) and Year Eight (aged 11–13) children, or any other ages. The proficiency tests that were available were mainly for internationally dominant languages such as English, Spanish, and French. These dominant languages are not at risk or in need of revitalisation. Also available were proficiency tests for adults learning languages such as English as a second or foreign language. These would not have been suitable, as pointed out by Leeman (1981, p. 125), who says "A test that is reputable and widely used for adults may be inappropriate for children simply because the tasks are too complex and too demanding".

To compound the team's difficulties, there were many other issues. For example, the students did not fit the standard testing profiles of first, second, or foreign language speakers of Māori, the target language of the test. What the team did know was that the children would come from schools funded at Level One by the Ministry of Education. The ideal would be to use tests geared specifically to the context within which they were to be used, or in the event of there being none available, instruments with norms established on children from the same cultural background could possibly be utilised (Leeman, 1981). However, even if such instruments were available for Māori, other problems could have arisen in the New Zealand context. For example, Hollings et al. (1992) point out the dearth of Māori children who are also proficient speakers of Māori on whom tests could be standardised; district variability in dialect and levels of Māori language proficiency; and the catch twenty-two situation whereby the team lacked the methods by which to determine the best children on whom to establish norms of reference.

Notwithstanding the issues identified above, the Kaiaka Reo Team still felt that a proficiency test was essential. The tests of the year 2000, together with the initial test development undertaken in 1999, defined language proficiency in general terms as involving knowledge of language (not knowledge about language) and the ability to make use of that knowledge in performing a range of communicative activities (Crombie, Houia, & Reedy, 2000). Proficiency was conceptualised, according to Bachman's framework (1990), as involving a combination of operational competence and pragmatic competence, with operational competence relating to grammatical competence and textual competence, and pragmatic competence relating to illocutionary competence and sociolinguistic competence.

Creating a test instrument in *te reo Māori* (Māori language) was not an easy task. In listening, a decision was made to use the proficiency descriptors that had been piloted in 1999. With Year Five and Year Eight Level 1 Māori medium students in mind, the development team designed the test(s) with culture and language being of central importance. They were mindful that familiar and culturally appropriate materials were more likely to result in a demonstration of behaviour that accurately represented children's real language abilities (Armour-Thomas, 1992). The team selected and adapted the texts of the stories to reflect our testing objectives in consultation with the external consultant on human development, who set out the cognitive skills that could be expected for the targeted age levels and with the expert on universal proficiency descriptors for listening and reading.

Just as the conceptualisation and operationalisation of the tests were created by Māori, so were the test materials. Māori writers were actively sought out and invited to submit stories that they considered appropriate for the intended age levels. The stories had to be original, written in Māori, and not translations of English stories. The artists who illustrated the stories also had to have a good working knowledge of Māori or close acquaintance with a native speaker so that they could appropriately interpret the intended meanings of the test developers and story writers.

In the case of the productive skills (speaking and writing), the Kaiaka Reo Team, together with the Advisory Group who comprised Māori educators, Māori linguists, Māori applied linguists, and practicing teachers in Māori medium contexts, decided that it was important to create test items that would stimulate children to produce open and creative linguistic compositions. These compositions would provide insight into the language that the children had acquired over time either as a first language (L1) or a second language (L2). Although the achievement objectives of *Te Reo Māori i roto i te Marautanga o Aotearoa* (The Māori Language in the New Zealand Curriculum) provided a guide to the level of expectancies for speaking and writing for the age levels, at that time no research had been conducted that indicated whether the students' language actually reflected those levels or not.

Kaiaka Reo Year Eight test for writing

A single test was used initially to measure the writing proficiency of the Year Eight students. The test itself consisted of a sequence that comprised 16 pictures representing the life cycle of the *tuatara* (see Figure 1), a lizard-like reptile of ancient lineage that is native to New Zealand.

During the piloting of the 2001 test materials, this picture sequence elicited the broadest range of language. *Te reo māori i roto i te marautanga o Aotearoa* [The Māori language in the New Zealand curriculum] (Ministry of Education, 1996, p. 87) states that students at level four should be capable of expressing their ideas and of providing supporting information; furthermore these students will have, at some time, studied the life cycle of a living creature in science. Therefore, the test developers were fairly confident that the Māori-medium students at Year Eight would be capable of writing about the life cycle of a creature such as the tuatara, or write creatively based on the pictures of the tuatara.

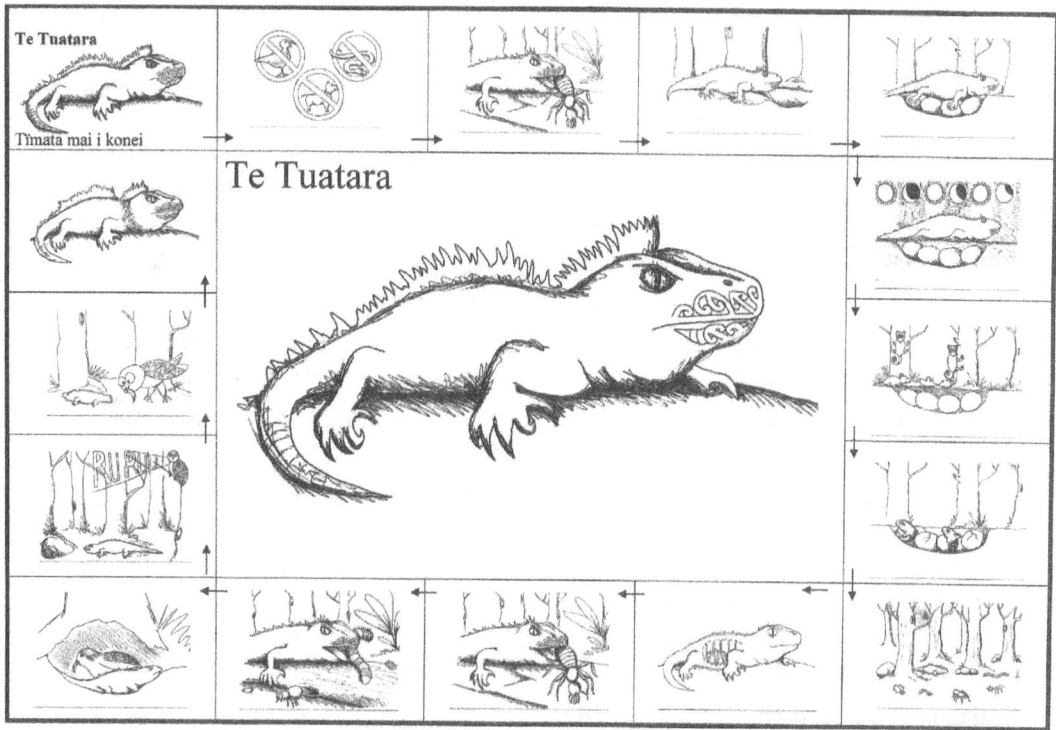

Figure 1. Te tuatara pictorial prompt for the Kaiaka Reo Year Eight writing test.

The Kaiaka Reo Team purposely chose not to define or constrain the construct of proficiency at this point of the proceedings by the parameters of the *Te Reo Māori i roto i te Marautanga o Aotearoa*. While there was a general acceptance of Bachman's model of language competence (1990), the Kaiaka Reo Team wanted the language of the students in Māori-medium themselves to inform the construct of Māori language proficiency in writing for Year Eight. The team received guidance from practicing teachers who were informants to the project and was confident that the test prompts were capable of eliciting language that required the students to express meanings and general notions such as time, quantity, duration, and location. Moreover, the items were tested informally on some of the children of Te Pua Wānanga ki te Ao staff, who in the afternoons would arrive after attending their local kura kaupapa Māori. The children happily sauntered in and out of the team's office, responding spontaneously in Māori to any questions asked of them. They readily engaged in conversation and just as readily left if there were more interesting happenings elsewhere. Perhaps the presence of a generous *kuia* (respected female elder) who was part of the team encouraged them as well; she was always prepared to listen to the tales, trials, and tribulations of their day and on occasion shared after school treats with them (with parent permission of course).

The test materials were, in the main, developed by a small team. Two of its leading members were retired native speaking Māori educators who the team was extremely lucky to have working on the project. Both had been primary school teachers, and over their professional lives, had worked at all levels of Māori education. Their language was impeccable, their standards daunting. Their attention to detail was unfailing and they would work tirelessly on items until the intention of the test specification was achieved in the simplest and most appropriate Māori language that might bring forth language from the intended test-takers, Year Eight children. They were exacting mentors who were determined that the integrity of the Māori language and its attendant culture was not to be compromised; they are referred to here as the *pakeke* (respected elders) of the team.

During the preparation of the writing test based on the tuatara, the two pakeke tested out many linguistic possibilities for responding to the test prompts. The development team was confident that the prompts had the potential to elicit a wide range of language. For example:

Picture 1   Tuatara sitting on a rock: *He tuatara tēnei*…[subject in focus, factual discourse—identification, descriptive discourse]

Picture 2   Several signs signaling non allowance of the things in the picture: *Ehara/kaua/kāore* [negation, verbal nominal, imperative]

Picture 3   The tuatara preparing to eat: *Engari*…[contrary to expectation, connective clauses]

Picture 4   The tuatara preparing to lay its eggs: *Kei te*…[present progressive, explanation genre].

The students were provided with a practice activity that required them to consider the pictures and write about them. They were then directed to consider the page with the 16 picture prompts that represented the life cycle of the tuatara and respond in a similar fashion. The number corresponding to each picture was set out on a separate piece of paper.

Kaiaka Reo diagnostic writing schedule

The diagnostic writing marking schedules (Appendices B & C) that were created during the pilot phase of the programme and used subsequently with minor alterations, assessed Māori grammar, Māori discourse, Māori vocabulary, proficiency in written conventions, and interlingual interference of English. The scripts were marked independently, using the diagnostic writing schedule, by practising teachers who were actually in the classroom, or were in in-school support roles providing support services to teachers in Māori immersion classrooms. They were either native speakers of Māori or native-like second language speakers. It was important to the Kaiaka Reo Team that the process was to be a positive experience, and therefore, the students were not to be harshly penalised unnecessarily by an over-emphasis on error. Errors were to be identified, correct usage was to be acknowledged, and creativity and excellence was to be commended. Moreover, the team was most interested in the potential or *predictive* language of the students.

In the marking of the scripts, the Kaiaka Reo Team were very conscious that teachers in Māori medium settings were not trained in the teaching of Māori[1] as a first, second, or foreign language. Therefore, the Kaiaka Reo Team devised diagnostic marking schedules (see Appendices B & C) that they felt the teachers would be able to use effectively and efficiently. A number of teachers had already indicated at an earlier meeting their lack of confidence in assessing the grammatical and Māori discourse features of the Māori language. With regard to grammar, the teacher markers were first shown how to categorise the sentences into phrases, and obtain a potential score for the phrase(s) produced by the children. For example, at the simple sentence level, within the Māori phrase, there is generally a verb or nominal marker + the verb or noun and maybe a modifier. It was demonstrated to the

---

[1] Teachers who teach in the medium of Māori are not trained to teach Māori language, either as a first, second, or foreign language. Therefore, professional development for the teachers occurred at every phase of the testing programme, especially with regard to the language features the development team were interested in. For example, teachers were taught the parts of a Māori sentence such as the phrase

teachers concerned how to recognise: (a) the cluster of markers that carried linguistic meaning and refer to them as *function words* (FW); (b) the verb or noun as the *main word* (MW) and; (c) all other modifiers as *other bits* (OB). Each part of the phrase was to receive a score, that is: MW=2, FW(s)=2, initial OB=2, and all subsequent OB's within each phrase=1.

In the following example, a response to picture prompt No. 4, the potential scores and actual scores using the above scoring guide would have been analysed as follows:

E hīkoi haere, e tipitipi haere tenei tuatara engari ehara i te tuatara noiho, he moko tā tenei tuatara.

Phrase (Phr)		Phrase potential	PhrPot
Phr 1	[e] [hīkoi] [haere] is going along	[FW+MW+OB]	2+2+2=6
Phr 2	[e] [tipitipi] [haere] is wandering along	[FW+MW+OB]	2+2+2=6
Phr 3	[tēnei] [tuatara] this tuatara	[FW+MW]	2+2=4
Phr 4	[engari] but	[MW (conjunction)]	2
Phr 5	[ehara] isn't	[MW (conjunction)]	2
Phr 6	[i te] [tuatara] [noiho] only a tuatara	[FW+MW+OB+OB]	2+2+2+1=7
Phr 7	[he] [moko] a moko (tattoo on the face)	[FW+MW]	2+2=4
Phr 8	[tā tenei] [tuatara] has this tuatara.	[FW+MW]	2+2=4

The child's phrase potential (PhrPot) score, for this item would be 35. However, in the phrase *E hikoi haere* the pre-posed verb marker *e* requires that the post-posed marker *ana* follow the verb modifier *haere* to realise the aspect of *going*. Therefore the Function Words (FW) for Phrase 1 (Phr 1) would be deducted from the score. The same applies to Phrase 2 (Phr 2). Note that in Phrase 6 (Phr 6) there are two Other Bits (OB's), because *noiho* is contemporarily usually written as *noa iho*; however, in older texts it is commonly seen as one word. In Phrase 8 (Phr 8), the child has used the possessive marker *tā* instead of *tō*, but more importantly, we can see that the child is aware of the use of the possessives in Māori, and moreover he/she is aware of the *t* class possessives. The scores for Phrase Potential would now look like the following:

Phrase (Phr)		Phrase potential	PhrPot
Phr 1	[e] [hīkoi] [haere] is going along	[FW+MW+OB]	2+2+2=6 (–2)
Phr 2	[e] [tipitipi] [haere] is wandering along	[FW+MW+OB]	2+2+2=6 (–2)
Phr 3	[tēnei] [tuatara] this tuatara	[FW+MW]	2+2=4
Phr 4	[engari] but	[MW (conjunction)]	2

Phr 5	[ehara]	[MW (conjunction)]	2
	isn't		
Phr 6	[i te] [tuatara] [noiho]	[FW+MW+OB+OB]	2+2+2+1=7
	a tuatara only		
Phr 7	[he] [moko]	[FW+MW]	2+2=4
	a moko		
Phr 8	[tā tenei] [tuatara]	[FW+MW]	2+2=4 (–2)
	has this tuatara.		

The second part of the assessment, Phrase Order (PO), sets out to evaluate the order of the phrases within the sentence, awarding a score of one to each phrase correctly ordered. In the above example the child uses eight phrases therefore the potential score is 8, although strictly speaking the first phrase should not be counted because there would only be one possible order. However, to simplify procedures each phrase was awarded a score of 1. With respect to our example the phrases are in the correct order, no deductions are required, and therefore, the child would retain a score of 8 for Phrase Order (PO) on this particular item.

The next aspect to be assessed was the child's use of conventions of print, which was simply labelled Written Conventions (WC). The curriculum statement *Te Reo Māori i roto i te Marautanga o Aotearoa* was used as a guide as to what conventions could be expected of the students at Year Eight, such as, spelling, punctuation, macron[2] usage. The goal was not to overly penalise students, so a ceiling was set on the maximum number of errors a child could receive for this section. For example, for each item where there were no errors the child received a total score of two. For 1–3 errors the score would be one, four plus errors received zero. In this manner, the over-penalising of students' repeatedly spelling a particular word incorrectly would be avoided. In addition, written conventions were not something the team were overly concerned with, since teachers had confidence with this aspect of writing, and therefore this aspect would be dealt with elsewhere in the curriculum and not as part of the testing programme.

The Kaiaka Reo Team was also interested on the impact of English interlingual interference. A deduction of one point was made each time a clearly English interlingual event occurred, such as the use of an English word.

The next aspect assessed was referred to as *bonus*. In this area, the student was awarded one point for the use of Māori discourse structures, Māori idioms and proverbs and the like, as appropriate; the appropriate use of macrons[3]; punctuation features beyond that expected of this level and other features that distinguished the student writing as Māori.

The last scoring category was related to vocabulary. Initially, the intention was to distinguish lexical items and functional items; however, this became too onerous for the teachers, so each new word was counted as a token and added to the total of the overall score (see Edmonds, 2008 Appendix G for a sample of the vocabulary elicited).

Kaiaka Reo teacher marker competence

A random review of the scores allocated by the teacher markers indicated that our intuitions about teacher confidence, and/or lack of confidence with regard to their knowledge of grammar were correct. Generally, the teacher's assessments were correct but they had difficulty describing errors and very often this section on the marking schedule was ignored.

---

[2] According to the *Encarta Dictionary: English* (Soukhanov, 1999), a macron is a short horizontal line placed over a vowel sound to indicate that it is long or stressed.

[3] On each new usage, not repeatedly for the same word.

Most or the teacher markers found it easier to guess what the child was trying to say based on what was written. The teachers recorded their guesses to signal an awareness that errors had occurred although they were not sure how to categorise or describe the error.

The diagnostic writing schedule described above was used to determine and assign scores to the scripts of the 202 students, including those of the sample of forty analysed in this chapter. The scheme had no inbuilt maximum because it included scope for the production of a varying number of phrases. For these skills, notional maxima were derived by considering the actual marks achieved and the relationship to expected maximum performance. The marks were converted to percentages of the notional maxima and the average score for each child calculated. (The scores that were reported included only those students whose data were complete.) Four grades, A, B, C, or D, were calculated, so that 25% of the cohort fell into each grade (Figure 2).

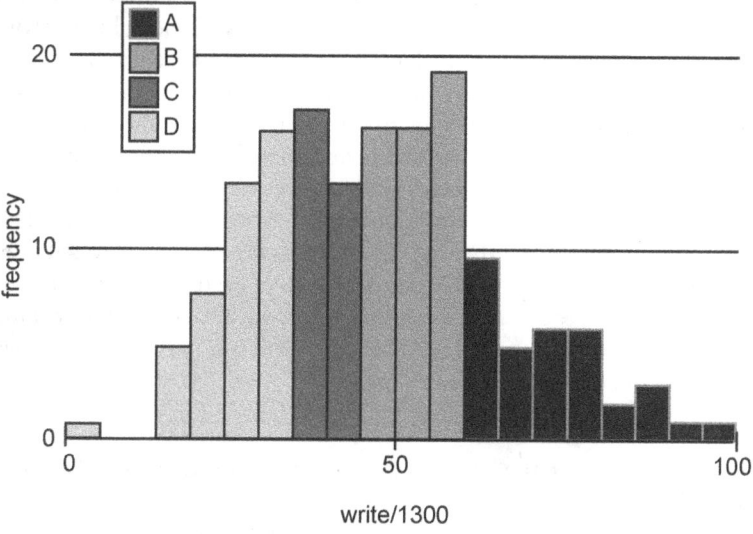

Figure 2. Year eight test results for writing (165 students – Kaiaka Reo 2001.

At the end of the process, while there was general satisfaction with the marking schedule that had been developed and its usefulness as a diagnostic tool, the language produced had still not been described in any useful manner for the teachers. A score that provided the students a percentile ranking could be assigned, but given the time constraints, an analysis and full description of the language based on actual performance at the various levels had not been produced. Moreover, a statistical analysis for reliability and validity was to be carried out by an external institution, namely, the New Zealand Council of Education Research (NZCER). However, as stated earlier, the New Zealand Council of Education Research decided against the statistical analysis due to their lack of Māori language, a decision that was consistent with the kaupapa Māori philosophy of Kaiaka Reo.

This chapter will complete that stage of analysis by examining the data generated by the sample of forty students who obtained scores nearest the midpoint averages for each grade (A, B, C and D), taken from the test population of 202. This information forms the basis of the analytical rating scale developed and used to investigate the reliability and validity of the test instrument Kaiaka Reo Year Eight Writing.

Kaiaka Reo phase two

Kaiaka Reo Phase Two specifically involves the methodology and process used to determine the reliability and validity of the Kaiaka Reo Year Eight Writing test at the centre of this study. The student participants of the study will not be described again except to reiterate that they are the sample of forty students who obtained near midpoint averages for each grade (A, B, C and D), as previously stated. The other significant participants of the study are the raters who rated the scripts of our sample using the analytical rating scale specially created for this purpose. Details of the rating scale, raters, and the rating process, that is, the methodology used to collect the data, are described below.

Analytical scale

Each of the original scripts was re-scored according to the diagnostic writing schedule (Appendices B & C), the language features identified and the errors noted. The scripts were then transcribed and Wordsmith software for corpora (available at http://www.lexically.net/wordsmith/) was used to assist in the identification of linguistic features that contribute to proficiency. It became evident that students made similar kinds of errors across all levels. For example, grammatical errors related to the passives in Māori were not restricted to those who scored low; they were spread across all band quartiles. There were also a number of positive features in their writing, such as idiomatic usage of Māori and range of vocabulary. What was of interest during the transcription process was that, despite errors in their language, the students applied the experiences of their Māori world to tell their story of the tuatara and portrayed Māori conceptualisations of events. For example, with regard to the pictorial prompt of the tuatara foraging for its food, a student used a commonly used Māori expression for going *pig-hunting*. The expression is *te haere ki te whakangau poaka*. The following is the student's transcribed example:

> *Ka haere te tuatara ki te whakangau wētā*

Went the tuatara to cause the biting of the weta (tree insect native to New Zealand). (See Appendix D)

High quality expressions, such as the one above, were awarded *bonus* points in the scoring, in recognition of typical Māori discourse in student writing. The marking procedure described in Appendix B showed that knowledge of the Māori phrase and the number of different tokens (words) used accounted for a large part of the students' initial score. The student scripts were marked in detail, and that diagnostic information was used to inform this study. However, a thorough analysis of those findings was not carried out, and therefore not included here.

The analytical rating scale was adapted from the *Analytic Scale for Rating Composition Tasks* by Brown and Bailey (1984) and the categorisation of the language features derived from the analysis of the scripts of the sample of forty. Brown and Bailey's (1984) analytical scale for rating composition tasks include:

- Organization: Introduction, Body and Conclusion
- Logical Development of Ideas: Content
- Grammar
- Punctuation, Spelling and Mechanics
- Style and Quality of Expression

The final rating scale (Figure 3) was an adaptation of the above, resulting in the following features:

- Organisation and Ideas (O&I)
- Grammar and Accuracy (G&A)
- Punctuation, Spelling and Mechanics (PSM)
- Style and Quality of Expression (SQE)
- Māori Discourse Intelligibility (MDI)

Notice, that a new feature, Māori Discourse Intelligibility (MDI) was added to the scale. This new aspect of the rating scale, among other features, distinguishes the analytical scale as a rating schedule specifically for the Māori language. It was accepted that the features of Organisation: (Introduction, Body and Conclusion and Logical Development of Ideas), and Punctuation, Spelling, Mechanics (PSM) were generic and necessary features of proficient writing. Grammar and Accuracy (G&A) and Style and Quality of Expression (SQE) were also deemed necessary features although these would be expressed in Māori. Also added to the scale was a summary statement that provided an overall impression of written language proficiency based on all components. The qualifying statements for levels on the various aspects from Brown and Bailey (1984) were also adapted as appropriate for the Māori language. The scale was also reduced from their five levels to four levels as a result of feedback by teachers during the piloting of the analytical scale in 2007.

The analytical scale in Figure 3 that was finally used to assess the scripts was piloted by teacher markers involved in three different national professional development programmes (*Whakapiki Reo* Providers[4], *Whakapiki Reo Waikato*[5], *Ngā Taumatua*[6]) for Māori immersion teaching. These teachers applied the descriptors to the sample of forty scripts using the rating form shown in Appendix E.

The feedback from the teachers involved in the professional programmes Whakapiki Reo and Ngā Taumatua determined the final scale that was used to re-assess the forty scripts at a two-day meeting. This meeting was funded by the Ministry of Education to facilitate doing the ratings of the forty scripts. Contact was made with the schools that had previously been involved in the proficiency testing programme of 2000/2001. It was hoped that the group of raters would comprise practicing teachers from Māori medium schools and hopefully equal numbers of native speakers of Māori and second language speakers of Māori. The Ministry of Education official who facilitated the meeting made contact with the schools and made arrangements for all concerned to meet in Wellington. This meeting took place at the Brentwood Hotel in Wellington on 17th and 18th of December 2007.

---

[4] Whakapiki Reo are professional development programmes funded by the New Zealand Ministry of Education for teachers in Māori medium settings. The programmes focus on the language proficiency, knowledge and skills for teaching in the medium of Māori. Currently there are six providers in New Zealand.

[5] Whakapiki Reo based at the University of Waikato.

[6] Ngā Taumatua is another provider funded by the Ministry of Education to provide in-service teacher education for teachers in Māori medium settings. Their focus is on Māori language literacy.

levels	organisation: introduction, body and conclusion, logical development of ideas, content	grammar & accuracy	punctuation, style and mechanics	style and quality of expression	Māori discourse intelligibility	overall impression
1 poor/ limited	development of ideas inappropriate to function, text type and communicative goal; ideas are haphazard and writing does not reflect careful thinking or was written offhandedly and hurriedly; minimal phrases	numerous serious grammar problems interfere with communication of the writer's ideas; cannot understand what the writer is trying to say	serious problems with format; parts of writing not legible; errors in sentence, i.e., obvious capitals missing, no margins, severe spelling problems; split words, joined words	poor expression of ideas; problems with vocabulary; lacks variety of structure; text maybe simple, showing little development; isolated words or short stock phrases only; very short text	can convey basic meanings in Māori with some difficulty; vocabulary is limited, code switching; English conceptualisation strong; English interferes strongly and affects reader	limited writer: rather difficult to follow in Māori
2 adequate	development of ideas is minimally appropriate to function, text type and communicative goal; ideas are not complete or writing is somewhat off the topic; sentences usually have only one idea	ideas getting through to the reader, but grammar problems are apparent and have a negative effect on communication; run-on sentences or fragmentation present	uses general writing conventions but has errors; spelling problems distract the reader; punctuation errors interfere with ideas	some vocabulary misused; lacks awareness of register; maybe too wordy or not enough words; moderate level of subtlety and flexibility	able to convey meanings in Māori; interlingual interference of English clearly apparent although able to communicate meaning speaking English in Māori	moderate writer: fairly easy to read and understand; text minimally organised
3 good	the writing is generally appropriate to function, text type and communicative goal but misses some points; ideas could be more fully developed; some extraneous information is present; good sentence structure; ability to write using paragraphs evident	good proficiency in Māori grammar; some grammar problems but they do not influence communication although the reader is aware of them	some problems with writing conventions or punctuation; occasional spelling errors; left margin correct; paper is neat and legible	attempts variety; good vocabulary; not wordy; register good; style fairly concise; good range of grammatical structures and vocabulary; can generally write spontaneously	generally communicates meanings effectively in Māori; occasional inappropriate use of Māori vocabulary; able to use Māori cohesive devices; occasional interlingual interference of English	good writer: easy to read from start to finish; text generally well organised
4 advanced	the writing is mainly appropriate to function, text type and communicative goal; ideas are concrete and thoroughly developed; no extraneous material; writing reflects thought; writes using paragraphs	native-like fluency in Māori grammar; no fragmentation or sentences; sentences cohesive and coherent	correct use of Māori writing conventions; left and right margins, all needed capitals, macrons, paragraph conventions used as appropriate; punctuation and spelling very neat	precise vocabulary usage; use of parallel structures, paraphrases; concise; register good (language appropriate to the context; an excellent range of grammatical structures and vocabulary, subtlety, and flexibility	communicates meaning competently and effectively; can be understood without difficulty; able to conceptualise and communicate competently and effectively in Māori; idiomatic usage is appropriate and effective	excellent writer: can write well within general and own special purpose areas; able to produce well organised, coherent and cohesive discourse

Figure 3. Kaiaka Reo: Analytical scale–description of Māori writing performance levels–Tuhituhi year eight.

Rater training

A total of fifteen Māori educators working across the spectrum of Māori medium education attended the rater meeting. They were experienced professionals whose roles in Māori language revitalisation ranged from teachers in universities, retired teachers who had returned to teaching, practising teachers in the classroom, *Resource Teachers of Māori*,[7] school principals, *iwi* (tribal) education administrators, Ministry of Education officials, a *kaumātua* (respected elder) still actively involved in teaching at a university, a Māori language applied linguist, and the author of this chapter. The last three had particular roles. The kaumātua provided support and guidance on the Māori language and culture, and the applied linguist on the area of second language. The three of us were native speakers of Māori. All the participants shared many common characteristics: they were Māori, fluent speakers of Māori, fully trained primary teachers, and committed to the survival of the Māori language.

The *hui* (meeting) began with a *mihi whakatau* (semi-formal Māori welcome speeches) by *tangata whenua* (Māori tribal representative/s of the region), who happened to be a Ministry of Education attendee, followed by a response by one of the visiting raters, as appropriate for a Māori hui. Each rater was invited to talk about who they were and where they were from. Māori protocol at situations such as these includes the sharing of food and the coming together as a group under one purpose. In a practical sense, this was welcomed by some of the raters, especially those from distant country schools, who would have arisen at 4:00 o'clock in the morning to travel up to two hours to catch a flight at the nearest town for Wellington.

The formal part of the meeting began with an outline of the purpose of the meeting by the Ministry of Education representative. Following this, a review of the 2000/2001 Kaiaka Reo development process was presented. Rater training began after lunch and research procedures were discussed including the following: confidentiality with respect to student scripts was imperative; the declaration of possible conflict of interest; and each rater was to sign an agreement of participation. The raters were assigned rater numbers, and then asked to complete the rater form, which asked for details like the number of years teaching (see Appendix F). We collected these forms at the end of the session.

Each rater was walked through the analytical scale and its implementation. The analytical scale was distributed to each participant and a shared reading process took place; that is, a round-the-table reading was undertaken with accompanying explanations of the analytical scale, as appropriate. The raters were then encouraged to become familiar with the analytical scale, and to ask questions and discuss issues from their shared and individual perspectives of the scale. The raters understood that consensus was important and that they should work within the parameters of the scale. Each rater was then provided with the same copy of an original anonymous script to conduct a practice rating. Some of the raters asked whether they could assign half marks but they were advised to keep to the scoring schedule of one to four whole number points for each of the five categories (Organisation and Ideas; Grammar and Accuracy; Punctuation, Spelling and Mechanics; Style and Quality of Expression; and Māori Discourse Intelligibility) outlined in the scale. This was followed by the completion of the scoring sheet for the student, which included the student's individual number, the date, and the assigning of the score for each category and an overall impression as indicated on the scoring sheet based on the total score. The scoring procedure was completed by filling in the rater identification number, signature, and date. A discussion

---

[7] Resource Teachers of Māori provide support services for learning and teaching in Māori.

took place afterwards sharing their ideas and experience of applying the analytical scale. The raters were then asked to use the analytical scale on a minimum of four more scripts, selecting one from each of four individual piles that—unbeknownst to them—represented the A, B, C and D quartiles from the first assessment. These did not include the scripts of the students who are discussed in this study. This further practice continued until they felt confident to take on the actual research samples. Although this was a practice run, the raters were asked to apply themselves seriously to their tasks in preparation for scoring the scripts of the selected sample. The meeting concluded with a *karakia* (prayer) and an invitation to return to the meeting room after dinner for an hour if the raters felt the need for further assistance.

Day two opened with *karakia*, and then the raters were reminded of the following: the research ethical procedures; the importance of completing all parts of the scoring sheet; and the importance of respecting and marking each of the forty scripts. They were then given the opportunity to raise any concerns that had arisen since the practice period the day before and reminded that they should direct all their questions to the main facilitator (the author of this chapter). This was followed by a re-run of the scoring procedures and an opportunity to ask last minute questions regarding their task. In total, ten raters of the fourteen attendees carried out the assessments. The author of this chapter was excluded from this process as were the Ministry of Education officials and the applied linguist. Five of the raters identified themselves as native speakers and the other five as second language speakers of *te reo Māori*. Rating continued throughout the day until all the scripts had been rated by each of the ten raters. As the raters completed the assessment of each individual script they were asked to mark this on a schedule of scripts provided to reduce the possibility of marking the same student twice. All the scripts were then collected and prepared for data analysis.

Results

This section presents the statistical results of the study. Analyses by the *SPSS*™ statistical programme and the *Excel*™ spreadsheet programme provide the descriptive statistics and multifaceted Rasch analysis was performed using Bond and Fox (2007) and *Facets* version 1.0.0 (Linacre, 1997).

Descriptive statistics

The data were specified as having three facets, namely, the ability of the students, the severity of the raters, and the difficulty of the categories. Each will be discussed in turn.

Table 3 presents the descriptive statistics for the scores achieved by the students according to the 10 raters on five categories (language traits) as already determined by Māori medium educators. The maximum score of 20 (a rating of 4 points in each of the five categories) was assigned three times: once to one student and twice to one other. However, this is not immediately apparent because the *maximum* column in Table 3 only indicates the individual student's average score not the number of times that an individual student may have received a particular score. Two students received a maximum of 20 and four students received the lowest score of 5. The mean for all the student scores was 12.03 with a standard deviation of 2.18, and the range was 7.25.

Table 4 presents the descriptive statistics for rater performance. Raters 1, 2, and 6 each awarded the maximum of 20 and similarly the lowest score of 5 points was assigned by Raters 6, 8, and 10. This does not mean that only three students received a five, instead the statistics tell us which raters assigned a score of five. The scores of the most lenient rater (Rater 4) had a range of 11.00 and a standard deviation of 2.38. Rater 7 who was one of the most severe rater had a range of 11 and a standard deviation 3.12. The other severe rater (Rater 9) had a range of 9 with a standard deviation of 2.86.

Table 3. Descriptive statistics of scoring for students

ID	Mean	SD	Minimum	Maximum	Range
1	7.90	2.61	5.00	10.00	5.00
2	12.40	4.04	9.00	16.00	7.00
3	11.00	3.59	7.00	15.00	8.00
4	10.30	3.38	8.00	15.00	7.00
5	10.10	3.33	6.00	15.00	9.00
6	14.70	4.70	11.00	17.00	6.00
7	12.80	4.10	10.00	16.00	6.00
8	11.40	3.69	7.00	15.00	8.00
9	13.00	4.18	10.00	15.00	5.00
10	9.30	3.05	6.00	12.00	6.00
11	11.20	3.76	7.00	18.00	11.00
12	14.40	4.62	11.00	17.00	6.00
13	12.40	3.98	9.00	15.00	6.00
14	15.10	4.83	12.00	19.00	7.00
15	12.80	4.09	10.00	16.00	6.00
16	15.90	5.09	12.00	20.00	8.00
17	15.70	5.12	10.00	20.00	10.00
18	15.40	4.90	12.00	19.00	7.00
19	9.90	3.21	7.00	13.00	6.00
20	11.60	4.10	6.00	19.00	13.00
21	8.80	2.91	5.00	12.00	7.00
22	11.60	3.89	7.00	16.00	9.00
23	11.40	3.76	7.00	16.00	9.00
24	15.00	4.88	10.00	19.00	9.00
25	12.80	4.25	7.00	17.00	10.00
26	13.10	4.23	10.00	16.00	6.00
27	11.70	3.90	8.00	17.00	9.00
28	9.60	3.29	5.00	14.00	9.00
29	11.80	3.89	8.00	15.00	7.00
30	13.50	4.35	9.00	16.00	7.00
31	11.70	3.74	10.00	15.00	5.00
32	8.70	2.79	7.00	10.00	3.00
33	11.70	3.94	7.00	15.00	8.00
34	12.70	4.06	10.00	15.00	5.00
35	11.70	3.76	9.00	14.00	5.00
36	7.70	2.55	5.00	10.00	5.00
37	10.20	3.26	8.00	13.00	5.00
38	10.50	3.48	6.00	15.00	9.00
39	14.10	4.65	9.00	18.00	9.00
40	15.60	4.97	12.00	19.00	7.00
total	12.03	2.18	5.00	20.00	16.00

Table 4. Descriptive statistics of scoring for raters

	rater									
	1	2	3	4	5	6	7	8	9	10
Mean	12.30	13.45	12.58	10.40	10.93	11.25	13.80	10.58	13.65	11.38
SD	3.38	2.54	2.64	2.38	2.10	3.47	3.12	3.31	2.86	3.38
Minimum	7.00	8.00	7.00	6.00	6.00	5.00	8.00	5.00	9.00	5.00
Maximum	20.00	20.00	19.00	17.00	15.00	20.00	19.00	16.00	18.00	17.00
Range	14.00	13.00	14.00	12.00	10.00	16.00	12.00	12.00	10.00	13.00

Table 5 presents the descriptive statistics for the language categories overall. Punctuation, Spelling and Mechanics (PSM) were scored most severely with a mean of 91.20, while Organisation and Ideas (O&I), the most leniently scored had a mean of 100.60. Grammar and Accuracy (G&A) had the largest range with a minimum of 76.00 and a maximum of 118, a difference of 43 although there is only a 1 step difference to that of Punctuation, Spelling, and Mechanics (PSM) which had a minimum of 70 and a maximum of 111, a difference of 42.

Table 5. Descriptive statistics of scoring for categories overall

	O&I	G&A	PSM	SQE	MDI
Mean	100.60	96.78	91.20	92.70	100.30
SD	11.79	14.12	15.04	10.49	10.50
Minimum	84.00	76.00	70.00	78.00	84.00
Maximum	117.00	118.00	111.00	107.00	115.00
Range	34.00	43.00	42.00	30.00	32.00

Multifaceted Rasch analysis

The Rasch model is a logistic latent-trait model of probabilities which allows student ability, rater severity, and category difficulty (a multi-faceted model) to be analysed independently, but compared on a common scale called a logit scale (see Chapter 4, for more information about Rasch analyses). The analytical rubric in this study was used by ten raters who were Māori medium educators to analyse year eight student writing samples in Māori. The scale assigned one of four grades to each of the five category subscales: Organisation and Ideas; Grammar and Accuracy; Punctuation, Spelling and Mechanics; Style and Quality of Expression; and Māori Discourse Intelligibility.

Some of the raters (eight) had forgotten or double scored some of the students' scripts. In total, eight raters missed at least one script (2.25% of the scripts) and three raters' double scored scripts (.75% of the scripts). In the case of missing data, these were filled by averaging the scores of the particular student concerned. Where there was a double scoring, the first score was taken to be the intended score. Therefore, there were considered to be zero cases of missing data and the computer programme recognised four hundred data points equalling two thousand valid responses.

In this study, three facets were used: the ability of the students, the severity of raters, and the difficulty of the categories. The analysis also places all the facets in what is called a vertical ruler on a common logit scale for easy comparison, enabling the researcher to see how the students, raters, and categories performed in terms of the relative student ability, relative rater severity (or leniency), and relative category difficulty. The analysis also produces fit statistics to identify misfitting persons, raters, or categories. Each of the tables produces its own list of elements and estimates for each arrangement of each facet.

A higher score equalled a positive logit, that is, a higher measure; similarly, a lower score equalled a negative logit, that is, a lower measure. The extreme score measurement was set at 0.3 for the Rasch estimation. Convergence was set at the default for FACETS, which is 0.5 score points, half the smallest observable difference between raw scores and 0.01 logits, the smallest useful difference. The analysis achieved convergence after forty-four iterations, permitting the construction of an unambiguous measurement system.

A visual depiction of how the facets relate to each other is shown in the vertical ruler in Figure 4, which shows the measures for student ability, rater severity, and category difficulty. The figure presents the logit scale in the first column. The logit scores represent a "true interval scale" (Brown, 2005, p. 56), unlike raw test scores in which the distances between intervals may not be equal (Henning, 1987, p. 129). Figure 4 also provides information on the three facets of interest. Notice that it is possible to determine the variation in student ability ranging from –2.00 to +3.00 on the logit scale, and the scale score a student is likely to obtain when evaluated on a single category of average difficulty (a category with 0 difficulty estimate on the logit scale) by a rater of average severity (a rater whose severity estimate is 0 on the logit scale). For example, the student whose ability estimate was 3.00 logits on the logit scale is likely to get almost all correct on their raw scores when the student is assessed by an average-severity rater.

In a similar manner, one can also determine the severity variation among the raters as well as the independent overall difficulty of each of the categories. The scale in the first column shows the logit measures, which represent the range of scores on the true interval scale, where the mean is 0 and, as is the case in this study, the scores range from –2.00 to +3.00.

The second column shows the ability variation among the students and where each student (marked with an asterisk *) sits on the scale. The students are ordered with the most able at the top of the scale, indicating higher ability, and the bottom of the scale indicating those of lower ability. The students are spread out along the measure, with slightly more than half (twenty-two) of the forty students above 0.00 logits, and slightly less than half (eighteen) situated at or below 0.00 logits.

Column three shows rater severity. Half of the raters (five) are situated below 0.00 logits, indicating that they tended to rate the student scripts leniently. Half of the raters are situated above 0.00 logits, the more severe end of the scale. The most severe rater was at the top and the least severe rater at the bottom.

```
|Measr|Student |Rater        |Category| PSM | SQE | G&A | MDI | O&I |
     |Ability  Severity      Diff.
+  3 +*       +              +       + (4) + (4) + (4) + (4) + (4) +
     |                                 ---                 ---
     |
     |
     | **
     |
+  2 +
     | *
     | *
     |                                        3     3
     | **                              3                  3     3
     | *
+  1 +       + Rater 7 Rater 9+        +     +     +     +     +     +
     | *     | Rater 2
     | **
     | **
     | ***** | Rater 3       | PSM
     |       |               | SQE
     |       | Rater 1       |          ---    ---
*  0 * **    *               * G&A     *     *     *     *     *
     | *     |
     | ***   |               | MDI
     | **    | Rater 10      | O&I
     |       | Rater 6
     | *     | Rater 5
     |       | Rater 8
+ -1 +*      + Rater 4       +         +     +     +     +     +     +
     | *
     |
     |                                              2          2
     | **                                     2          2           2
     | *
+ -2 +*      +               +         +     +     +     +     +     +
     |
     |
     |
     |
     |                                        ---
+ -3 +       +               +         + (1) + (1) + (1) + (1) + (1) +
```

Figure 4. Vertical ruler with partial credit scoring for categories.

Column four shows the variation in category difficulties. This column has the least variation of all, with all the categories clustered around the mean 0.00 logits. Punctuation, Spelling and Mechanics (PSM), Style, Quality and Expression (SQE) are slightly more difficult than the other categories, while Grammar and Accuracy (G&A) sits on the mean. Māori Discourse Intelligibility (MDI) and Organisation and Ideas (O&I) are the easiest of the categories.

Columns 5–9 show the raw four-step rating scales for the five categories and how they relate to the logit scores (i.e., distances between step on each scale adjusted to the true interval logit scale). These indicate what the Year Eight student writers at any given ability level on the scale are likely to receive. For example, a writer at a 1.00 logit ability level has a probability of receiving a 3 on a particular category from a rater at a 0.00 logit severity level. The numbers 1, 2, 3, and 4 within the vertical rulers of PSM, SQE, G&A, MDI, and O&I depict the threshold levels, as discussed earlier. These show the logit scores required to reach each of the scores for each particular category. For example, the threshold level 3 for each of the categories is not too distant, each falling within the logits of +1 to +2. The same applies to the threshold level 2 for each of the categories, each falling within –1 to –2. If these were too far apart, it would indicate that it would be harder to score a 3 in some categories than in others.

In addition to the summary map provided in the vertical ruler shown in Figure 4, detailed information is presented in separate tables (Tables 6, 7, and 8) for each of the individual facets: student ability, rater severity, and category difficulty.

Student ability

Table 6 provides a detailed measurement report of the students' ability performances. From the left, the columns show student identification (IDs); the students' ability logit measures;

and then error and infit and outfit values (as mean square values and as standardized *z* values). Column 1 presents us with the order of the students according to the measure of ability in column 2. Column 2 indicates that the ability span between the highest scoring student (Student 36) and the lowest scoring student (Student 16) was 5.01 logits. The differences in ability ranged from –2.03 to 2.98 logits (a little over 5 logits). Column three shows that the standard error (SE) ranged from 0.25 to 0.27.

The infit statistics of the remaining columns indicate the extent to which the data representing individual responses was not predicted accurately which as a general rule (for fit statistics), the infit and outfit mean squares should be >0.75 and <1.3. Values greater than 1.3 show significant misfit and values lower than 0.75 indicate significant overfit. For example, if we take the infit statistics of students over 1.3, that is, students 20 (1.81), 29 (1.65), and 25 (1.38), we see that these are very high and not performing as the model predicted, thus the responses are said to be misfitting and could not necessarily be said to be accurately predictive of student ability (McNamara, 1996). In contrast, the overfitting responses of students under 0.75, that is, students 32 (0.69) and 3 (0.65), for example, were too good to be true, or in Rasch terms too deterministic, therefore the scores may not be good predictors of their ability. Overfit may indicate a lack of local independence, that is, the items are not working independently of each other. For example, it could be that the overfitting students have particular content knowledge that creates lack of independence among items for those students.

These statistics indicate that the performance of the students should be examined for what might account for their non-predictive behaviour. It would be possible to eliminate students whose data appear as misfitting or overfitting the model. However, elimination at this point is not an option because that would reduce the number of students in this study from 40 closer to 30, and this in itself might be the reason for the misfit and overfit. Misfitting or overfitting does not necessarily mean that the students, raters, or categories are not good; it just means that the students did not perform according to the model, or they performed too well within the model.

Table 6. Student measurement report

student	measure	model SE	infit MnSq	Zstd	outfit MnSq	Zstd
36	2.98	0.27	0.87	–0.7	0.87	–0.7
1	2.84	0.27	0.90	–0.5	0.92	–0.4
32	2.29	0.26	0.69	–1.8	0.68	–1.9
21	2.22	0.26	0.87	–0.6	0.86	–0.7
10	1.90	0.25	0.94	–0.2	0.92	–0.3
28	1.71	0.25	1.26	1.3	1.28	1.3
19	1.52	0.25	1.03	0.1	1.00	0.0
5	1.40	0.25	0.82	–0.8	0.80	–1.0
37	1.34	0.25	0.69	–1.7	0.70	–1.5
4	1.27	0.25	0.88	–0.5	0.84	–0.7
38	1.15	0.25	1.00	0.0	0.99	0.0
3	0.85	0.25	0.65	–1.9	0.65	–1.9

continued...

Table 6. Student measurement report *(cont.)*

student	measure	model SE	infit MnSq	Zstd	outfit MnSq	Zstd
11	0.73	0.25	1.05	0.3	1.03	0.2
8	0.61	0.24	0.88	−0.5	0.88	−0.5
23	0.61	0.24	0.89	−0.5	0.88	−0.5
20	0.49	0.24	1.81	3.3	1.78	3.2
22	0.49	0.24	1.30	1.4	1.33	1.5
27	0.43	0.24	1.33	1.5	1.35	1.6
31	0.43	0.24	0.55	−2.6	0.54	−2.7
33	0.43	0.24	1.08	0.4	1.12	0.6
35	0.43	0.24	1.30	1.4	1.27	1.3
29	0.37	0.24	1.65	2.8	1.68	2.8
2	0.02	0.24	1.04	0.2	1.02	0.1
13	0.02	0.24	0.58	−2.4	0.60	−2.3
34	−0.15	0.24	0.96	−0.1	0.94	−0.2
7	−0.21	0.24	1.04	0.2	1.05	0.2
15	−0.21	0.24	0.83	−0.8	0.82	−0.9
25	−0.21	0.24	1.38	1.8	1.37	1.7
9	−0.33	0.24	0.47	−3.3	0.46	−3.4
26	−0.38	0.24	1.08	0.4	1.07	0.3
30	−0.62	0.24	0.64	−2.1	0.64	−2.0
39	−0.96	0.24	1.23	1.1	1.24	1.2
12	−1.14	0.24	0.82	−0.9	0.81	−1.0
6	−1.31	0.24	0.62	−2.2	0.61	−2.3
24	−1.49	0.24	0.95	−0.1	0.94	−0.2
14	−1.55	0.24	0.84	−0.8	0.83	−0.8
18	−1.73	0.24	0.81	−0.9	0.83	−0.9
40	−1.85	0.25	1.34	1.6	1.36	1.8
17	−1.91	0.25	1.52	2.4	1.53	2.5
16	−2.03	0.25	1.03	0.2	1.04	0.2
Mean	0.26	0.25	0.99	−0.1	0.99	−0.2

note: SD=1.29; Reliability=0.96

Standardised z scores (Zstd) are interpreted in a similar way to the infit mean squared, statistics. The measurement for misfit should be<2, and for overfit>−2. For example Student 9 has an infit value of 0.47 and the standard Zstd value of −3.3 (showing significant overfit). Some students are also high, such as student 17, who also has a high outfit value of 1.52 standardised to Zstd 2.4.

These results from either the mean square values or the Zstd values are not too alarming and could be due to the small sample. Also, the reliability estimate of 0.96 tells us how well the testing procedures are differentiating among the persons on the measured variable; it estimates the replicability of a person placement across other items measuring the same construct.

Note that this type of reliability estimates the degree to which the testing procedures consistently separate the students. It is analogous to Cronbach alpha in that "the fraction of observed response that is reproducible" (Bond & Fox, 2007, p. 284). High reliability refers to the extent to which students differ and not the extent to which raters agree (McNamara, 1996). The infit statistic gives more weight to the performances of persons closer to the item value, and it is argued that this gives more sensitive insight into the students' performances. The outfit statistic is not weighted and therefore remains more sensitive to the outlying scores. Users of the Rasch model routinely pay more attention to infit values than to the outfit values because aberrant infit scores usually cause more concern than large outfit statistics (Bond & Fox). Therefore the discussion that follows will refer only to the infit statistics although the Zstd outfit statistics will be displayed in the tables.

Rater severity

The rater measurement report (see Table 7) presents information in a similar way to the student report. From the left, the columns show rater identification (IDs), rater severity, then error and fit statistics. Column 1 presents the order of the raters according to the measure of severity in column 2. Column 2 indicates that the severity span between the most lenient rater (Rater 4) and the most severe raters (Rater 7 and Rater 9) was 2.03 logits. The standard error range was 0.12 to 0.13.

The differences in severity ranged from −0.98 to 1.05 logits (almost two logits). At 0.65, Rater 2 is overfitting because the infit mean square is less than the minimum 0.75. In other words Rater 2 is not performing according to the model's specifications. It is possible that Rater 2 is not working independently on the items, a situation that Rasch analysis can accommodate by adjusting for rater characteristics. For example, it is possible to eliminate Rater 2 from the analyses or investigate further Rater 2's performance. It happens that Rater 2 is the only rater who, although he had similar experiences to the other raters with respect to length of time in teaching and teaching experiences, was also the only person working in teacher education at university level. His involvement with students on a day-to-day basis was less than that of the other raters and might account for the overfit. This, however, is unlikely to affect the overall results because, despite Rater 2's response pattern, the raters are still behaving independently with a reliability of 0.97 and a separation index of 6.23. Lower might have been better, but considering that this is a first time rating, it is satisfactory.

Table 7. Rater measurement report for ten raters

rater	measure	model SE	infit MnSq	Zstd	outfit MnSq	Zstd
7	1.05	0.12	1.06	0.6	1.05	0.5
9	0.97	0.12	1.15	1.5	1.14	1.4
2	0.85	0.12	0.65	−4.1	0.66	−4.0
3	0.33	0.12	1.07	0.7	1.06	0.6
1	0.17	0.12	1.07	0.7	1.05	0.5
10	−0.39	0.12	0.83	−1.8	0.82	−1.9

continued...

Table 7. Rater measurement report for ten raters (cont.)

rater	measure	model SE	infit MnSq	Zstd	outfit MnSq	Zstd
6	−0.46	0.12	0.99	−0.1	0.98	−0.1
5	−0.66	0.12	0.90	−1.0	0.89	−1.1
8	−0.88	0.12	1.11	1.1	1.10	1.0
4	−0.98	0.13	1.10	1.0	1.13	1.2
Mean	0.00	0.12	0.99	−0.1	0.99	−0.2

note: SD=0.77; Reliability=0.97

The chi-square of 357.49 with 9 df (degrees of freedom) was significant at p<0.00 (probability is less than 0.00) and therefore, the null hypothesis that all raters are equally severe must be rejected. These indicators of the magnitude of severity differences among raters indicate that significant variation in severity did exist among the raters. Rater 6 was slightly but more consistently lenient than the other raters, and Raters 7 and 9 were slightly more severe than Rater 2, but consistently more severe than all other raters.

Overall, apart from Rater 2, the fit values for all raters were within the range of two standard deviations from the mean. In other words, all the raters were self consistent in scoring. In summary, although one of the raters showed misfit outside of the model's expectations, the vast majority of the student responses were well within the model's expectations and given the high reliability, we can be confident that the raters performed to expectations.

In practical terms, it would appear that the raters consistently scored neither severely or leniently across the persons and items. However, their ratings remained close to the mean, in fact within one logit on either side of the mean, indicating, perhaps, that the raters were reluctant to assign extreme low or high scores. It is possible that extending the scale from 4 points to a 6–point scale might resolve this issue (see Discussion for further comment on this point).

Category difficulty

The category difficulty measurement report for five categories (see Table 8) is presented in the same way as the student ability and rater severity reports. From the left, the columns show category identification, variance in category difficulty, error, and fit statistics. Column 1 presents the order of the categories according to the measure of difficulty in column 2. Column 2 indicates that the difficulty span between the most leniently scored item (O&I) and the most severely scored item (PSM) was small, 0.72 of a logit. The differences in category difficulty ranged from 0.38 to −0.34 (0.72) of a logit. Column three shows that the standard error ranged from 0.08 to 0.09. All the items were within the acceptable range of 1.30 and 0.75 with no misfitting or overfitting data. Although the difference in category difficulty is small, the reliability is 0.93 shows that the items are performing consistently independent of each other. The chi-square of 54.1 with 4 df was significant at p<.00 and, therefore the null hypothesis that all categories were equally difficult must be rejected. All of these indicators taken together suggest that these five scoring categories did not vary greatly, and none of the items showed any significant misfit or overfit, suggesting that the analytical scale is behaving as the model might expect.

Table 8. Difficulty measurement report for five categories

categories	measure	model SE.	infit MnSq	Zstd	outfit MnSq	Zstd
3 PSM	0.38	0.09	0.91	−1.3	0.90	−1.4
4 SQE	0.26	0.08	0.90	−1.5	0.90	−1.5
2 G&A	−0.01	0.09	0.96	−0.05	0.96	−0.5
5 MDI	−0.28	0.09	0.96	−0.06	0.96	−0.6
1 O&I	−0.34	0.09	1.23	3.1	1.23	3.1
Mean	0.00	0.09	0.99	−0.2	0.99	−0.2

note: SD=0.31; Reliability=0.93

Scale step analysis

Item-by-item analysis of scale step structure helps us understand the structure of rating scales in judgement tasks (McNamara, 1996). It is of particular use because it enables us to examine the scoring structure of scales such as the one we have here which results in an overall score awarded to each student (see vertical ruler in Figure 4).

To a certain extent, *rating scale validation* can be argued by checking the statistics and the probability curves (see Figure 5). The category statistics show the range of step difficulties, which should advance by at least 1.4 but less than 5.0 logits (Bond & Fox, 2007). When step difficulties advance by more than 1.4, then the rating scale can be theoretically "decomposed" into a series of independent dichotomous items, which indicates that "a rating of *k* implies successful leaping of hurdles" (Linacre, 1997), indicated by the threshold levels where, for example, achievement moves from Level 1 to Level 2. When step difficulties are too far apart (greater than 5.0 logits), then a category is too wide and there is less statistical information available from the item, indicating a need for more categories.

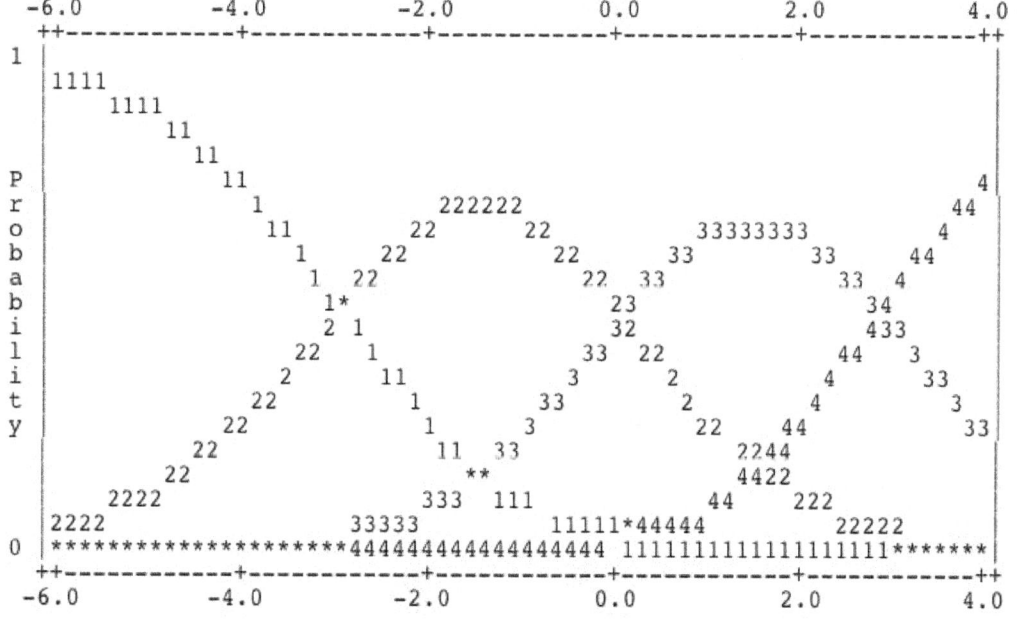

Figure 5. Overall category probability curves.

An examination of the step calibration measures for the overall category probability statistics shows that two of the four step difficulties are outside of the acceptable range of 1.4 but less than 5.0 logits (see Table 9). These outfitting statistics and frequencies suggest that the four-step scale should be reconsidered. Generally, the remedy would be to collapse the problematic categories into adjacent, better-functioning categories, and then reanalyse the data (Bond & Fox, 2007). However, given the category probability statistics aforementioned, Figure 5 confirms that we would end up with only two categories because we have a need to collapse those two that are outside of the acceptable range. The option that makes most sense, from those recommended, would be to review the rating scale to determine new pivot points to provide distinct category definitions as suggested by Bond and Fox (also see Wright, 1996; Wright & Linacre, 1992).

Table 9. Overall category probability statistics

category score	counts used	average measure	step calibrations measure	SE
1	206	−2.03		
2	912	−0.84	−2.95	0.081
3	746	0.60	0.08	0.061
4	136	1.68	2.87	0.101

The step structure above was extended by Wright and Masters (1982) to handle data from rating scales and items scored using partial credit scoring as follows:

> That the step structure of the rating scale, or the step structure of partial credit items, might vary from item to item or from one aspect of performance to the next...Partial credit "allows item by item analysis of step structure with items involving rating scale steps of any kind. In addition to making it possible to understand the structure of rating scales in judgement tasks more finely, a Partial Credit analysis enables us to examine the scoring structure of individual items which have partial credit scoring (cited in McNamara, 1996, p. 255).

The variation identified by Wright and Masters (1982) is evident in the present study where it can be seen that the probability curves show the probability of occurrence for scale scores, with the extreme categories always approaching 1.0 for corresponding extreme measures. They also show how the thresholds for a set of rating scale items can be depicted as the intersection of item probability curves for each response option.

In addition to the partial credit variation (across categories treated as items), the probability curves show how the thresholds for a set of rating scale items, can be depicted as the intersection of item probability curves for each response option. These thresholds represent the intersections at which persons are likely to be scored at the next highest level. Thus, as ability level increases on the logit scale, the probability increases of achieving the next highest score ranking. For example, Figure 6 shows, for Intelligibility, that the threshold for choosing Category 2 over Category 1 occurs at approximately −3.0 logits; the threshold for choosing Category 3 over Category 2 at 0.0 logits; and the threshold for choosing Category 4 over Category 3 at 3.0 logits. The x-axis expresses the difference between person ability (B_n) and item difficulty (D_i). For example, a student who scores 4 logits lower than the endorsability of the item as a whole ($B_n-D_i=-3$), has a greater than 80% chance of scoring in Category 1. If however a person's agreeability is, for example, greater than 4 logits higher than the endorsability of the item (Bn–Di=–3), scoring in Category 4 is clearly the one most likely to be endorsed.

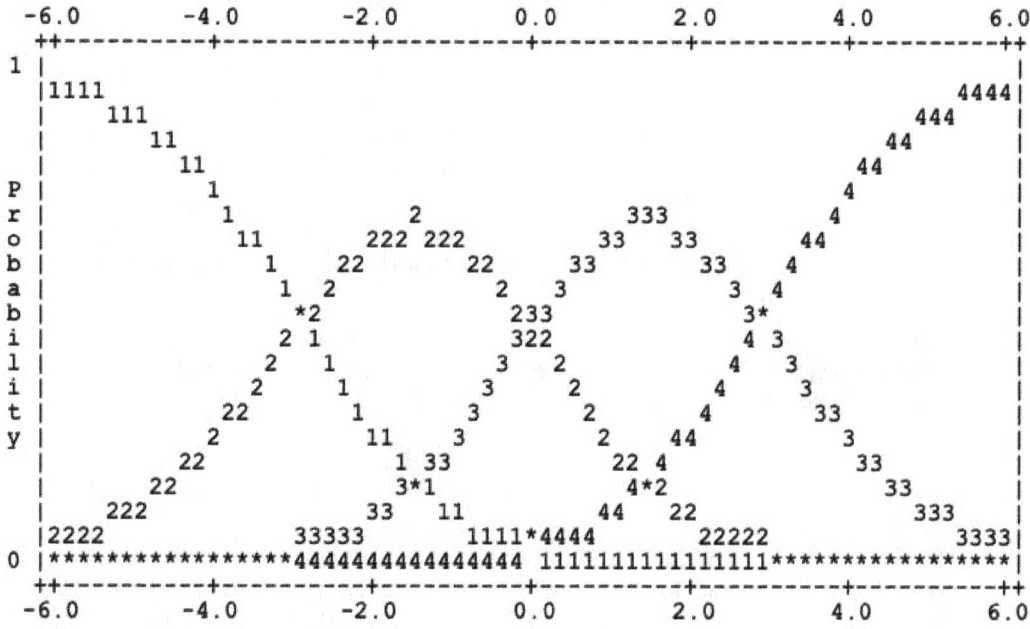

Figure 6. Category probability curves for the Māori discourse intelligibility rating scale.

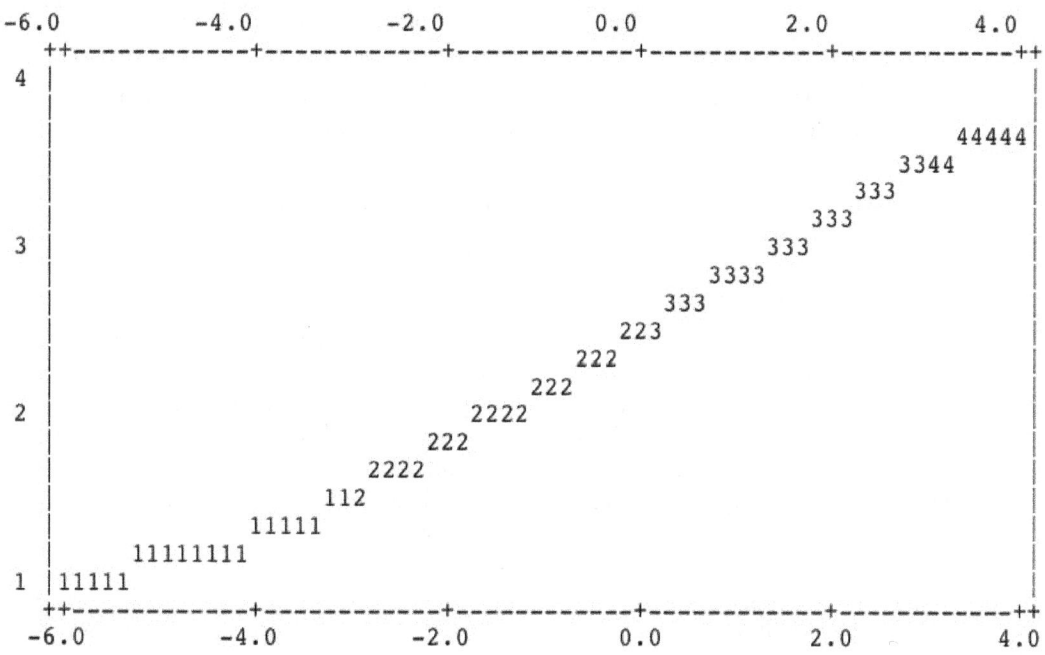

Figure 7. Overall category item characteristic curve.

Overall category item characteristic curve

The relationship between student ability, category difficulty, and probability of a correct score is a function of the difficulty of the category relative to student ability (see Figure 7). The expected score ogive[8] (model ICC) shows an Item Characteristic Curve (ICC) for the overall categories. The probability of a correct response on the item, represented on the y-axis, is a function of the ability of the individual taking the item, represented on the x-axis. The discrimination of the item is represented by the slope of the curve, that is, the steeper the slope of the ICC item, the higher the item discriminates. For example, the overall item characteristic curve (Figure 7) has a very moderate level of discrimination. Therefore, the chances of getting a high score on that category increases only gradually. In addition, the analysis shows that the model successfully separated all the facets into levels.

Item characteristic curves for the categories of Organisation and Ideas; Grammar and Accuracy; Style and Quality and Expression; Māori Discourse Intelligibility; and Punctuation, Spelling and Mechanics were also analyzed (see Edmonds, 2008).

Discussion

As stated much earlier in this chapter, the purpose of the study was to investigate the reliability and validity of the Kaiaka Reo Year Eight test in writing that was developed *by Māori for Māori in te reo Māori*, in 2000–2001. The study maintained that *Kaupapa Māori* principles are paramount, and therefore it is important that the investigations uphold the integrity of the student participants, the teacher raters, and the Māori language and culture that the Kaiaka Reo Team refused to compromise during Kaiaka Reo Phase One. With this in mind, the author set out to answer the following three research questions:

1. To what degree is the Kaiaka Reo Year Eight writing test a reliable assessment tool for assessing the Māori language proficiency of year eight students in Māori medium settings?

2. To what degree is the Kaiaka Reo Year Eight writing test a valid assessment tool for assessing the Māori language proficiency of year eight students in Māori medium settings?

3. How will the study improve the Kaiaka Reo Year Eight writing test?

This section will address each of those questions in turn.

Reliability of Kaiaka Reo Year Eight writing

Earlier, it was stated that a strategy that could be used to estimate the reliability of the Kaiaka Reo Year Eight test was that of internal consistency, where only internal information from the single administration of a test is necessary. That has been the case here. The student writing that was analysed came from the one and only nationwide administration of the Kaiaka Reo Year Eight test in writing of 2000–2001. Initially, the student scripts were marked according to a language analysis schedule that required a communicative performance (in writing) depicting the life cycle of the tuatara. The language analysis included a grammatical analysis by phrase and sentence, the use of written conventions in Māori language writing, the presence of English interlingual interference, the Māori discourse features in writing, and the range of vocabulary used (both lexical and linguistic).

---

[8] *Ogive* is a statistical term for a graph or curve that represents the cumulative frequencies of a set of values.

The language features evident from this analysis were then assumed to represent the language of year eight students in Māori medium settings in 2000–2001.

Let us return to Figure 4 and look at how the three facets (student ability, rater severity, category difficulty) performed according to the Rasch model. At a quick glance, this figure showed the overall performances of the students and the range of ability among them. Although the raters did not assign scores at the lower end of the scale it is still possible to see that the students' performances are fairly well spread out over 5 logits, and that there are cutoff points that distinguish ability among the students. For example, two students were close to +3 logits at 2.98 and 2.84, nine between 2.22 and 1.15, twenty between 0.85 and –0.62 logits, five at –0.96 and –1.55, four between –1.73 and –2.03.

With respect to the reliability of student performance, the student ability measurement report showed that the students' scores were fairly well distributed and although several of their responses were outside the model's expectations, the vast majority were well within expectations. The reliability index on the student measurement was very high at 0.96 which indicates that it is highly likely that the students' would perform in a similar order if they were given another set of items, of the same number and distribution that purported to measure the same construct (Bond & Fox, 2007, p. 40). However, it is fair to say that one possible shortcoming with this analysis could be that the number of students was only 40 even though the analysis does demonstrate a "hierarchy of ability/development (person separation) on this construct" (p. 41). To reiterate, the analysis does show that there is high person reliability where some of the students have scored higher and some lower and that there is consistency in these inferences.

Overall, the rater measurement report (Table 7) showed that the raters were also consistent in their ratings. Their performances were not as widely spread as those of the students (2 logits, +/–1 from the mean). Although one of the raters demonstrated misfit, the vast majority of the ratings were well within the model's expectations. It is important to note that the high reliability index (0.97) does not indicate the extent to which raters agree, but the extent to which they really differ in their level of severity, not in their ranking of students but in the actual levels of scores assigned to the students (McNamara, 1996). In other words, the raters would probably perform in a similar way given similar circumstances. According to McNamara, these indices tend to indicate that one of the aims of rater training (eliminating rater differences) was not achieved, something that he claims is neither achievable nor desirable. Our raters then, despite the training, and similar teaching backgrounds performed to the model's expectations.

Although one-half of the raters indicated that they were native speakers and one-half second language Māori speakers, the author is personally aware that there was great variation among them. Four of the native speakers, for example, were all from the same tribal region where Māori is still strong in the home and community but even among them there were distinct differences in age, current positions in the profession and experiences. During the training session, two of these raters indicated that Māori Discourse Intelligibility was very important to them. One was interested in how well the students crafted their compositions, another was interested to see if the students of the sample performed as she would expect her students in her class to perform. The retiree wanted the students' efforts to be recognised, and she thought that they were to be commended for their efforts. The two youngest raters in the team (both second language learners of Māori) quickly assessed the tasks before them and wasted no time in assessing the student scripts. They were interested in the students' communicative competence (i.e., whether or not the students effectively responded to the tasks put before them and could be understood by the raters). As far as they were concerned, communicating meaning was more important than accuracy or depth of expression. One rater was concerned with what one could expect in the writing of a year 8 student. Up until this time, she had not seriously given consideration to the language proficiency of the students. As far as she was concerned, they should have been able to perform the tasks required of them. The last two raters, both very competent native-like speakers of Māori who claimed second language status probably gave each category equal attention for each student. They were probably, in the author's view, the most balanced of the raters in terms of educational and language background. One of these raters' was Rater 2, whose ratings were not well predicted by the model. An analysis for rater bias (which was not conducted here), by analysing the residuals (the values one gets that are not expected) might have shown further sub-patterns in rater behaviour. For example, perhaps the differences among raters were associated with certain tasks, or certain students, or even certain candidates on particular tasks.

Category difficulty concentrated around the mean at approximately +0.5 and –0.5. Punctuation, Spelling, and Mechanics was the most severely scored and Organisation and Ideas the most leniently scored and the least consistent of all the categories. These results are not too surprising since most of the teacher raters were most confident in rating Punctuation, Spelling, and Mechanics and since the nature of the test prompts directed the organisation of the ideas for the written compositions.

After the scoring process, the teacher raters commented that they felt the scale did not cope very well in cases where the students' scripts were of a high standard in every category, but the script was too short and did not respond to all the prompts. Conversely, some students had lengthy but what some raters called *messy* scripts that had many errors, were difficult to read, or contained simple sentences. Yet they felt compelled to provide a high score because the student had responded to each prompt, and it was to Organisation and Ideas that they generally directed this score. Although Organisation and Ideas was less consistent than the other categories, there was little variation in difficulty among the five categories and the values are not so different from those of the other scales to be of concern. Overall, category reliability remained fairly high at 0.93, indicating a high probability that these categories were reliably separated from each other and that they would perform in a similar way under similar circumstances.

The analysis, however, indicates that the four-step scale of the rating scale did not provide sufficient distance between each step to indicate "a successful leaping of k hurdles" (Linacre 1997) or to use the more common phrase a successful *jumping through the hoops* from one level to the other. This is not surprising. Teachers who piloted the scale as well as the teacher raters who applied the scale to student scripts all expressed a wish to have a five step scale, or the freedom to use +/- 0.5. This, they thought would make it easier to score a script when they were uncertain whether the score was definitely a 1, a 2, a 3 or a 4. Amongst themselves, however, they thought that +/- 0.5 or a middle score of 3 might induce them to be more generous or take the easy way out, and therefore decided to keep the four-step scale. This issue will be taken up again in implications for the future.

It is certain, however, that each of the facets (student ability, rater severity, and category difficulty) indicates high replicability, and we can be fairly confident at 0.96, 0.97, and 0.93 that the estimates are consistently separating out each facet.

Validity of Kaiaka Reo Year Eight writing

Because the scores of student ability indicated a high degree of reliability, it appears that the writing portion of Kaiaka Reo Year Eight has satisfied an important and necessary precondition of validity, that is, in order for a test to be valid it must be reliable (Bachman, 2003; Brown, 2005; Brown & Hudson, 2002; Cronbach, 1971a, 1971b, 1988; Messick, 1980, 1989, 1995, 1996).

In this study, the validity of the Kaiaka Reo Year Eight writing test has been assessed, not only with respect to its behavioural function of assessing for Māori language proficiency, but also in the context of political and explanatory perspectives. At the fore, has been the right of Māori to be self-determining and include arguments from socio-linguistic approaches that validate the testing process.

Bachman (2003) suggested that the different kinds of validity, such as content, criterion, and construct, can be more appropriately viewed as complementary types of evidence that must be gathered. Content relevance relates to the behavioural domain and the specification of the content as defined by Cronbach (1971b, p. 449):

> [a] validation study examines the procedures as a whole. Every aspect of the setting in which the test is given and every detail of the procedure may have an influence on performance and hence on what is measured. Are the examiner's gender, status, and ethnic group the same as those of the examinee? Does he put the examinee at ease? Does he suggest that the test will affect the examinee's future, or does he explain that he is merely checking out the effectiveness of the instructional method? Changes in procedure such as these lead to substantial changes in ability—and personality—test performance, and hence in the appropriate interpretation of test scores… The measurement procedure being validated needs to be described with such clarity that other investigators could reproduce significant aspects of the procedure themselves.

Did the Kaiaka Reo Year Eight in writing satisfy the conditions of Cronbach's test method facets and procedures stated above? For both Kaiaka Reo Phase One and Kaiaka Reo Phase Two, the test developers' and examiners' gender, status, and ethnicity (Māori) were the same as those of the year eight students in Māori medium settings in our sample. The testing was conducted in the students' usual classroom environment by their teacher. The procedures were carefully read and each student was given the opportunity to ask questions before the testing took place. In fact, the teachers followed the instructions provided and reported that they were clear and easy to follow.

The second aspect proposed by Bachman (1996) is that of content coverage. The Kaiaka Reo Team carefully considered this, ensuring that the tasks required of the students were appropriate for their level. This, first, included an investigation of the cognitive tasks that could reasonably be expected of year eight students of the ages 11–13 years. For example, students at this level should be able to combine a number of ideas within a logical system (see Appendix A). Secondly, the task was a curriculum writing task that the students at year 8 were capable of, for example, "ko te whakamātau me te whakapakari i ēnei momo tuhituhi, arā, te tuhi whakaihiihi, te tuhi ruri, te tuhi arotake" (to test and strengthen their expressive, poetic and critical writing skills) (Ministry of Education, 1996, p. 87). Thirdly, as much as possible the task enabled the students to show off their language ability in writing without prior content knowledge. The pictures depicting the life cycle of the tuatara promised test stimuli that were ethnically appropriate and open to interpretation by the students. The life cycle of the tuatara was also well within the writing experiences of the students, all of whom would have studied the life cycle of some other living creature, prior to reaching year eight in their schooling. Specifically, the students could express in writing their knowledge and use of grammar, vocabulary, and discourse features of the Māori language.

During Kaiaka Reo Phase Two, the development of the analytical scale helped refine the construct of Māori language proficiency. Māori are firmly of the view that the Māori language encapsulates their own world-view within its language system. The development and use of the marking schedule (Kaiaka Reo Phase One) made more explicit the intuitive knowledge of the native Māori speakers by detailing aspects of grammar, vocabulary or Māori discourse that were present in the students' writing. A measure was needed that could estimate how much of something the students displayed or possessed. The basic question of construct validation according to Messick (1975, p. 957) is "What is the nature of that something?" Toward this end, an analytical scale was created that provided descriptions of the students' Māori language proficiency according to their performance on the Kaiaka Reo Year Eight writing test. Rasch analysis has verified these descriptions to be reasonably reliable and valid.

How will the study improve the Kaiaka Reo Year Eight writing test?

First, the study has given the Kaiaka Reo Year Eight test legitimacy and credibility in the field of language proficiency testing. Secondly, the study has identified several aspects that would improve the test. Because of the study, the test now has its own set of descriptors which are satisfactory, although additional work is required to develop and trial a five or six-step scale. Technically, the quality of the test materials should be upgraded and finished professionally. For example, the picture prompts depicting the life cycle of the tuatara need improvement. The author would like to see further Rasch analysis that focuses specifically on the language proficiency aspects of Grammar and Accuracy, Quality, Style and Expression, and Māori Discourse Intelligibility. The author would also like to spend time with a group of Māori teachers to study how the scale could be improved to assist them to distinguish among the levels. Furthermore, this process has identified many exciting features of language use (right and wrong) that require a thorough language analysis so that the knowledge gained from testing can be of practical use in the classroom environment and Māori language revitalisation.

This process has given the author confidence that, if the other Kaiaka Reo tests that were developed in 2000–2001 for year five writing and years five and eight oral language were subjected to a similar process to that carried out in this study, they would also prove to produce reliable and valid scores.

Conclusions

A brief review of the events that caused the decline of the Māori language, since 1840, shows that Māori must be vigilant and continue to assert their *tino rangatiratanga* today to restore the numbers of proficient speakers of Māori to ensure its survival.

The colonization of *Aotearoa* by a major foreign power in the 1800s meant that the indigenous people, Māori, became a minority. The decimation of numbers also led to rapid language loss. Education accelerated the indoctrination of Māori into the prevailing social, political, and cultural order, displacing and marginalising the people. These practices dismissed the Māori language as a tool of daily communication, the result being that English emerged as the sole language of instruction in schools. However, that suppression of the language and culture has transformed schooling into contested sites of struggle to the extent that a significant number of students engage in learning through the medium of Māori today.

Kōhanga reo and *kura kaupapa Māori* have radically redefined schools for their learners. Participants in these movements, young and old, validate and legitimize Māori knowledge, culture, and language on a daily basis. The impact on education has been that Māori are no longer passive participants in education. Systems are in place whereby learning through the medium of Māori, where Māori culture and values are practised, is accessible throughout the state education system.

The restoration, revitalisation and maintenance of the Māori language and its attendant culture, plus gaining the cognitive benefits of learning in one's indigenous language, remain key goals in Māori medium education. These goals were central to the development of the Kaiaka Reo proficiency tests with which this chapter is concerned. Those goals and the Kaiaka Reo Team associated with that development were factors that motivated a large number of Māori medium schools to participate in the research. The teachers and the school communities perceived the development of an assessment tool that was developed *by Māori, for Māori in te reo Māori* as extremely valuable and worthwhile. The high participation rate, of forty-four of sixty eight schools, is an attestation of their faith that the Kaiaka Reo Team would develop a Māori language proficiency tool that would advance and enhance their goals.

It was against this background that the test at the centre of this study, Kaiaka Reo, was born and the need for an instrument to measure the Māori language proficiency of students in Māori medium settings was recognized.

At the time that the 2000-2001 tests were developed, there was no instrument available for teachers in Māori medium primary educational settings to assess the Māori language proficiency of their students. The value of an instrument for Māori medium learning contexts that focussed on Māori language proficiency instead of literacy was identified.

This study has achieved its objective: it has shown the scores on the Kaiaka Reo Year Eight test in writing to be reasonably reliable and valid. The model used here could readily be adapted to determine the reliability of the remaining tests of Kaiaka Reo Year Eight test in speaking (oral language), Kaiaka Reo Year Five test in writing, and the Kaiaka Reo Year Five test in speaking (oral language).

This study has also identified the value of an indigenous instrument for assessing language proficiency. It also demonstrates a process of development that other indigenous groups might like to adopt and adapt for their own indigenous language and cultural revitalisation purposes. The success of the Māori community in developing a test that produces reliable and valid scores for its language provides an indigenous precedent, and an adaptable model, for other indigenous groups who feel the need to test for indigenous language proficiency.

The development of the test *by Māori, for Māori, in te reo Māori* demonstrates that it is possible to provide assessments of Māori language proficiency for Māori students that meet both kaupapa Māori philosophy criteria and international standards for the investigation of reliability and validity.

References

Armour-Thomas, E. (1992). Intellectual assessment of children from culturally diverse backgrounds. *School Psychology Review, 21*(4), 552–565.

Bachman, L. (1990). *Fundamental considerations in language testing*. Oxford: Oxford University Press.

Bachman, L. (2003). *Fundamental considerations in language testing*. Oxford, UK: Oxford University Press.

Bishop, R. (1996). *Whakawhanaungatanga: Collaborative research stories.* Palmerston North: Dunmore.

Bond, T., & Fox, C. (2007). *Applying the Rasch model: Fundamental measurement in the human sciences.* Mahwah, NJ: Laurence Erlbaum Associates.

Brown, J. D. (2005). *Testing in language programs.* New York: McGraw-Hill.

Brown, J. D., & Bailey, K. M. (1984). A categorical instrument for scoring second language writing skills. *Language Learning, 34,* 21–42.

Brown, J. D., & Hudson, T. (2002). *Criterion-referenced language testing.* Cambridge, UK: Cambridge University Press.

Crombie, W., Houia, W., & Reedy, T. (2000). Issues in testing the proficiency of learners of indigenous languages: An example relating to young learners of Māori. *Journal of Māori and Pacific Development, 1*(1), 10–26.

Cronbach, L. J. (1971a). Construct validation after thirty years. In R. L. Thorndike (Ed.), *Educational measurement.* Washington, DC: American Council on Education.

Cronbach, L. J. (1971b). Test validation. In R. L. Thorndike (Ed.), *Educational measurement* (2nd ed.). New York: Harper and Row.

Cronbach, L. J. (1988). Five perspectives on validity argument. In H. Wainer & H. I. Braun (Eds.), *Test validity.* Hillsdale, NJ: Lawrence Erlbaum Associates.

Durie, M. H. (1998). *Te mana, te kāwanatanga: The politics of self-determination.* Auckland: Oxford University Press.

Edmonds, C. A. (2008). *The reliability and validity of the Maori Language Proficiency in Writing Test: Kaiaka Reo Year Eight.* Unpublished doctoral dissertation. Hilo, Hawai'i: University of Hawai'i at Hilo.

Henning, G. (1987). *A guide to language testing: Development, evaluation, research.* Cambridge, UK: Newbury House.

Hollings, M., Jeffries, R., & McArdell, P. (1992). *Assessment in kura kaupapa Māori and Māori language immersion programmes: A report to the Ministry of Education.* Wairarapa: Wairarapa Community Polytechnic.

Leeman, E. (1981). Evaluating language assessment tests: Some practical considerations. In J. B. Erickson & D. R. Omark (Eds.), *Communicating assessment of the bilingual bicultural child.* Baltimore, MD: University Park Press.

Linacre, J. M. (1997). Guidelines for rating scales. MESA research note #2 Retrieved November 11, 2008, from http://www.rasch.org/rn2.htm

Littler, R. (2001). *Report on Kaiaka Reo data.* Waikato, NZ: University of Waikato.

McNamara, T. (1996). *Measuring second language performance.* London: Longman.

Messick, S. (1975). The standard problem: Meaning and values in measurement and evaluation. *American Psychologist, 30,* 955–966.

Messick, S. (1980). Test validity and the ethics of assessment. *American Psychologist, 35,* 1012–1027.

Messick, S. (1989). Validity. In R. L. Linn (Ed.), *Educational Measurement* (pp. 13–104). New York: Macmillan.

Messick, S. (1995). Validity of psychological assessment. *American Psychologist, 50*(9), 741–749.

Messick, S. (1996). Validity and washback in language testing. *Language Testing, 13*(3), 741–749.

Ministry of Education (1996). *Te reo Māori i roto i te marautanga o Aotearoalc.* Wellington, NZ: Te Pou Taki Kōrero

Ministry of Education (2000). *Tikanga a Iwi i roto i te Marautanga o Aotearoa* [Māori social sciences in the New Zealand curriculum]. Wellington, NZ: Learning Media.

Ministry of Education (2008). *Is there a place for you in primary teaching: Teacher education qualifications 2009.* Retrieved October 13, 2008 from http://www.teachnz.govt.nz/thinking-of-becoming-a-teacher/maori/help-to-consider-teaching.

Soukhanov, A. (1999). *Encarta world English dictionary.* New York: St. Martin's Press.

Wright, B. D. (1996). Comparing Rasch measurement and factor analysis. *Structural Equation Modeling, 3*(1), 3–24.

Wright, B. D., & Linacre, J. M. (1992). Combining and splitting of categories. *Rasch Measurement Transactions, 6*(3), 233–235.

Wright, B. D., & Masters, G. N. (1982). *Rating scale analysis.* Chicago: MESA.

Appendix A: Cognitive competencies

	8–10 year olds		11–13 year olds
1	cognitive activity is focused on the concrete world not the abstract; the focus is on the real, physical and observable	1	beginning to work through logical systems in a systematic manner
2	no longer tied to their visual perception of objects or events; can evaluate or check up on their perceptions of the physical world	2	thinking becoming hypothetical and abstract not necessarily tied to the real concrete world of space and time
3	can decentre by focusing on more than one feature of a visual array, coordinating different centrations	3	interest develops in the ideal, the probable and the non physical
4	can reverse their thinking mentally to an original array that is not present because its appearance has changed	4	can combine a number of ideas within a logical system
5	realises that the identity of an object doesn't change when only its appearance has been changed	5	egocentrism takes the form of an imagined audience and a personal fable as personal identity is sought
6	can classify objects and numbers by set and subset and seriate them in order	6	verbal reversibility in thinking becomes internalized, not necessarily related to concrete but also abstract ideas
7	can coordinate spatial perspectives from two or four positions other than their own perspective, depending on the relevance of the experimental materials to their own experience	7	thinking now deductive and inductive, able to generate a number of possible solutions to problems
8	egocentric language is internalized; uses inner speech to verbally rehearse ideas related to physical objects and events in the visual concrete world	8	thought becomes more internalized so that one can think about one's own thinking
9	social egocentrism still evident in dealing with more than two aspects of social events; can put oneself in another person's position unlike when younger	9	thought becomes more propositional considering possibilities beyond the real world, developing a number of propositions to their logical conclusion
10	can reason deductively from general to a specific solution but has difficulty with a number of solutions	10	even faster at processing information and better at memory strategies like rehearsal
11	faster at processing information and better at memory strategies like rehearsal	11	even more complexity in scripts and efficiency in meta-cognitive strategies
12	more complexity in scripts and efficiency in meta-cognitive strategies	12	greater idealism in social and moral cognition
13	focuses on intentions as well as consequences in judging social and moral situations	13	can combine action, image, and word at a more advanced thinking level than previously
14	conventional rules now regarded as arbitrary and changeable	14	can mentally represent several spatial perspectives from points of view other than their own

15	less dependent on parents and teachers when making social and moral judgments	15	more advanced knowledge of the social system, conventions now not part of a rule system but a social system and as such changeable, arbitrary and only social expectations
16	growing conformity to peer group expectations and ideas	16	moral rule transgressions even more serious than conventional rule transgressions
17	moral rule transgressions more serious than conventional rule transgressions	17	care and justice reasoning may be used in judging social and moral situations; boys may choose justice and girls care type reasoning
18	social system knowledge developing, conventions now arbitrary rules, no longer sacrosanct but arbitrary and changeable	18	more than two different social and moral perspectives can now be considered
19	both care and justice reasoning may be used in judging social and moral situations; boys may prefer justice and girls may prefer care type reasoning	19	even more cognitive independence from parents and teachers; adolescent peer group however an even stronger influence on social and moral cognition; respect for law and emergence of social contract ideals in social and moral issues

Appendix B: Diagnostic marking schedule A

abbreviation	meaning	example	value	
kura/tamaiti	school number and the child number	01/01		
pic		picture number		
phr pot	phrase potential	FW/MW/OB	each	2
FW	function word(s)	at the beginning of the phrase e.g., *i, ki te, i te, kei te, e ... ana, ko, kua, he, hei*		2
MW	main word	the word that is following the function word (usually a noun or a verb)		2
OB(s)	other bit(s)	the word or words in that phrase that qualify, modify or add to the meaning of the main word (adjectives, directionals, emphasisers)		2
Ddn1	deduction 1 (error/s)	if the function word at the beginning of the phrase is wrong, inappropriate, omitted, incomplete	for each aberration above	2
PO pot	phrase order potential	tally at the end of marking each response to test stimuli the total of phrases used and correct order of phrases. *please check the no. of phrases and phrasing	1 phrase= 2 phrases= 3 phrases= n phrases=	0 2 3 n, etc.
Ddn 2	deduction 2 (error/s)	if there is a phrase/or phrases in the wrong order	count the total no. of phrases and deduct those that are in the wrong order. apply the above values	n
WC	written conventions	the mechanics of writing. spelling, punctuation etc. year five. upper case/lower case, full stops award a bonus if the comma and speech marks are used appropriately	for each separate response to test stimuli: 0 errors= 1–3 errors= 4+ errors=	2 1 0
ET Ddn 3	English transfer	when a word or phase is accurate but not the correct way of saying something in Māori e.g., *kei ahau he waero* (is grammatically correct but not the appropriate way (in Māori) to say "I have a tail;" this does not include transliteration	deduct for the phrase/s (i.e., each complete expression)	–2

bonus	bonus points	award for correct use of macrons, commas, speech marks, paragraphing, appropriate idioms	each, however do not award repeatedly if the item is the same e.g., macron on *kōtiro* if the same word is used again the correct use of the macron has already been awarded	1
kupu	vocabulary	each different word used (these have been identified and are on an attached sheet – count at the end)	per item but do not count again if used again in the same way i.e., award only when first used	1
total	total marks		
reason	reason for deduction		
correction	correction		

Appendix C: Diagnostic marking Schedule B

kura/ tamaiti	pic	phr pot	ddn1	PO pot	ddn 2	WC	ET ddn 3	bonus	*kupu*	total	reason

Appendix D: Kaiaka Reo: ID 38

1. Ko te ingoa o tenei tuatara ko Tama e toru ona tamariki no te XXXXX ia ko nga ingoa o tona tamariki ko Tane, Hone, Tama, ko te Potiki ko Tama.

2. Ko te ingoa o te manu ko Naomi. Ko te ingoa o te noke ko Paki kote ingoa o te Kuri ko Hone. Te XXXXX ratau.

3. Ko Paki te ingoa o tenei tuatara kei te kai ia i tetahi pungawerewere irunga i te rakau kauri i roto i te ngahere.

4. Ko Hone te ingoa o tenei Tuatara kei te haere ki te whakangau pungawerewere i roto i te ngahere

5. Ko Tama te ingoa o tenei tuatara e waru ona tau kei te haere ia ki te kainga mo te kai.

6. Ko Honore te ingoa o tenei tuatara. ko XXXXX raua ko XXXXX ona matua no XXXXX ia kei te haere i ki Waikato
7. Ko XXXXX me XXXXX tera no XXXXX raua he hoa tino pai raua.
8. He heki enei e wha nga heki ko nga ingoa o nga heki ko XXXXX, XXXXX, XXXXX, XXXXX. No XXXXX
9. e ono nga rakau e kauri ratou kei te noho ratou ki roto i te ngahere o XXXXX
10. Ko Paerau tenei tuatara kei te tatari ia mo tona mama i roto i te wharepaku
11. Ko Tama tenei inaianei e iwa ona tau i Tiki ia he pungawerewere.
12. Ko Honore tenei i whitu ona tau kei te kai ia he noke.
13. Ko XXXXX raua ko XXXXX kei te moe raua i whitu te pakeke a XXXXX.
14. Ko Ruru To nga ingoa i nui o nga whatu i tekau o nga tau no Waikato ia.
15. Ko matua tōna ingoa no XXXXX ia i whitu o nga tau no XXXXX ia.
16. ko XXXXX ia kei te waiata ia i te waiata e Honore i whitu o nga tau.

Appendix E: Kaiaka Reo: Whārite Whakatau: Tau Tuawaru (8)

Kura: _____ Tamaiti: _____ Rā: _____

	1	2	3	4	
organisation and ideas					
grammar/ accuracy					
punctuation, style and mechanics					
style and quality of expression					
Maori discourse intelligibility					
overall impression	0–4	5–9	10–14	15–20	PIRO _____
	beginner	elementary	intermediate	advanced	

He kōrero:
_____
_____
_____

Te tangata whakatau

Kura: _____ Tamaiti: _____ Rā: _____

Appendix F: Kaiaka Reo: Rārangi Tangata Whakatau

nama	ingoa	current position	years in teaching profession	years teaching in primary	years teaching in secondary	years teaching in tertiary	years teaching in immersion	years teaching in mainstream	Māori language

The Hawaiian Oral Language Assessment: Development and Effectiveness of the Scoring Rubric

Alohalani Housman
Kaulana Dameg
Māhealani Kobashigawa
University of Hawai'i at Hilo

James Dean Brown
University of Hawai'i at Mānoa

Introduction

This chapter[1] presents a shortened version of our full report on the development and effectiveness of the Hawaiian Oral Language Assessment (H-Ola). The full report is available in Housman, Dameg, Kobashigawa, and Brown (2011) which can be downloaded online at the URL provided in the references. In particular, for more information on the background of the Hawaiian language revitalization movement and Hawaiian language immersion program qualitative assessment efforts that were made over the years, see the full report. Similarly that report contains considerable information about the first systematic studies designed to investigate the effectiveness of the Hawaiian language immersion program (HLIP) in transmitting the Hawaiian language to a new generation of children, as well as about two related programs: the *Kaiaka Reo* project commissioned by the New Zealand Ministry of Education to develop a Māori language proficiency assessment tool in the form of proficiency tests (Edmonds, 2008; also see Chapter 5) and the Cherokee Immersion Language Assessment project (Cherokee Nation, 2003, 2009). Since the purpose of this chapter is to focus on the development and effectiveness of the H-Ola as an assessment tool rather than to explain its place in the larger set of language revitalization and testing issues, we will simply refer you to the full report for further information on those aspects of the project and provide essential background information here.

---

[1] This project was funded by the Native Hawaiian Education Program of the USDOE, CFDA Number: 84.362A (8/1/2007 to 7/31/2010).

Housman, A., Dameg, K., Kobashigawa, M., & Brown, J. D. (2012). The Hawaiian oral language assessment: Development and effectiveness of the scoring rubric. In J. D. Brown, (Ed.), *Developing, using, and analyzing rubrics in language assessment with case studies in Asian and Pacific languages* (pp. 131–167). Honolulu: University of Hawai'i, National Foreign Language Resource Center.

Hawaiian language immersion program (HLIP) education came into existence in the Hawaiʻi public school system over 23 years ago. In the 1989–1990 and 1990–1991 school years, the first systematic study to investigate the effectiveness of the HLIP in transmitting the Hawaiian language to a new generation of children was conducted. Even though the study only included the language excerpts of students from one school, the information that Warner (1996) collected during his research is invaluable in that it provides the first analysis of grammatical structures produced by HLIP students in the early elementary grades. In more recent years, especially since the No Child Left Behind Act was written, the Department of Education (DOE) has translated or created standardized assessment tests to evaluate students' abilities in the area of reading, writing, and math. However, to date, no formal oral language assessment in the Hawaiian language has been developed by the State office. Since no formal oral language assessment is available, individual HLIP schools and/or teachers have attempted to assess their students informally within the classroom setting. This type of informal assessment aids in evaluating students' abilities can than be used to inform instruction, but in order to ensure consistency between schools, it is imperative that a statewide standard be established to determine language proficiency levels of students across the board in the HLIP.

The Hale Kuamoʻo Hawaiian Language Center located at the University of Hawaiʻi at Hilo received a Native Hawaiian Education grant from the federal government in 2007. The central goal of the grant project, entitled ʻŌlelo Ola (the Living Language), is to develop a high level of Hawaiian language oral proficiency among Hawaiian language immersion students enabling them to meet and exceed standards in Hawaiian. There are five main objectives of the grant (*Ka Haka ʻUla O Keʻelikōlani*, 2007, p. 6):

1. To investigate current research on oral language development and proficiency that benefits Hawaiian language immersion students in grades K–3.

2. To develop assessment resources and curricula that support Hawaiian oral language development and proficiency for K–3 HLIP students.

3. To conduct ongoing assessment of the Hawaiian language oral proficiency of K–3 HLIP students by expanding and adapting research.

4. To strengthen the oral language proficiency of K–3 HLIP students by providing teacher preservice and inservice training.

5. To support families of K–3 HLIP students, and other interested community members, in developing Hawaiian language oral proficiency and literacy skills within the home environment.

This report in its entirety focuses on the first three objectives of the grant. The research team also completed the last two objectives, however, they will not be covered in this document. The first objective will be addressed in the Review of Literature. The second objective will be explained in the Methodology section. The third objective will be described in the Methodology and Results sections.

The first task of the research grant team was to investigate current research on oral language development and proficiency. Housman, et al. (2011) describe the five assessments that provided major contributions to the construction of the Hawaiian Oral Language Assessment (H-OLA) and the rubric that was used to score the language proficiency level of HLIP students. These assessments were chosen based on the similarities of language revitalization goals found amongst indigenous people as well as their relevance to an immersion educational context.

A central objective of the ʻŌlelo Ola project was to develop a detailed and comprehensive oral language proficiency assessment to collect baseline data on the oral language proficiency levels of HLIP students in grades 1–3 at seven participating schools. This was to be accomplished through the creation and utilization of a standards-based assessment tool and an oral language proficiency rubric.

It is important to note that the oral proficiency level of teachers in the classroom is directly related to the language development and proficiency of the students. This is highlighted in the HLIP Program Guide (Office of Instructional Services, General Education Branch, 1994). It emphasizes the importance of teacher oral proficiency and also the connection between oral proficiency and literacy by stating the following:

> A skilled, highly proficient teacher can provide the best model of appropriate Hawaiian language usage as well as design curriculum that optimizes language learning for the new speaker of Hawaiian. This enhances students' skills in all aspects of language use—speaking, reading, and writing—as well as minimizes the need to spend time correcting inappropriate use of Hawaiian in subsequent years. (p. 7)

Therefore, of central importance to the ʻŌlelo Ola project is the capacity for the assessment instruments developed to provide continuous feedback for improvement in teaching and learning, as well as a summative evaluation to provide a quantitative measure of systemic program growth.

Since its inception in 1987, the HLIP has grown significantly and the issue of oral language proficiency has not been sufficiently addressed. Thus the ʻŌlelo Ola team posed the following three research questions:

1. What are the most important aspects of oral language development that should be assessed?
2. What is the Hawaiian oral language proficiency level of Hawaiian Language Immersion Program (HLIP) students in grades 1–3?
3. Once baseline data is collected, what can be done to improve the Hawaiian language proficiency level of students?

The ʻŌlelo Ola team chose to focus on the oral language proficiency of grades 1–3 not only because of the stipulations of the federal grant with which it was funded, but also to be able to assess and intervene to improve the students' proficiency level at a critical stage of oral language development. It was decided that kindergarten level students would not be assessed due to the length of the test and their developmental limitations. Also, in order to complete the project in accordance with the timetable outlined in the grant, the project would assess a broad representative sample of students from various schools on the different islands rather than attempting to assess all prospective study participants. The sample selected would be drawn from the three types of schools in the HLIP: charter, laboratory, and DOE public schools.

Methodology

This section is divided into four major categories: (a) participants, (b) procedures of test development, (c) materials, (d) test administration steps, and (e) rating steps.

Participants

The participants in this project were 270 students from seven HLIP schools located on four different islands. They ranged in age from 7 to 10 with a mean of 7.93 years and standard deviation of .85 years. In terms of gender, 123 were male and 147 were female. They were in grades 1 (*n*=110), 2 (*n*=86), and 3 (*n*=74). Seventy attended laboratory schools, 100 were in charter schools, and 100 were in other DOE immersion schools. The seven schools were coded anonymously here 1 to 7, but the distribution of students in schools was as follows: 1 (*n*=75), 2 (*n*=45), 3 (*n*=25), 4 (*n*=8), 5 (*n*=17), 6 (*n*=53), and 7 (*n*=47). A total of 109 students had previous *Pūnana Leo* (Hawaiian immersion pre-school) experience, while 161 did not. The numbers of years in Hawaiian language schools were as follows: 1 year=8, 2 years=74, 3 years=66, 4 years=83, 5 years=27, 6 years=8, and 7 years=3 (data in this category was not provided for one student). The amount of Hawaiian language use in the home was rated on a 1–6 scale (where 1=low and 6=high), but there was one zero given, so there were seven different ratings overall: 0 (*n*=1), 1 (*n*=63), 2 (*n*=77), 3 (*n*=77), 4 (*n*=35), 5 (*n*=11), and 6 (*n*=6). The language levels of the students were rated by their teachers on a 1–3 scale (where 1=*low* and 3=*high*), but there were two zeros given, so there were four ratings overall: 0 (*n*=2), 1 (*n*=60), 2 (*n*=154), and 3 (*n*=54).

There were five raters in this study. Two were professors of *Ka Haka ʻUla o Keʻelikōlani* College of Hawaiian Language and three were members of *Hale Kuamoʻo's ʻŌlelo Ola* grant team. The raters were the same people who wrote, developed, and revised the tests investigated in this project. In their roles as raters, each administered the test to between 47 and 65 students and scored the same students for both the Extended Response Items and the Short Oral Response (SOR) items. These raters were coded as: rater 1 (*n*=47), rater 2 (*n*=52), rater 3 (*n*=65), rater 4 (*n*=47), and rater 5 (*n*=59).

Procedures of test development

The ʻŌlelo Ola team was made up of individuals who specialize in Hawaiian language immersion education, and/or Hawaiian language and culture. In order to develop an effective assessment tool, it was essential that an advisory committee consisting of experts on language assessment, linguistics, and Hawaiian language and culture be invited to participate with the ʻŌlelo Ola team in the development of an assessment tool appropriate for the target grade levels from its draft stages until its finalized version.

An important part of the process in developing the Hawaiian Oral Language Assessment (H-OLA) tool along with an appropriate scoring rubric was looking at other oral language assessment instruments that were developed by other experts. The ʻŌlelo Ola team benefited from the fact that Katarina Edmonds was completing her doctoral thesis in Hilo during the same time that the Hawaiian assessment was being developed. The team gleaned insights from her knowledge, experience, and expertise regarding Māori immersion, linguistics, and assessment. Katarina played a significant role as the project manager in the development of the *Kaiaka Reo Māori* Language Assessment. The oral language section of the Kaiaka Reo laid the foundation for the development of the Story-telling Picture Series (described in the Materials section) of the Hawaiian Oral Language Assessment (H-OLA). In addition, the Kaiaka Reo analytical scale was analyzed in the process of developing a scoring rubric for the Hawaiian assessment.

The H-OLA development team felt it was also necessary to include a short response section of the test, which looked at specific components of Hawaiian grammar. Therefore, a close examination of the Cherokee Kindergarten Immersion Language Assessment (C-KILA) was undertaken. The Cherokee assessment inspired the development of items included in the short response section of the Hawaiian assessment such as identifying objects (nouns), identifying actions (verb, verb marker, pronoun), using locatives, and following commands.

Lastly, the development team investigated the Student Oral Proficiency Assessment (SOPA) developed by the Center of Applied Linguistics (CAL). Several team members were familiar with the SOPA due to a class offered to Hawaiian language professors and immersion teachers in Spring 2007. During the semester class, Dee Tedick and Tara Fortune from the Center for Advanced Research on Language Acquisition (CARLA) elucidated several assessments that could be used to assess oral language proficiency levels of immersion students. Based on the age and task appropriateness of the SOPA, a similar task construct was created for the H-OLA. The finalized version of the H-OLA consists of four parts that comprise open-ended (Parts 1 & 4) and form-focused (Parts 2 & 3) oral prompts.

1. Introduction/Interview
2. Listening Comprehension & Short Response (identifying objects, pronouns, and location)
3. Listening Comprehension & Short Response (verbs, verb markers, personal pronouns)
4. Story-telling Picture Series (two series)

Test piloting

Piloting was done in March 2009 at two Hawaiian language immersion program sites, including one laboratory school and one charter school. Teachers of grades 1–3 from the participating schools were asked to select three students from their class to participate in the pilot study, one from each level of oral language proficiency (low, average, and high). There were 21 students that participated: nine laboratory school students and 12 charter school students. All five evaluators participated in the pilot testing, individually assessing at least one student from each grade level and each level of proficiency.

Test revisions

During pilot testing, three picture series were used: the Lei Series, the Slipper Series, and the Beach Series. This was done to determine which two of the three picture series would elicit the most language from students and would produce the most similar results. It was decided that for the formal test, the Lei Series and the Slipper Series would be used. Each series was used to elicit extended oral responses from approximately half of the students during the first assessment with all seven schools in spring 2009 with the understanding that during the follow-up assessment one year later, each student would be evaluated using a different series from the prior year to ensure that students would not memorize the pictures.

One section of the pilot test, oral story retelling based on a wordless book, was removed from the assessment. It was apparent that not all students were familiar with the story chosen, so instead of retelling the story, students had to create a storyline, and those familiar with the story had an unfair advantage. Furthermore, pilot testers observed that the wordless book prompt elicited basically the same type of response as the Story-telling Picture Series prompt. However, during the formal testing, when time permitted, students were asked to tell the story of the wordless book using the best language possible. This information was not scored, but was used in an error analysis report that included the grammatical strengths and weaknesses found in testing. An individual report for each school was given to participating schools and teachers.

In the pilot study, testing was done over two consecutive days in two sessions (approximately 20 minutes per session). Due to time constraints, some revisions were made to shorten the length of the test, keeping the most valuable, reliable or challenging items, and removing duplicate items. To aid in the selection of items to be removed, the form-focused sections of the test were scored and data analysis was done to determine items that were unreliable or not essential to the outcome of the test. Some items were too easy, and therefore unnecessary, and some items were too difficult, and deemed unreliable for the assessment, and some duplicate items were evident. As a result of this analysis, a section used to build confidence was shortened from 14 to 5 items; a section identifying objects, pronouns, and locations was reduced from 30 to 18 items; and a section testing verbs, verb markers, and pronouns were removed, reducing that section from 48 to 27 items). Using the revised test, the administrators were able to complete each assessment in a single 15–30 minute session.

Materials

The Hawaiian Oral Language Assessment (H-OLA) includes materials for long response and short response sections of the test. The long response sections were developed to elicit open-ended responses that would demonstrate the language being used by students in the target grades. The short response sections were developed to test the students' knowledge of specific sentence structures and parts of speech categories.

The long response section of the test includes two different Story-telling Picture Series tests. Each picture series consists of a set of six laminated, color-illustrated picture cards produced by a professional graphic artist following the conceptual guidance of the test development team. Used as prompts for open-ended oral storytelling, the two sets of cards are referred to by the development team as the Lei Series and the Slipper Series. In addition, a set of three color-illustrated laminated picture cards (referred to as the birthday series) was used for practice with the students in preparation for the official independent storytelling assessment.

The short response section of the test includes an array of manipulatives, selected to assess familiarity with nouns, and a set of laminated, color-illustrated action pictures, which are organized as a spiral bound flip chart.

An instruction booklet was developed by the team to ensure consistency during the administration of the test. Each booklet included detailed instructions on test administration, a script for evaluators, a list of needed supplies, and established goals for each task.

Each assessment started with introductions between the test administrator and the student. The test administrator introduced him/herself (name, names of immediate family members including sibling relationships foreign to the English language, age, place of birth and residence, pets, and favorite activity). The student was then asked to introduce him or herself in the same manner without prompts. If the student could not complete the entire task independently, the administrator would assist the student with scripted prompts. The test administrator then asked follow-up questions to check for understanding of Hawaiian sibling relationship terminology. Finally, an attempt was made to engage the student in casual conversation with the goal of eliciting as much language as possible while putting the student at ease and establishing comfort and rapport with the administrator.

The next unscored section of the assessment was a simple task that required students to point to familiar objects on the table. This was included to help students feel comfortable and confident about their ability to complete the assessment.

In the first part of the Short Oral Response section of the test, students were asked to first identify an object using the correct noun and pronoun and then identify its location in relation to a plastic box. The objects used for this section (spoon, shark, lei, etc.) were selected for their likely familiarity to students in these grade levels. Nine practice items, which were not scored, preceded the 18 formal items of this portion, including six items each for nouns, pronouns, and locatives. Practice items were used to ensure that students understood what was expected of them in the task in order to get a true assessment of students' language abilities.

In the second part of the Short Oral Response section, students were shown successive color illustrations and asked to state what action was being done (using the appropriate Hawaiian pronoun) in each picture. Following the set of pictures, the student and/or administrator performed simple actions (e.g., waving, clapping, building a house from blocks). For each action, the student was asked to state the action being done and by whom (using pronouns). Nine practice items preceded the 18 formal items, including six items each for verbs, verb markers, and pronouns.

The extended oral response sections of the test included the introductions described in the first task as well as a Picture Series prompt that was used in the last task of the formal assessment. For the Picture Series prompt, students were asked to tell a story about six picture cards arranged in a consecutive series, using the best language possible. From the two picture series that were determined following the pilot testing, one was randomly assigned to each student. A three-picture series was used as practice for this section of the test. Administrators provided coaching as needed, only during the practice series. Students were also asked to predict what would happen after the last picture for both the practice series and the formal assessment prompt that followed the practice.

Test administration steps

Students were randomly assigned to an administrator fluent in the target language and tests were conducted individually, with one administrator and one student. It was decided that students would be tested individually so that each student could interact with a test administrator without being interrupted or dominated by another student, or feel uneasy about responding to questions in front of another student.

The test was administered in a quiet room, free from distractions, but due to limited room availability at some school sites, in some instances, from two to five administrators conducted tests in a large spacious but undisturbed room, such as the cafeteria. This proved challenging at times, but students were still able to successfully complete testing in a satisfactory environment.

In most cases, all testing was completed between the times of 8:00 AM to 11:00 AM when the students were most attentive and the school sites tended to be more quiet and conducive to learning. During a designated time slot, students were individually called from class by an administrator and escorted to an assigned room away from the classroom. They were seated directly across from the administrator to create a formal testing atmosphere in the least distractive sitting arrangement possible.

Digital audio recorders were used during the administration of the test. Audio files were transcribed and revisited at a later time during scoring. It was decided that test administrators would not do any evaluations (rating, scoring, writing notes) at the time of testing to prevent the students from becoming nervous or apprehensive. A table of student names with numerical codes was provided and used to identify students in digital recordings while helping to maintain anonymity in file names.

Rating steps

In order to assess oral language proficiency, the ʻŌlelo Ola team had to develop a method for rating the collected data. The two form-focused, Short Oral Response sections of the test were given a 1 for a correct response and a 0 for an incorrect response on the 45 items. Because the Introduction and Story-telling Picture Series tests used open-ended oral language prompts, they could not be rated in this manner, and therefore an assessment rubric was needed.

The ʻŌlelo Ola team, with the guidance of experts on language assessment, collectively developed a Hawaiian oral language proficiency assessment rubric to rate the Introduction and Story-telling Picture Series portions of the test. This rubric would represent Hawaiian oral language proficiency as defined by this team. See Appendix A (Hawaiian version of the rubric) and Appendix B (English version of the rubric).

The assessment rubric was developed with three levels of proficiency (novice, intermediate, and pre-advanced), in seven proficiency domains: communicative skill, vocabulary, grammar, pronunciation, fluency, language steadfastness, and cultural and linguistic authenticity.

Using a number of student examples from the data collection conducted in May 2009, after the initial interviews had been completed, the ʻŌlelo Ola team and language assessment experts tested the initial draft of the rubric. Through experimentation, and resulting discussions, the team was able to improve the clarity and efficacy of the rubric, and build inter-rater reliability.

Students were rated on only the first two minutes of the Introduction, and then rated on the entire Story-telling Picture Series test. By listening to the audio file and using a transcription of these sections as reference, the rater used a 1–3 scale (where 1=*novice*, 2=*intermediate*, and 3=*pre-advanced*) to rate students in each of the seven proficiency domains mentioned above. Each rater scored each of the students with whom they conducted the oral language test.

The entire Introduction, Story-telling Picture Series, and story-telling using the wordless book section, was later analyzed by all raters and used to create a personalized report for participating schools and teachers on the grammatical strengths and weaknesses of their school. Schools were also shown a box and whisker plot revealing the level of proficiency demonstrated by the students in their school in comparison to the students in other participating schools. The anonymity of the other schools was maintained in all documents.

Results

This section presents the results of the study. The analysis of the oral language assessment data is broken down into several categories, which include: (a) the descriptive statistics of the open-ended long response test and the short response test, (b) an item analysis of individual subtests in the assessment, (c) correlational analyses, and (d) a multifaceted Rasch analysis.

Descriptive statistics

Table 1 shows the descriptive statistics for the total scores for the Open-Ended Oral Response sections (including the Introduction and either the Lei or Slipper series) and the form-focused Short Oral Response sections of the H-OLA assessment. Notice that 270 students took the Introduction and Short Oral Response Tests. The Lei and Slipper Picture Series tests were each taken by approximately half of the students: the Lei Series was taken by 137 examinees and the Slipper Series by 133. Note also that the means, medians, and midpoints are very similar for the Introduction, Lei Series, and Slipper Series with all of them falling between 13 and 14. Since these indicators of central tendency are based on a test with a total of 21 points possible, the scores are reasonably well centered. The high, low, range, and standard deviation indicate that the scores for the Introduction, Lei Series, and Slipper Series are also fairly widely dispersed around the central tendency with room for at least two standard deviations above and below the mean in all cases. All of this indicates that the distributions of these three measures were reasonably normal in shape. The Total Series combines the Introduction and Lei Series scores with the Introduction and Slipper scores (as though two forms of the test were combined). Naturally, these statistics (based on 270 students and 42 points possible) also indicate that the scores are well centered and dispersed. The reliabilities for the Introduction, Lei Series, and Slipper Series were moderate at .80, .74, and .69, respectively, meaning that the seven series category ratings taken together were 80%, 74%, and 69% reliable and 20%, 26%, and 31% unreliable, respectively.

The 45 items of the Short Oral Response sections were also completed by 270 students. The pattern of high to low for the indicators of central tendency (median=36.00, mean=33.90, and midpoint=26.00) and the fact that there is not room for two standard deviations above the mean in the distribution indicate that the distribution is somewhat skewed. In this case, it appears that this section of the test is a bit too easy for these students. Put another way, the short response items would probably function better if some of the easy items were eliminated and more difficult items were added. The reliability for the form-focused Short Oral Response section of the test turned out to be a moderately high .87 meaning that the 45 items taken together were 87% reliable and 13% unreliable.

Table 1.   Descriptive statistics for the Introduction, Lei Series, Short Oral Response test totals

statistic	Introduction	Lei Series	Slipper Series	total for open-ended oral response items	total for SOR items
Number	270	137	133	270	270
total Possible	21	21	21	42	45
Mean	13.25	13.46	13.83	26.89	33.90
Median	13.00	14.00	14.00	27.00	36.00
Midpoint	14.00	13.50	13.50	27.00	29.00
High	21	20	19	40	45
Low	7	7	8	14	13
Range	15	14	12	27	33
SD	2.93	2.41	2.30	4.82	6.62
Cronbach alpha reliability	.80	.74	.69	NA	.87

Tables 2, 3, and 4 show the descriptive statistics in a different way for the Introduction, Lei Series, and Slipper Series, respectively. Here the statistics are given separately for each of the seven categories that raters were scoring. The categories were Communicative

Skill (Com), Vocabulary (Voc), Grammar (Gra), Pronunciation (Pro), Fluency (Flu), Steadfastness (Ste), and Cultural Authenticity (Cul). The means in the tables can be used to determine which categories on which series were scored highest and lowest. For example in Table 2, Steadfastness (Ste) was scored the highest with a mean of 2.41, and Cultural Authenticity (Cul) was scored lowest with a mean of 1.27. Interestingly, the pattern of highest and lowest categories is the same in Tables 3 and 4. In any case, such comparisons of categories may help in deciding, on the basis of difficulty, which categories to keep and which to abandon.

The high and low statistics in all three tables are all 3 and 1, respectively, indicating that the full range of possible points was used by the raters in doing the scoring. The standard deviations indicate which categories spread the students out most and least. For instance, in Table 2 the Communicative Skill (Com) category had the highest standard deviation of .79, while Pronunciation (Pro) had the lowest at .53. Such comparisons of the standard deviations for categories may help in deciding, on the basis of score variation, which to keep and which to abandon.

Table 2. Descriptive statistics for the Introduction categories, totals, and averages

statistic	com	voc	gra	pro	flu	ste	cul	total	average
Number	270	270	270	270	270	270	270	270	270
Mean	2.01	1.84	1.69	2.27	1.77	2.41	1.27	13.25	1.89
Median	2.00	2.00	2.00	2.00	2.00	3.00	1.00	13.00	1.86
Midpoint	2.00	2.00	2.00	2.00	2.00	2.00	2.00	14.00	2.00
High	3	3	3	3	3	3	3	21	3
Low	1	1	1	1	1	1	1	7	1
Range	3	3	3	3	3	3	3	15	3
SD	.79	.63	.60	.53	.56	.67	.54	2.93	.42

Table 3. Descriptive statistics for the Lei Series categories, totals, and averages

statistic	com	voc	gra	pro	flu	ste	cul	total	average
Number	137	137	137	137	137	137	137	137	137
Mean	2.23	1.85	1.70	2.25	1.73	2.51	1.20	13.46	1.92
Median	2.00	2.00	2.00	2.00	2.00	3.00	1.00	14.00	2.00
Midpoint	2.00	2.00	2.00	2.00	2.00	2.00	2.00	13.50	1.93
High	3	3	3	3	3	3	3	20	3
Low	1	1	1	1	1	1	1	7	1
Range	3	3	3	3	3	3	3	14	3
SD	.65	.55	.53	.51	.51	.64	.42	2.41	.34

Table 4. Descriptive statistics for the Slipper Series categories, totals, and averages

statistic	com	voc	gra	pro	flu	ste	cul	total	average
Number	133	133	133	133	133	133	133	133	133
Mean	2.29	2.05	1.74	2.24	1.83	2.52	1.15	13.83	1.98
Median	2.00	2.00	2.00	2.00	2.00	3.00	1.00	14.00	2.00
Midpoint	2.00	2.00	2.00	2.00	2.00	2.00	1.50	13.50	1.93
High	3	3	3	3	3	3	2	19	3
Low	1	1	1	1	1	1	1	8	1
Range	3	3	3	3	3	3	2	12	3
SD	.66	.57	.53	.55	.56	.60	.36	2.30	.33

Table 5 gives similar information about the six subtests on the Short Oral Response (SOR) sections of the test. Notice that all 270 students completed the 45 items of these sections of the test. The high statistic supports the fact that the first three subtests had six items in each and the last three subtests had nine items in each. Note also that some students answered all six or all nine items correctly in each subtest. The means for the Noun, Locative, Marker, Verb, and Pronoun subtests were all fairly high. The fact that the means, medians, and midpoints vary considerably for the Total SOR scores and the fact that there is not room for two full standard deviations above the mean, probably indicate that there are some problems with normality in the distribution of total scores as well as in most of the subtests. Clearly, Table 5 presents the statistics of a test (and subtests) in need of revision.

Table 5. Descriptive statistics for the Short Oral Response subtests and totals

statistic	noun	dem. pronoun	locative	marker	verb	pronoun	total SOR
Number	270	270	270	270	270	270	270
Mean	5.29	3.54	4.47	6.57	7.34	6.70	33.90
Median	6.00	4.00	4.00	8.00	8.00	7.00	36.00
Midpoint	4.00	3.00	3.00	4.50	5.50	4.50	29.00
High	6	6	6	9	9	9	45
Low	2	0	0	0	2	0	13
Range	5	7	7	10	8	10	33
SD	.89	1.56	1.14	2.79	1.40	1.80	6.62

Item analysis

The best strategy to use in revising all of these tests and making them function more efficiently is to conduct item analysis. Here we will examine the item statistics for the original versions of the Introduction, Lei Series, and Slipper Series tests as well as the original Short Oral Response Test, in terms of which categories/items should be kept and which could be deleted. Much later in the report, we will consider what revised, shorter versions of all these tests would probably look like statistically if they were administered to the same sorts of students.

Table 6. Item statistics for the original versions of the Introduction, Lei Series, and Slipper Series

subtest description	Mean	r	SD	SD²
Introduction				
communicative skill	2.01	.76	.79	.62
vocabulary	1.84	.77	.63	.39
grammar	1.69	.79	.60	.36
pronunciation	2.27	.53	.53	.28
fluency	1.77	.79	.56	.32
language steadfastness	2.41	.49	.67	.45
cultural authenticity	1.27	.59	.54	.29
total (rubric scores)	13.25	.43	2.93	8.59
average of rubric scores	1.89		.42	.18
Lei Series				
communicative skill	2.23	.65	.65	.42
vocabulary	1.85	.72	.55	.30
grammar	1.70	.72	.53	.28
pronunciation	2.25	.55	.51	.26
fluency	1.73	.72	.51	.26
steadfastness	2.51	.55	.64	.41
cultural authenticity	1.20	.50	.42	.17
total (rubric scores)	13.46	.58	2.41	5.80
average of rubric scores	1.92		.34	.12
Slipper Series				
communicative skill	2.29	.64	.66	.43
vocabulary	2.05	.76	.57	.32
grammar	1.74	.71	.53	.28
pronunciation	2.24	.51	.55	.30
fluency	1.83	.65	.56	.32
steadfastness	2.52	.49	.60	.35
cultural authenticity	1.15	.34	.36	.13
total (rubric scores)	13.83	.51	2.30	5.27
average of rubric scores	1.98		.33	.11
intro & series prompts total	26.89		4.82	23.23
intro & series prompts average	1.92		.34	.12

Original versions of the Introduction, Lei Series, and Slipper Series
Table 6 shows the means, correlation coefficients (r), standard deviations (SD), and variances (SD^2) separately for each of the seven rating categories in the Introduction, Lei Series, and

Slipper Series. The means tell us about the relative difficulty (or severity) of the ratings given in each category. The correlation coefficients (r) indicate the degree to which each category is related to the total scores for each measure, or put another way, these coefficients indicate how well each category spreads the students out relative to the way the total scores spread them out. The standard deviation (SD) and variance (SD^2) are two slightly different ways of looking at how much the scores varied in each category.

What does all of this mean? To begin with, notice that the lowest means in all three sets of seven rating categories are for the Cultural Authenticity category at 1.27, 1.20, and 1.15, respectively, and that the highest means are for the Language Steadfastness category at 2.41, 2.51, & 2.52, respectively. This simply means that the raters were consistently giving their lowest ratings on average for Cultural Authenticity and their highest for Language Steadfastness. This pattern is interesting in itself, but taken together with the rest of the means, it seems that the raters were using these categories (low to high) in similar ways relative to each other in each of the three sets of seven rating categories.

The correlation coefficients indicate the degree to which each rating category spread the students out in a manner similar to the total scores for that set of seven categories. Because more observations are most often more reliable than fewer, the total scores on any test are taken to be more reliable than any single item or scoring category that contributes to that score. For this reason, we calculated the category/total correlation coefficients as an indication of how well each category is discriminating among the students in the same way that the total scores discriminated. We can use such information in trying to decide which categories we might want to eliminate in future versions of the test. For example, if we wanted to trim the number of categories used and thereby make the rating job easier, we might want to eliminate the lowest discriminating categories (Pronunciation, Steadfastness, and Cultural Authenticity) which discriminated as follows: for the Introduction, .53, .49, and .59, respectively; for the Lei Series, .55, .55, and .50, respectively; and for the Slipper Series, .51, .49, and .34.

Notice also that the same statistics are given for total scores and averages in each case. In addition, three of the correlation coefficients (r) are in bold-faced type. (These are the correlations for the total scores on each of the Introduction, Lei Series, and Slipper Series with the Introduction combined with whichever Series each student took). These indicate that the total Introduction scores correlated somewhat at .43, the total Lei Series scores a bit better at .58, and the total Slipper Series scores less and better than the other two at .51.

Original Short Oral Response

Table 7 also shows the means, point biserial correlation coefficients, standard deviations, and variances separately for each item of the Short Oral Response sections of the test that all examinees took. Notice that the items are organized into six items each (and subtotals) for Nouns, Demonstrative Pronouns, and Locatives, as well as nine items each (and subtotals) for Verb Markers, Verbs, and Pronouns. The means for each item tell us about the relative difficulty (or severity) of the items. The correlation coefficients indicate the degree to which each item is related to the total scores for each subtest, or put another way, these coefficients indicate how well each item spreads the students out relative to the way the subtest scores spread them out. The standard deviation and variance are two slightly different ways of looking at item variance.

What does all of this mean? To begin with, notice that the lowest mean is Verb: Wave=.19, which can be interpreted in this case (where the scoring is right/wrong) as the item facility, or proportion of examinees who answered correctly. By moving the decimal point two places to the right, we can interpret this as a percent (in this case, .19 becomes 19%). This means that, in this case, 19% of the examinees answered correctly. In other words, this was a difficult item for these examinees. After all, 81% got it wrong. However, two of the items had means (or item facility values) of .99 (Locative: Inside of and Verb: Sleep), which means that these two items were very easy for the examinees with 99%, or virtually everybody, answering them correctly. Good items for a placement or proficiency test are those that have item facility values around .50, say from .30 to .70.

Table 7. Item statistics for the original version of the Short Oral Response test

subtest description	Mean	r_{pbi}	SD	SD^2
noun				
shell lei	.88	.52	.32	.10
spider	.90	.55	.30	.09
octopus	.91	.49	.28	.08
spoon	.90	.43	.29	.09
shark	.77	.49	.42	.18
elephant	.93	.33	.26	.07
subtotal	**5.29**	**.48**	**.89**	**.80**
demonstrative pronoun				
kēla	.73	.29	.44	.20
kēia	.51	.62	.50	.25
kēnā	.54	.62	.50	.25
kēla	.72	.38	.45	.20
kēnā	.47	.63	.50	.25
kēia	.55	.66	.50	.25
subtotal	**3.54**	**.53**	**1.56**	**2.42**
locative				
on the side of	.62	.54	.49	.24
on top of	.95	.27	.22	.05
behind	.41	.72	.49	.24
under	.97	.28	.17	.03
inside of	.99	.35	.12	.01
in front of	.53	.75	.50	.25
subtotal	**4.47**	**.48**	**1.14**	**1.29**
verb marker				
ke...nei	.85	.73	.36	.13
ke...nei	.77	.80	.42	.17
ke...nei	.74	.79	.44	.19
ke...nei	.72	.75	.45	.20
ke...nei	.80	.81	.40	.16

ke...nei	.83	.81	.37	.14
ke...nei	.64	.75	.48	.23
ua	.64	.55	.48	.23
e...ana	.56	.53	.50	.25
subtotal	6.57	.84	2.79	7.78
	verb			
laugh	.93	.42	.26	.07
paddle (canoe)	.77	.67	.42	.18
sleep	.99	.25	.10	.01
converse (on the telephone)	.93	.48	.26	.07
cook	.86	.59	.35	.12
eat/picnic	.96	.33	.20	.04
wave	.19	.50	.39	.15
clap	.90	.53	.29	.09
build	.83	.60	.38	.14
subtotal	7.34	.76	1.40	1.96
	pronoun			
they (2)	.81	.62	.39	.16
they (3+)	.93	.56	.26	.07
he/she	.86	.58	.34	.12
they (2)	.73	.62	.44	.20
he/she	.90	.47	.30	.09
they (3+)	.93	.41	.26	.07
you	.70	.60	.46	.21
us (2)	.22	.40	.42	.17
I	.62	.51	.49	.24
subtotal	6.70	.78	1.80	3.26
SOR test total	33.90		6.62	43.85

Items in that range will also typically have relatively high point-biserial correlation coefficient (r^{pbi}). The correlation coefficients in this case (where the data were coded 0 for wrong and 1 for right) are point-biserial coefficients. In situations like this these can also be called discrimination indexes. Whatever name they are given, these values indicate the degree to which each item is spreading the students out in a manner similar to the subtest scores. We can use such information in trying to decide which items we might want to eliminate in future revised versions of the test. For example, if we wanted to trim the number of items in each subtest to five (making the test 30 items long instead of 45 items long, we could eliminate the one item with the lowest r^{pbi} value in each of the Nouns, Pronouns, and Locatives subtests, as well as the four items with the lowest r^{pbi} value in each of the Verb Markers, Verbs, and

Pronouns subtest. The resulting 30–item revised version of the test should not only be 15 items shorter than the original 45–item test, but also equally or more reliable than the .87 reliability found for this original version. Thus, the revised test should be much more efficient than the original version—being equally reliable, but quicker to administer.

Notice also that the same statistics are given for the six sets of subtest total scores (in **bold**). In addition, six of the correlation coefficients are in bold-faced italics type. These are the correlations for the subtest scores with the total test scores. These indicate that the subtests correlate with the total scores as follows: Noun/Total and Locative/Total are low at .48, Pronoun/Total is a bit better at .53, while Verb Marker/Total, Verb/Total, and Pronoun/Total are all moderately correlated at .84, .76, and .78., if we decide to cut the number of subtests, any of the first three subtests might be candidates for elimination.

Correlational analyses

Table 8 shows all possible correlation coefficients for the Introduction, Lei Series, Slipper Series, Introduction and Series combined, as well as for the Noun, Pronouns, Locative, Verb Marker, Verb, Pronoun, and Total Short Oral Response Test scores. Notice that all but three are significant at $p<.01$. This simply means that there is only a 1% probability that these coefficients occurred by chance alone. However, the degree to which the individual correlation coefficients are interesting is a separate issue. Notice for instance that the Introduction, Lei Series, Slipper Series, as well as the Introduction & Series combination all correlate with each other at between .637 and .929. Thus these correlations indicate that the various sets of scores go together from somewhat to a great deal, depending on the pairing involved. Put another way, the overlapping variances between the sets of scores ranged from 40.6% overlap to 86.3%, as indicated by r^2 (i.e., where $r=.637$ above, $r^2=.405769 \approx .406$, a proportion equivalent to 40.6%; similarly, where $r=.929$ above, $r^2=.863041 \approx .863$, a proportion equivalent to 86.3%). For ease of interpretation, the squared values for each correlation coefficient are shown in Table 9.

Table 8. Pearson product-moment correlation coefficients (extended and Short Oral Response sections)

	intro	Lei Series	Slipper Series	intro & series	noun	dem. pronoun	locative	verb marker	verb	pronoun	total SOR
intro	1.00	.637*	.673*	.929*	.202*	.132	.258*	.337*	.366*	.404*	.432*
Lei Series		1.00	**	.886*	.434*	.224*	.332*	.410*	.585*	.481*	.577*
Slipper Series			1.00	.891*	.093	.139	.289*	.459*	.390*	.456*	.513*
intro & series				1.00	.263*	.169*	.310*	.417*	.463*	.475*	.531*
noun					1.00	.110	.170*	.303*	.368*	.319*	.482*
dem. pronoun						1.00	.168*	.259*	.242*	.341*	.531*
locative							1.00	.266*	.350*	.226*	.482*
verb marker								1.00	.560*	.552*	.837*
verb									1.00	.552*	.764*

pronoun									1.00	.783*
total SOR										1.00

note: *p<.01
**no overlapping data, that is, half the students took each series, but no students took both

Table 9. Coefficients of determination (extended and Short Oral Response sections)

	intro	Lei Series	Slipper Series	intro & series	noun	dem. pronoun	locative	verb marker	verb	pronoun	total SOR
intro	1.00	.406	.453	.863	.041	.017	.067	.114	.134	.163	.187
Lei Series		1.00	**	.785	.188	.050	.110	.168	.342	.231	.333
Slipper Series			1.00	.794	.009	.019	.084	.211	.152	.208	.263
intro & series				1.00	.069	.029	.096	.174	.214	.226	.282
noun					1.00	.012	.029	.092	.135	.102	.232
dem. pronoun						1.00	.028	.067	.059	.116	.282
locative							1.00	.071	.123	.051	.232
verb marker								1.00	.314	.305	.701
verb									1.00	.305	.584
pronoun										1.00	.613
total SOR											1.00

note: **no overlapping data, that is, half the students took each series, but no students took both

In addition, the correlations shown in Table 8 for Verb Marker, Verb, and Pronoun subtest scores with the Total Short Oral Response (SOR) scores are moderately high at .837, .764, and .783, respectively. These results make sense given that the correlations of subtests within the Short Oral Response sections are themselves part of the total scores (and sets of numbers correlate with themselves perfectly, thus raising any correlation involving the set of numbers and another set of which they are part). But why are these three more highly correlated with the total scores than the Noun, Pronoun, and Locative are? Perhaps this difference occurs because the Noun, Pronoun, and Locative only have six items in each subtest, while the Verb Marker, Verb, and Pronoun subtests have nine items each; the latter three subtests are therefore contributing a larger proportion of the variance to the total scores than the former. Alternatively, the Verb Marker, Verb, and Pronoun subtests appear to be somewhat more highly related to each other, correlating at between .552 and .560 with each other, while the correlations involving the Noun, Pronoun, and Locative subtests are lower ranging from .170 to .368; this could lead to the Verb Marker, Verb, and Pronoun subtests working more closely together in their contribution to the total scores, which would in turn probably increase their correlation with those total scores.

Multifaceted Rasch analysis

Multifaceted Rasch analysis (calculated in the FACETS computer program, see Linacre, 2009) is used to examine the degree to which variables and levels of those variables produce different scores relative to each other—all on the same scale called a logit scale. In this study, we were interested in the degree to which different raters are severe or lenient and rating categories are difficult or easy.

Table 10. Preliminary results for the FACETS analysis for Introduction, Lei Series, Slipper Series, and Short Oral Response items for appropriate facets

facet	# misfit	RMSE	separation	reliability	Chi-square (fixed)
		Introduction			
examinees	7	.89	2.50	.82	p=.00
raters	0	.12	.25	.06	p=.36
categories	0	.14	13.59	.99	p=.00
		Lei Series			
examinees	6	.91	1.85	.77	p=.00
raters	0	.18	1.28	.70	p=.02
categories	0	.21	11.79	.99	p=.00
		Slipper Series			
examinees	5	.87	1.70	.74	p=.00
raters	0	.17	.00	.00	p=.53
categories	0	.21	11.56	.99	p=.00
		Short Oral Response test			
examinees	13	.49	2.21	.83	p=.00
items	0	.22	6.67	.99	p=.00

Preliminary results

Table 10 shows the preliminary results for the four FACETS analyses conducted here (one each for the Introduction, Lei Series, Slipper Series, and Short Oral Response items). Notice that labels are given for five statistics across the top of the table: # Misfit, RMSE, Separation, Reliability, and Chi-square (fixed). Also notice in the first column that the rows are labeled with the four tests (along with the facets that are appropriate for each). Let's consider each of the statistics in turn.

The *# Misfit* indicates how many examinees, raters, categories, or items "did not fit the general pattern of responses in the matrix, and can thus be classified as relatively misfitting..." (McNamara, 1996, p. 171). Notice that there were 7, 6, 5, and 13 misfitting examinees for the Introduction, Lei Series, Slipper Series, and Short Oral Response items, respectively, and that there were no misfitting raters, categories, or items. All of this means that 7, 6, 5, and 13 students were not fitting the measurement model in this analysis due to response patterns that were not expected in all but two of the cases. Two of the students completing the Short Oral Response test items received perfect scores of 45, which in Rasch analysis means that the test was not appropriate for these two students because it could not estimate if they were higher than the 45 total possible.

RMSE stands for *root mean square standard error* (for all non-extreme measures). The RMSE is used to calculate the separation index discussed in the next paragraph. However, it also serves as an estimate of standard error. The lower the RMSE the better the data fit the measurement model. The *RMSE* values in Table 10, ranging from .12 to .91, are relatively high indicating that none of these facets are fitting the model as well as might be desired.

The *separation* index tells us the degree to which each facet spreads the examinees, raters, categories, or items relative to their precision (Linacre, 2008, p. 149). The higher the value is, the more each facet is spreading the elements that it includes. Notice that the separation indexes for categories and items tend to be higher than the other values and that the rest are relatively low. All of this indicates that the categories and items facets are high in terms of the spread of the estimates relative to their precision, while the other facets are not.

The *reliability* estimates shown in Table 10 would more accurately be labeled *separation reliabilities*. According to Linacre (2008, p. 217):

> This shows how reproducibly different the measures are. This may or may not indicate how "good" the test is in other respects. High (near 1.0) person and item reliabilities are preferred. This "separation" reliability is somewhat the opposite of an interrater reliability, so low (near .0) judge and rater reliabilities are preferred.

For example, a high reliability for examinees indicates that the examinees consistently differ from each other, which is generally viewed as "good" from a norm-referenced testing viewpoint. In contrast, high reliability for raters would not typically be viewed as "good" because it indicates that the raters are consistently different from each other in the severity or leniency of the ratings they assign. The degree to which consistent differences among categories or items is important is a different sort of issue. From our point of view, there is no problem if one category is consistently scored lower or higher than the others, or if some items are consistently lower or higher than others. All in all, these reliability estimates should be interpreted as just what they are: estimates of the degree to which the test is consistently separating its examinees, raters, categories, or items. In Table 10, all measures appear to be reasonably reliable or consistent with regard to examinees. These examinee estimates are similar to the more familiar Cronbach alpha estimates of reliability that are reported elsewhere in this report. The estimates in Table 10 for raters are zero in two cases and .70 in another. This means that raters do not vary consistently from each other in two cases, but do vary with moderately consistency on the Lei Series. Category and item reliabilities are .99 in all cases, meaning that the difficulties of categories and items are consistently varying from each other.

The *chi-square (fixed)* statistic tests the following hypothesis: "Can this set of elements be regarded as sharing the same measure after allowing for measurement error?" (Linacre, 2008, p. 180). Thus for the facets in this design, the following four hypotheses are being tested:

1. Can these examinees be thought of as equally able?
2. Can these raters be thought of as equally severe or lenient in their ratings?
3. Can these categories be thought of as equally difficult?
4. Can these items be thought of as equally difficult?

The chi-square statistics in this study were found to be significant (at $p<.01$), except for the raters' facet on the Introduction, Lei Series, and Slipper Series. We cannot reject the null hypothesis that these raters are equally severe or lenient in their ratings. Hence we can only accept the hypothesis the raters are giving ratings of similar severity or leniency. All of the other hypotheses should be rejected, that is, the differences between examinee, categories, and items can be said to be statistically significant.

Vertical rulers

Next we will display and interpret the vertical rulers from our FACETS analyses. Four of these are shown in total (see Figures 1a to 1d) for the Introduction, Lei Series, Slipper Series, and Short Oral Response items, respectively.

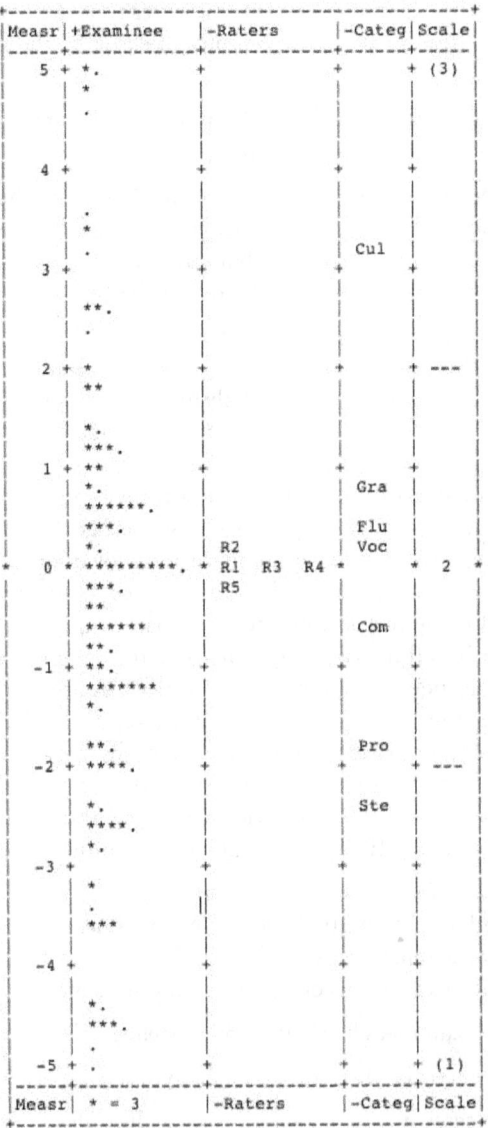

Figure 1a. Vertical ruler for the Introduction.

Focusing first on the oral tests, notice that the first column in the vertical ruler for the Introduction, Lei Series, and Slipper Series (Figures 1a–1c) is for measure, which represents the range of scores on a true interval logit scale where the mean is 0 and, in this case, the range is -/+ 5 or 6. The second column shows where the examinees were on the scale (with each asterisk equivalent to 2 or 3 examinees as labeled at the bottom of that column in each figure). The third column gives the averages for each of the five raters (R1, R2, R3, R4, & R5). The fourth column shows that the average ratings for each of the seven categories: Communicative Skill (Com), Vocabulary (Voc), Grammar (Gra), Pronunciation (Pro), Fluency (Flu), Steadfastness (Ste), and Cultural Authenticity (Cul). The final column shows the raw score equivalents along the same scale.

Figure 1a is the vertical ruler for the Introduction ratings. Notice that the examinees' scores range from –5 logits for the low scorers to +5 logits for the high scorers. This indicates reasonably wide differences in the performances/ratings of the students involved in this project. The third column shows that R2 was the most severe rater, and R5 was the most lenient rater with R1, R3, and R4 in between, but these differences were very small. The fourth column shows that the average ratings for Cultural Awareness (Cul) were suitable for students who scored slightly above +3 logits (i.e., the ratings were low on average). In stark contrast, the average ratings for Language Steadfastness (Ste) ratings were suitable for students who scored midway between –2 and –3 logits (i.e., the ratings were high on average). The other five categories in descending order of suitability for high scoring examinees to low were: Grammar (Gra), Fluency (Flu), Vocabulary (Voc), Communicative Skill (Com), and Pronunciation (Pro).[2] The last column to the far right shows how the raw ratings 1, 2, and 3 matched up to the true interval logit scores on the far left for the Introduction ratings overall.

Figure 1b is the vertical ruler for the Lei Series ratings. Notice that the examinees' scores range a bit more than those in the previous figure from –6 logits for the low scorers to almost +6 logits for the high scorers. This indicates reasonably wide differences in the performances/ratings of those who took this series. The third column shows once again that R2 was the most severe rater, but this time R1 was the most lenient with R3, R4, and R5 in between; these differences were a bit more substantial than those shown in the previous figure, but were still not very substantial. As with the pervious figure, the fourth column shows that the average ratings for Cultural Awareness (Cul) were suitable for high scoring students, in this case those who scored somewhat above +4 logits (i.e., the ratings were low on average). In stark contrast and also similar to the previous figure, the average ratings for Language Steadfastness (Ste) were suitable for students who scored low, this time below –3 logits (i.e., the ratings were high on average). The other five categories in descending order of suitability for high scoring examinees to low were: Grammar (Gra), Fluency (Flu), Vocabulary (Voc), Communicative Skill (Com), and Pronunciation (Pro). The last column to the far right shows how the raw ratings 1, 2, and 3 matched up to the true interval logit scores on to the far left for the overall Lei Series ratings.

Figure 1c is the vertical ruler for the Slipper Series ratings. Notice that the examinees' scores range less than those in the previous two figures from –5 logits to about +4 logits. This still indicates reasonably wide differences in the performances/ratings. The third column shows that R4 was the most severe rater, but this time R1 was the most lenient rater with R2, R3, and R5 in between;[3] these differences were small like those in Figure 1a. As in the previous two figures, the average ratings for Cultural Awareness (Cul) were suitable for high scoring students, in this case between +4 and +5 logits (i.e., the average ratings were low). Also

---

[2] While Grammar and Fluency appear to be exactly the same in the Figure as do Communicative Skill and Pronunciation, the order described in text is reflected in small differences in the actual logit scores for these categories.

[3] While R2 and R4 appear to be exactly the same in the Figure as do R1 and R3, the order described in text is reflected in small differences in the actual logit scores for these pairs of raters.

similar to the previous two figures, the average ratings for Language Steadfastness (Ste) were suitable for students who scored low, this time slightly above −3 logits (i.e., the average ratings were high). The other five categories are in the same general descending order of high to low examinee suitability with the exception of Pro and Com (which have switched positions): Grammar (Gra), Fluency (Flu), Vocabulary (Voc), Pronunciation (Pro), and Communicative Skill (Com). The last column to the far right shows how the raw ratings 1, 2, and 3 matched up to the true interval logit scores on to the far left for the overall Slipper Series ratings.

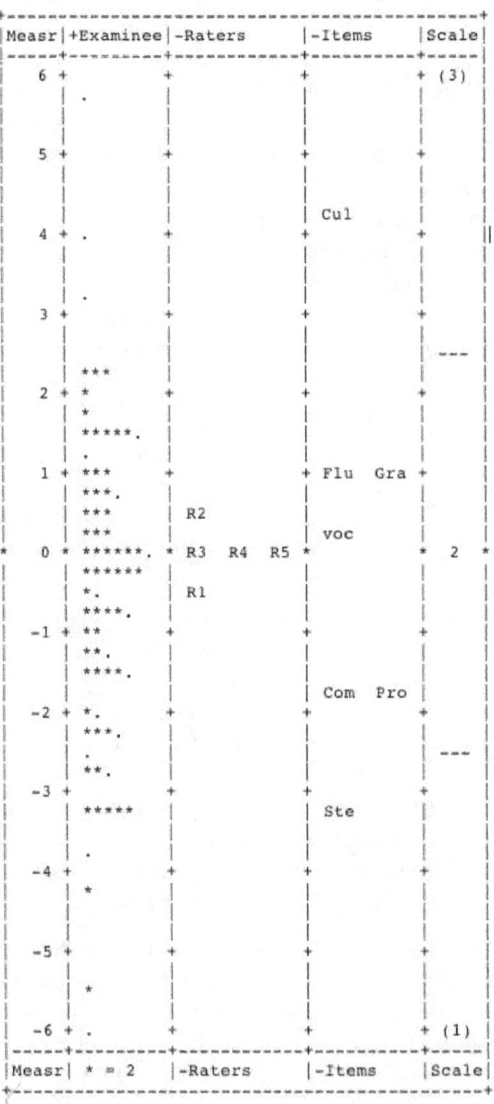

Figure 1b. Vertical ruler for the Lei Series.

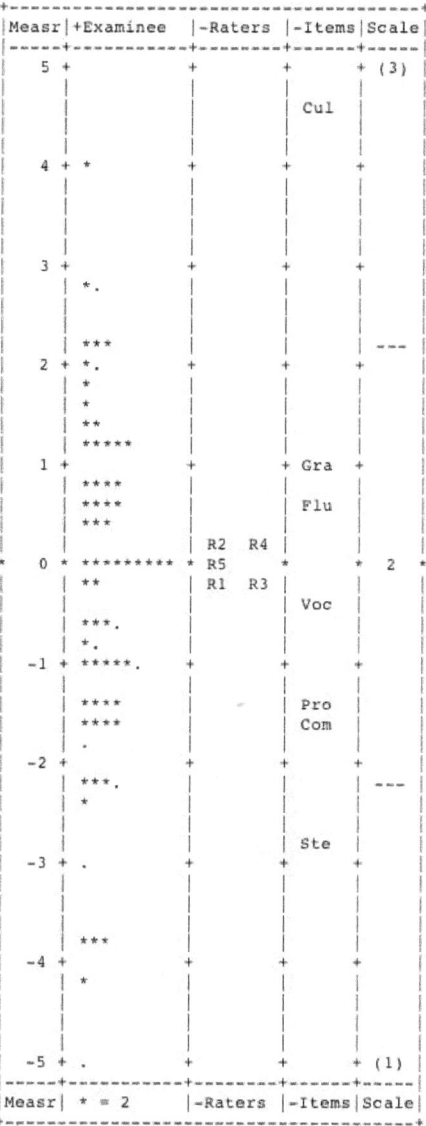

Figure 1c. Vertical ruler for the Slipper Series.

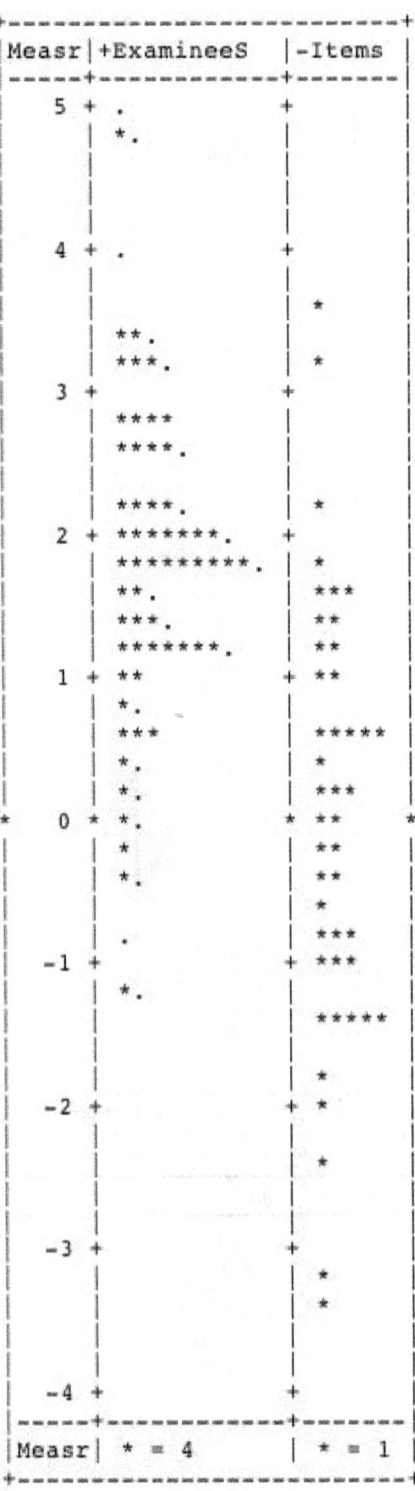

Figure 1d. Vertical ruler for the Short Oral Response test.

Figure 1d is the vertical ruler for the Short Oral Response items. Notice that the examinees' scores range less than those in the previous two figures from a bit lower than −1 logits to almost +5 logits. Because this test had no raters or categories, the only other column shown in the vertical ruler is for items. Notice that they range from a bit below −3 logits to a bit below +4. The mismatch between the examinee logits and item logits indicates that a number of the items were too easy for the examinees in this sample. More importantly there were no items difficult enough to be suitable for the very high performing students.

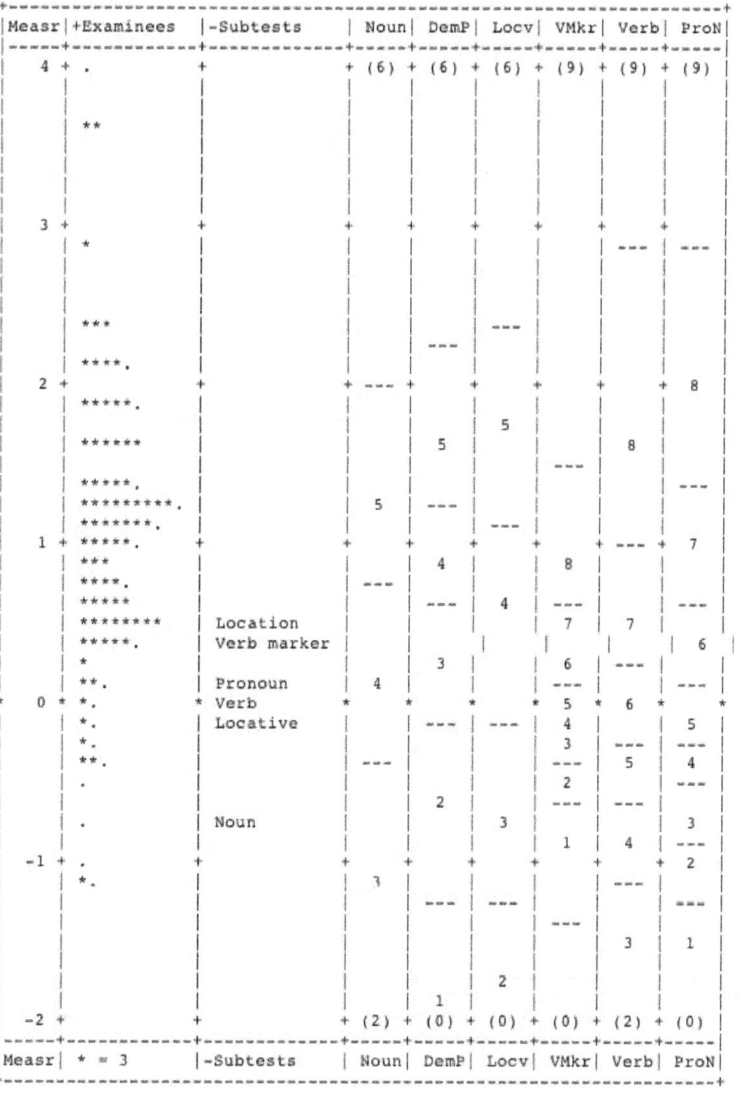

Figure 1e. Vertical ruler for the Short Oral Response test (partial credit model).

Figure 1e is the vertical ruler for the Short Oral Response items that resulted from what is called a partial credit analysis (for purposes of this analysis, each subtest was treated as a single item). Notice that the subtests range in suitability for high scoring examinees to low in the following order (from midway between −1 and 0 to midway between 0 and +1) as follows: Pronoun, Verb Marker, Pronoun, Verb, Locative, and Noun. Notice also the six columns to the right, one each for each subtest. These show how the raw scores on the subtests matched up with the logit scores. Notice how very different the suitability of the items was on each subtest for low to high scoring examinees.

Probability curves

FACETS analysis also provides information in the form of probability curves. These tell us about the degree to which the points on the rating scale are separate or overlapping. The probability curves for the three long response oral tests in this study are shown in Figures 1a to 1c. To understand such graphs, we need to keep in mind that ideal probability curves have a distinct *hill-like* look with little overlap between curves, in this case, one each for the three scores, 1, 2, and 3. Notice in Figures 1a to 1c that the curves for the Introduction, Lei Series, and Slipper Series scores are all reasonably steep and hill-like with some overlap. What overlap there is appears to be due to heavy use of the 2 score by raters.

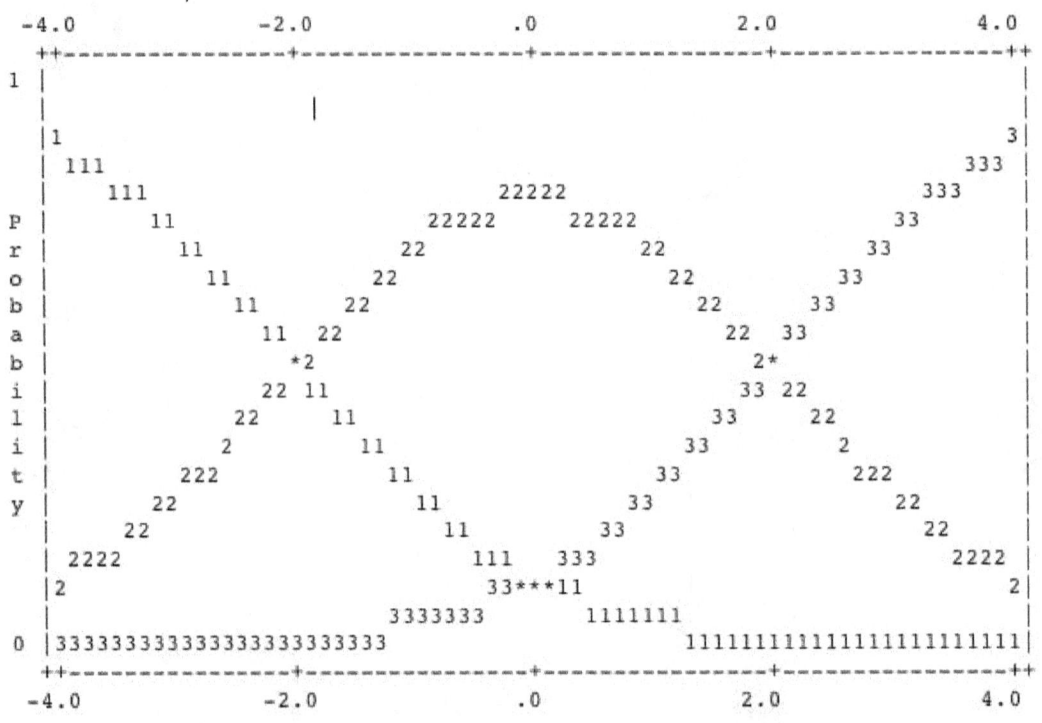

Figure 2a. Introduction Series probability curves.

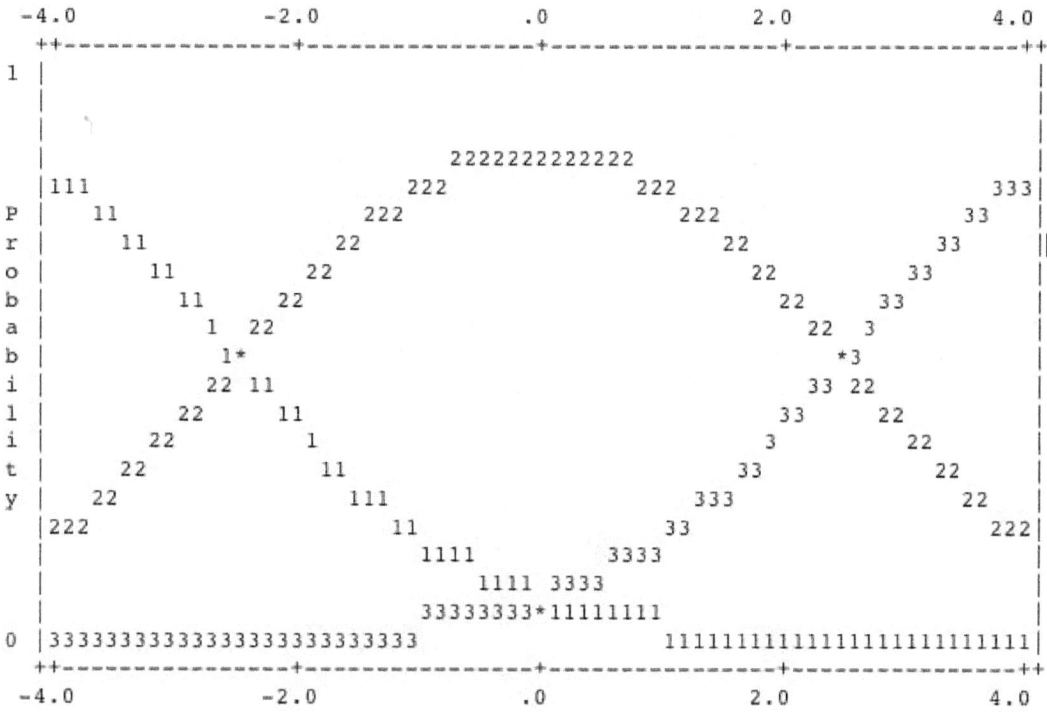

Figure 2b. Lei Series probability curves.

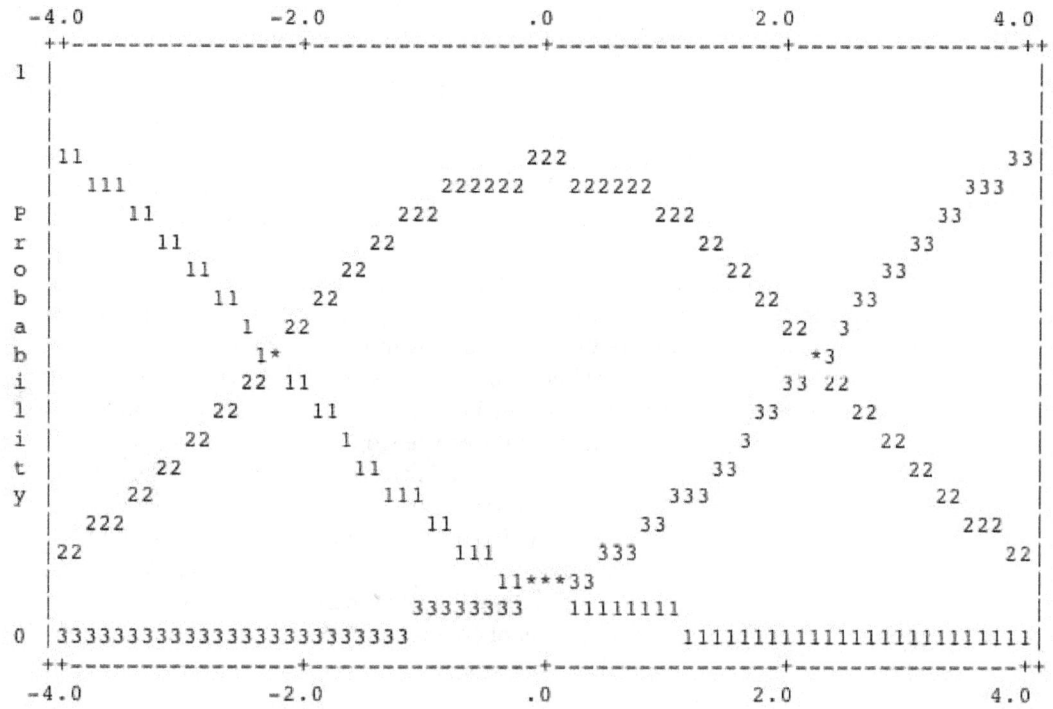

Figure 2c. Slipper Series probability curves.

Discussion

This section includes a discussion of the results of the Hawaiian Oral Language Assessment. An analysis of the open-ended long response sections (Introduction, Lei Series, and Slipper Series) and the findings from the Short Oral Response items will be presented. Figure 3 below shows the cumulative scores of the students' performance in the long response sections of the test in each of the seven proficiency domains: Communicative Skills, Vocabulary, Grammar, Pronunciation, Fluency, Steadfastness, and Cultural Authenticity. The seven domains will be addressed in order from the highest cumulative score to the lowest cumulative score, with the exception of the Grammar domain, which will be last. The Grammar domain is addressed last since the findings from the Long Response Test and the Short Oral Response items will be presented together in that section.

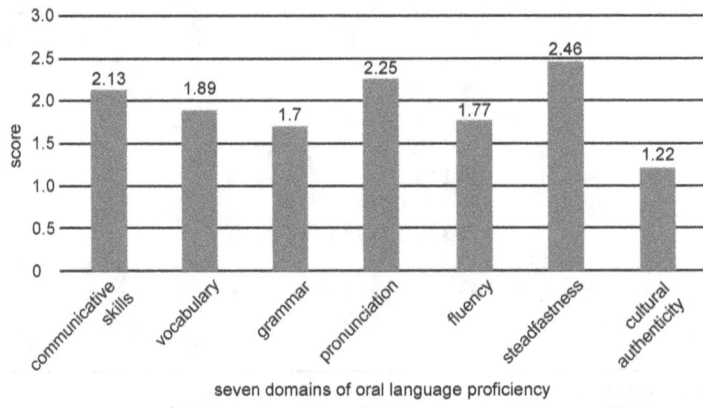

Figure 3. Cumulative scores of students in grades 1–3 for Introduction and Picture Series.

The results of the long response tests (Introduction, Lei Picture Series, and the Slipper Picture Series) showed that students scored the highest in the Steadfastness domain. In order to score a three, students had to consistently use Hawaiian during the assessment period, which typically lasted about 20 minutes. A score of two means that students used Hawaiian the majority of the time, but interjected English words when they were not sure of the Hawaiian vocabulary. A student was given a one if she or he frequently used English during the prompt. The Steadfastness score is 2.41 for the Introduction, 2.51 for the Lei Series, and 2.52 for the mean Slipper series. When these three scores are averaged, the resulting composite value is 2.46. It is interesting to note that the score for both the Lei Series and the Slipper Series are very close with a slight decrease for the Introduction. Perhaps the difference between the Introduction, Lei Series and Slipper Series prompts occurred since students followed the storyline that was evident in the sequence of the six pictures, whereas, during the Introduction section, students followed the basic sequence, but then also added more information regarding their home life and interests, perhaps using more vocabulary that they were not familiar with in Hawaiian. The evaluators of the oral language assessment found the Steadfastness domain to be a great strength of students in the Hawaiian language immersion program in grades 1–3. The result is an indication of a high level of commitment of students to maintain the Hawaiian language at all times and a demonstration of the high level of fluency that has been achieved in the early grades.

The second highest cumulative man score was found in the Pronunciation domain. The score is 2.27 for the Introduction, 2.25 for the Lei Series, and 2.24 for the Slipper Series. All of these scores are very similar, demonstrating the consistency of pronunciation between the prompts. The average of the three scores is 2.25. To score a three, students must consistently pronounce *hakalama* (consonant-vowel clusters), vowel blends, *ʻokina* (glottal stop), *kahakō* (macron), and phonemes correctly. A score of two means the student mispronounces some aspects of the items listed above. If pronunciation errors are frequent and obvious, a student will receive a score of one. Generally speaking, students did well in this domain. The most common mistake found is the insertion or deletion of the ʻokina and the kahakō. Another area of weakness to be addressed is vowel blends, which is most likely due to interference from the students' first language of English. Therefore, the basic rules for pronunciation mistakes should be explicitly taught and incorporated into lessons in the lower elementary grades, so that these types of errors don't become fossilized and difficult to change as students grow older.

The third highest cumulative mean score was the Communicative Skills domain. In this category, students were given a three if complete sentences were used, ideas were expressed in a clear and easily understood manner, most aspects of the task were included in the student's response, and communications were independently directed without relying on prompts or assistance from the evaluator. For a score of two, students sometimes spoke at the phrase level and sometimes at the sentence level, ideas expressed were mostly clear in meaning, some important aspects of the task were included in the student's independent response, and assistance in producing responses was required by the student. To score a one, the student spoke in brief and incomplete sentences sometimes involving only one word or phrase, ideas were unclear, few aspects of the task were included in the student's independent response, and assistance and prompts were often required. The mean score for the Communicative Skills domain is 2.01 for the Introduction, 2.23 for the Lei Series, and 2.29 for the Slipper Series. The composite mean score for this domain is 2.13. Again, we see a close similarity between the two Story-telling Picture Series, but a slight decrease in the Introduction score, suggesting perhaps that the task for presenting an independent introduction of oneself for two minutes is a slightly more difficult for younger children than looking at a sequence of pictures and then independently telling a story.

In the Vocabulary domain, the Introduction mean score is 1.84, the Lei Series score is 1.85 and the Slipper Series is 2.05 with a cumulative average score of 1.89. In this domain, the Introduction score and Lei Series score are more closely related than the Slipper Series score. The Introduction task deals with aspects of home life and interests at home, therefore students need to know vocabulary words that are typically used outside of the immersion school environment to successfully complete this task. The Lei Series also includes elements in the picture that take place in the community such as gathering flowers from a tree in the yard, putting flowers in a basket, making leis, driving to the airport, and giving leis to visiting grandparents. The setting of the Slipper Series, however, takes place at school with a situation that most young children experience: doing schoolwork in class, going to the playground when the recess bell rings, taking slippers off and leaving them on the side, playing kickball, returning to class when recess is over, being the last one to get your slippers and finding a pair of mix-matched slippers. The familiarity of the Slipper Series context and the likelihood of in-school Hawaiian language modeling and support for such a context is one possible explanation for a higher score in this domain. Since the majority of immersion students speak English at home, this creates an obstacle for teachers. Students tend to know *school vocabulary* very well because they use it everyday. However, when children need to use words that are more commonly used at home, evaluators discovered that many of the students didn't know those words, for example, *wahī* (to wrap a present), *'ie* (basket), *kahua ho'olulu mokulele* (airport), and *mānai* (needle for string leis). On the positive side, when students didn't know particular vocabulary words, they did use strategies to communicate their ideas. Although some students said the word in English because they didn't know the equivalent in Hawaiian, many others tried to find a similar word such as box or bag for the word *basket*, while others used circumlocution techniques to express their thoughts. Therefore, this challenge behooves teachers and parents to expose children to a variety of circumstances in which vocabulary can be learned. If we want students to be able to speak in Hawaiian in every context outside of school, vocabulary is one area that needs to be actively and explicitly taught to students.

In the Fluency domain, the Introduction mean score is 1.77, the Lei Series score is 1.73 and the Slipper Series is 1.83, with a composite average score of 1.77. All of the scores are somewhat similar, demonstrating consistency between the three separate tasks. This domain illustrates the students' proficiency in the phonological aspects of the language. These aspects include an ease and natural flow of speech in an authentically Hawaiian way, i.e., proper inflection, intonation, emphasis, rhythm, and appropriate pauses. The Fluency domain is another area of challenge for Hawaiian language immersion students for several reasons. First of all, outside of the Ni'ihau community, the students are rarely exposed to a native speaker. Secondly, almost all of the HLIP teachers are second language learners themselves and therefore may not be using authentic aspects of fluency in their own Hawaiian speech patterns. In addition, the students' first language of English often interferes with the correct flow of Hawaiian fluency. A glaring example that was heard over and over again during the interviews is the use of the word *um*. Native speakers will interject utterances such as 'Ō and 'Ā when thinking, but HLIP students have a tendency to fall back on English sounds. Another example is the rise of the voice in English at the end of a sentence when a question is asked. Many students tend to improperly use the same intonation when asking questions and even when making statements in Hawaiian. When HLIP schools first began, *kūpuna* (elders) were an integral part of the program. They provided excellent examples of native speech for the children to hear. Unfortunately, 23 years have passed since immersion began, so *mānaleo* (first-language Hawaiian speaking) *kūpuna* are often no longer available to work in HLIP schools. Since students don't have access to native speakers today, one idea is for teachers to use recordings of native speakers in their instruction so that students can hear and imitate authentic examples of proper fluency patterns.

Cultural Authenticity is the lowest scoring domain to be addressed. The Introduction mean score is 1.27, the Lei Series score is 1.20 and the Slipper Series is 1.15, with a composite average score of 1.22. In this domain, the students were evaluated on how well they used traditional features of speech and communication in their language. The Cultural Authenticity domain was included in this study because evaluators wanted to see if students were using Hawaiian thought and perspectives in the construction of language. Students were scored on their ability to use oratorical features such as reciting *mo'okū'auhau* (genealogy), complementary pairs, opposites, idioms, famous sayings, proverbs, along with using culturally correct phrases such as, *Aia lākou ma luna o ke ka'a.* (They are on the car), rather than the incorrect phrase, *Aia lākou ma loko o ke ka'a.* (They are in the car). Generally speaking, it seems that students are committed to speaking in Hawaiian, but English thinking sometimes interferes with sentence construction. However, several students did score high in this domain, but appeared to be students from only a few classes. Therefore it appears that certain teachers make a special effort to focus on rich language experiences in the classroom, which include memorized verses, phrases, and wise sayings taken from traditional stories and chants. It was also evident that certain classes continue to focus on family lineage and more elaborate memorized introductions and build upon the introductions that are first taught at the *Pūnana Leo* Preschools.

The last domain is the Grammar domain. The Introduction mean score is 1.69, the Lei Series score is 1.70 and the Slipper Series is 1.74, with a cumulative average score of 1.71. Out of all seven domains, the results of the Grammar domain are the most consistent between the three tasks. The Grammar domain had the second to the lowest score in the oral language assessment and therefore is an area that needs attention. In addition to the statistical analysis that was conducted to get an overall general idea in terms of performance in each of the seven domains, an error analysis of grammar was conducted. Students' recordings were transcribed, analyzed, and compiled in an individualized report for each school that participated in the study. Codes were created to summarize the strengths and weaknesses of 12 overarching categories and 48 subcategories of grammar. Along with each summary report, printed examples of students' language coinciding with the 48 subcategories were also given to teachers at the reporting meeting at each school, with the intention that teachers would create lessons to address the specific weaknesses of their students in the area of grammar. The analysis and examples of grammar are very comprehensive and too long to include in this paper and should be addressed in a separate paper focused solely on grammar. However, summarized below is a small sample of findings from the Short Oral Response items of H-OLA. The graphs show cumulative scores of the students' performance in the short response sections. The test measured proficiency in six different grammatical structures including nouns, pronouns, locatives, verb markers, verbs, and pronouns.

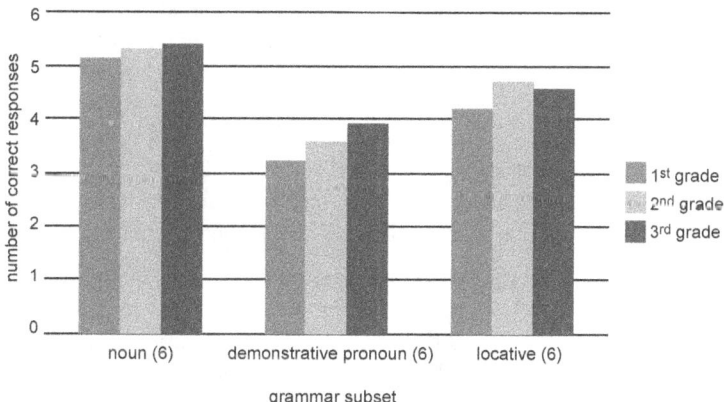

Figure 4a. Cumulative scores for short response (six-item subsets)

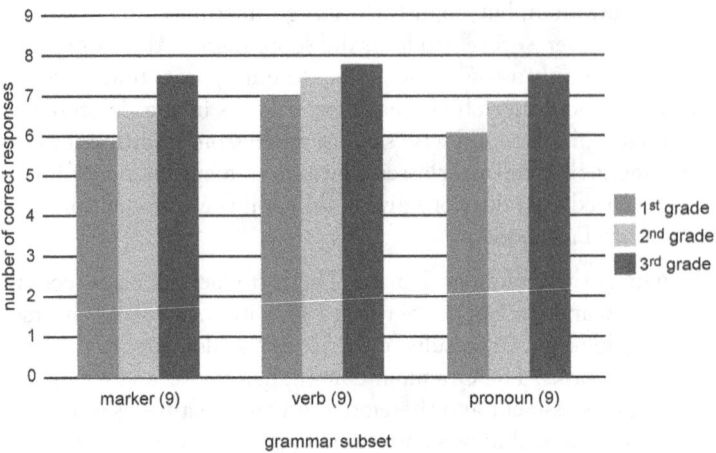

Figure 4b. Cumulative scores for short response (nine-item subsets).

Figure 4a shows structures in which subsets of six items were tested, while Figure 4b shows structures in which subsets of nine items were tested. It is interesting to note that although five out of six of the categories show a natural progression from year to year, it appears that in the *locative* category, students in grade two performed slightly better than those in grade 3.

Students did very well on the Noun section, however, some students struggled with the Pronoun section. Students consistently used the word *kēia* correctly, but did not consistently use *kēnā* and *kēlā* correctly. The distinction between these two words for *that* is difficult for many second language speakers of Hawaiian, as it involves a different way of thinking about space and location as opposed to the English equivalent. In English, there is only one word for *that*, however, in Hawaiian, the speaker must distinguish between *that* (by you, the person being addressed) and *that* (far from you).

Students generally did well in the Locative section, with the exception of the words for *mua* and *hope*. The student sat on one side of a box and the test administrator sat on the opposite side of the box. So when the test administrator placed an object either in front or in back of the box and asked where the object was in relationship to the box, the students sometimes gave an answer from the perspective of the student and sometimes gave an answer from the perspective of the test administrator. To alleviate the confusion, perhaps it would be best for the test administrator to sit next to the students instead of across from the student. It is possible that the scores for the Locative items were adversely impacted by this flaw in methodology as opposed to student ignorance of the meanings of these words.

Students did well in the Verb section, but results varied in the Verb Marker section from school to school. Students from certain schools knew the verb markers well, while students from other schools either dropped the markers altogether, dropped one half of the verb marker, or created interesting combinations of the different tense markers. Students from one particular school even created a new marker, *He* verb *nei*. The use of verb markers in the long response section was also analyzed to see if the findings were consistent with the short response section. However, evaluators found that students tended not to use verb markers in the Introduction or the Story-telling Picture Series. Therefore, verb markers are a weakness that needs to be looked at and addressed in the Hawaiian language immersion classroom.

In the Pronoun section, students know the singular pronouns (*au, 'oe, 'o ia*) well. However, confusion lies in the dual pronouns (*kāua, māua, 'olua, lāua*). Many students seem to categorize pronouns into two areas, singular and plural, and therefore tend to overuse plural pronouns and underuse dual pronouns. The pronouns *kākou* and *lākou* especially are used as general terms for *we* and *they*. This is another indication of the English language interfering with Hawaiian thinking and perspectives, since there is only one word to express these thoughts in English, but there are several specific choices in Hawaiian.

In summary, the findings of the Short Oral Response items of H-OLA manifest a natural progression in growth from Grade 1 to Grade 3. When all of the subtest scores of the Short Oral Response items from all seven schools are combined together by grade level, students in Grade 1 demonstrate an average accuracy rate of 31.53 out of 45 items, which is 70% accurate. Students in Grade 2 show an average accuracy rate of 34.57 out of 45 items, which is 76.8% accurate. Students in Grade 3 display an average accuracy rate of 36.65 out of 45 items, which is 81.4% accurate.

Conclusions

Overall, students in the Hawaiian language immersion program are performing very well in the Grades 1–3 levels. After assessing the proficiency levels of 270 students from seven different HLIP schools, the evaluators of the Hawai'i Oral Language Assessment are confident to say that the obvious strengths of the program are: (a) the students' steadfastness in using Hawaiian, (b) the correct pronunciation of words, and (c) and the high levels of communicative skills that are being demonstrated by the students in the early elementary grades. Students have the ability to express their thoughts through clear and descriptive Hawaiian without the need to code-switch to English or other languages. Therefore it appears that students are accomplishing one of the major goals of the program, which is to develop a high level of proficiency in comprehending and communicating in the Hawaiian language.

Students are also making progress in the areas of: (a) vocabulary, (b) grammar, and (c) phonological aspects of the language such as proper inflection, intonation, emphasis, rhythm, and appropriate pauses. However, the development of materials and the use of best-practice language acquisition teaching strategies, reinforced with excellent native speech examples and explicit instruction, would help to raise the proficiency levels of students in these three areas.

The greatest weakness that was found in the study is the area of cultural authenticity. Even though students are speaking in the Hawaiian language, this does not mean that they are automatically thinking and constructing language with Hawaiian thought and perspectives. This finding also has implications in other areas such as grammar for example. Many of the grammatical mistakes are due to the interference of the students' first language of English, such as in the case of pronouns and dual pronouns.

Students naturally follow the examples that are presented to them by their teachers and parents. Therefore, it is imperative that adult role models provide the foundation for Hawaiian thought and perspectives. The *Kumu Honua Mauli Ola* philosophy is one such model. There are other Hawaiian philosophical models that have also been developed by various groups. Whichever model is chosen, it is important for students to understand that Hawaiian thought plays an important role in perpetuating the traditional aspects of the language that have been passed down by ancestors for generations.

Limitations of the study

The developers and evaluators of the Hawaiian Oral Language Assessment would have preferred to be able to assess every student at all 15 HLIP elementary schools throughout the state. However, due to restrictions on financial resources, human resources, and time, it was not possible. Given the above limitations, the assessment team carefully planned and followed statistical guidelines to assess a representative sampling of students from Hawaiian language immersion laboratory schools, charter schools, and regular immersion schools located on four major islands. Therefore, the team feels that enough data was collected to make generalizations regarding the progress of HLIP students in the early elementary grades.

The results of this study were collected from a 20–30 minute session between one student and one test administrator. It is important to keep in mind, that the interview session is only a small snapshot in a larger timeframe in the life of a HLIP student. If a student had a bad day, then perhaps that might reflect in the sample interview collected. However, since 270 students were assessed, the research team still feels they have a good sample from which to draw conclusions.

Implications for future research

Funding for this study was only sufficient to assess students in Grades 1–3. In 1989–1990 and 1990–1991, Warner conducted the first systematic study of HLIP students in Grades K–4. It would be interesting to take a closer in-depth look at grammatical structures that were produced in this assessment and compare it to Warner's study to determine the progress that has been made over the past twenty years.

Hawaiian language immersion program students beyond the fourth grade level have yet to be assessed and studied. In order to truly understand the language acquisition of students from Kindergarten to Grade 12, a comprehensive study should be developed and administered. Through systematic and longitudinal studies, language benchmarks can be determined and used to provide targets in continuous language growth.

Another area of research that can be addressed is assessing the proficiency levels of Hawaiian language immersion teachers. The purpose of such a study should be to help teachers and should not be used for punitive measures. In addition, if a study were to be conducted, follow-up classes should be made available to teachers to foster the growth of language skills in areas of need identified by the assessment.

Final thoughts

This chapter only includes the results of the first assessment that was administered in April and May of 2009. The research team returned during the same months in 2010 to assess the same students (now representing Grades 2–4) for the second time. Since the scoring and statistical analysis of the second administration of the test is still ongoing, the longitudinal results of 2010 will be determined at a later time. Once the results of 2010 are complete, a comparison can be made between the two years of assessment.

As mentioned in the introduction of this paper, if the vision, mission, and goals of the Hawaiian language immersion program are to be realized, then several things need to transpire. For one, excellent language models need to be provided for children both at school and in the home. This can be accomplished by providing ongoing teacher training and parent classes or workshops. Secondly, additional materials both in print and non-print resources need to be developed and disseminated to schools and families. In order to produce language materials, funding needs to be made available. Lastly, assessment and evaluation for the purpose of improving instruction and raising the language proficiency levels of HLIP teachers and students needs to be ongoing. *E ola mau ka ʻōlelo Hawaiʻi* [May the Hawaiian language live on forever].

References

Cherokee Nation. (2003). *Ga-du-gi: A vision for working together to preserve the Cherokee language.* Report on DHS ANA Grant #90–NL–0189. Tahlequah, Oklahoma: Cherokee Nation.

Cherokee Nation. (2009). *Cherokee nation immersion school expands.* Retrieved on October 16, 2010 from http://www.cherokee.org/PressRoom/24146/Press_Article.aspx

Housman, A., Dameg, K., Kobashigawa, M., & Brown, J. D. (2011). Report on the Hawaiian Oral Language Assessment (H-Ola) development project. *Second Language Studies, 29*(2), 63–121. Retrieved on August 15, 2011 from http://www.hawaii.edu/sls/sls/?page_id=135

Edmonds, C. (2008). The reliability and validity of the Māori language proficiency in writing test: Kaiaka Reo Year Eight. *Dissertation Abstracts International,* (UMI No. 3336175)

Ka Haka 'Ula O Ke'elikōlani-University of Hawai'i at Hilo. (2007). *'Ōlelo Ola oral language proficiency project.* A grant proposal under the Native Hawaiian Education Program, US Department of Education, CFDA Number: 84.362A.

Linacre, J. M. (2008). *User's guide to FACETS: Rasch-model computer programs.* Chicago: Author.

McNamara, T. (1996). *Measuring second language performance.* London: Longman.

Office of Instructional Services, General Education Branch. (1994). *Long-range plan for the Hawaiian language immersion program: Papahana kaiapuni Hawai'i.* Hawai'i State Department of Education, RS 94–5555.

Warner, S. (1996). I ola ka 'Ōlelo i na keiki: Ka 'apo 'ia 'ana o ka 'Ōlelo Hawai'i e nā keiki ma ke kula kaiapuni. *PhD dissertation. Abstracts International,* (UMI No. 9629864)

Appendix A: Hawaiian oral language proficiency assessment rubric (ʻŌlelo Hawaiʻi)

PAKUHI ANALOI MĀKAU ʻŌLELO WAHA NO KA ʻŌLELO HAWAIʻI

	Pili i ka Manaʻo		Pili i ke Kani			Kuanaʻike Hawaiʻi	
	Mākau Hoʻokaʻaʻike	Huaʻōlelo	Pilinaʻōlelo	Puana	Poeko	Kūpaʻa ʻŌlelo	Ke ʻAno Hawaiʻi o ka hōʻike Hawaiʻi ʻana
3	1. Hoʻopuka ʻia nā manaʻo o ma nā hopuna ʻōlelo piha. 2. Mōakāka nō nā manaʻo o ke lohe aku. 3. Aia ma kāna pane ʻaeʻoia ka nui o nā ʻāpana o ia māhele o ka hōʻike. (hoʻolauna, pukaʻina kiʻiʻi) 4. Hiki ke hana nona iho, ʻaʻohe kaukaʻi i i ka mea loiloi ma ka hoʻoholo ʻana i ke kamaʻilio ʻana.	1. Lawa ka ʻikena huaʻōlelo e hoʻokō pono ai i ka hana hōʻike. Hoʻohana pū ʻia nā huaʻōlelo o nā pōʻaiapili ma ʻō aku. 2. Hoʻohana pololei mau ʻia nā huaʻōlelo. 3. Kākaʻikahi (ʻaohe paha) ka wā e pono ai e kū a noʻonoʻo ma ke koho ʻana i ka huaʻōlelo.	Hoʻohana ʻia nā pilinaʻōlelo like ʻole he nui. Kākaʻikahi ka wā e hoʻohana pololei ʻole ʻia ai ka pilinaʻōlelo.	Puana pono mau ʻia nā ʻāpana hakalama, nā huēwoela, nā ʻokina, ke kahakō, nā kāpana, a me nā hualeo.	Lohe maʻamau ʻia nā hiʻohiʻona poeko Hawaiʻi: • ka wali • ke kiʻina leo • ke kālele • ka pana (wikiwiki/mālie) • ke kū ʻana i ka wā kūpono. • ʻaʻole hoʻohana ʻia ka ʻōlelo "um"	Kūpaʻa mau i ka ʻōlelo Hawaiʻi.	Lohe ʻia 2 a ʻoi hiʻohiʻona o kēia analoi: 1. ka noʻonoʻo Hawaiʻi/ʻike kuʻuna ("kau" ma luna o ke kaʻa, "holoholo" ma kahi o "lawaiʻa") 2. loina/meiwi (kūpinaʻi, ʻekoʻa, helu, welina) 3. ʻikeoma, ʻōlelo kaulana, ʻōlelo noʻeau 4. kuanaʻike ʻohana
2	1. Hoʻopuka ʻia nā manaʻo o ma ka pae hopuna ʻōlelo a māmala ʻōlelo paha i ka hapanui o ka manawa. 2. Mōakāka ka nui o nā manaʻo ke lohe aku. 3. Aia ma kāna pane ʻaeʻoia kekahi hapa o nā ʻāpana o ia māhele. 4. Kaukaʻi iki ʻia ka mea loiloi ma ka hoʻoholo ʻana i ke kamaʻilio ʻana.	1. Lawa ka ʻikena huaʻōlelo e hoʻokō ai i ka hana hōʻike. 2. Hoʻohana pololei ʻole ʻia nā huaʻōlelo i kekahi manawa. 3. Kū i kekahi manawa e noʻonoʻo i ka huaʻōlelo a loaʻa iā ia nona iho i ka hapanui o ka manawa.	Hoʻohana ʻia nā pilinaʻōlelo like ʻole. Lohe ʻia kekahi mau hemahema pilinaʻōlelo.	Hemahema ka puana i ia mau hiʻohiʻona ʻōlelo o luna aʻe nei i kekahi manawa.	Lohe ʻia nā hiʻohiʻona poeko Hawaiʻi (i helu ʻia ma luna aʻe nei) a lohe pū ʻia ka hiʻohiʻona ʻōlelo ʻē, e like hoʻi me "um".	Kūpaʻa ma ka ʻōlelo Hawaiʻi i ka hapanui o ka manawa. Komo naʻe ka ʻōlelo ʻē i kekahi manawa.	Lohe ʻia 1 laʻana o nā ʻano Hawaiʻi o ke kamaʻilio ʻana i helu ʻia ma luna aʻe nei.
1	1. Mumuku ka ʻōlelo i hoʻopuka ʻia ma nā hopuna ʻōlelo piha ʻole a me nā huaʻōlelo a māmala ʻōlelo paha. 2. Mōakāka ʻole nā manaʻo o ke lohe aku. 3. Nele nō ka pane ʻaeʻoia i ka nui o nā ʻāpana o ia māhele o ka hōʻike. 4. Kaukaʻi nui ʻia ka mea loiloi ma ka hoʻoholo ʻana i ke kamaʻilio ʻana.	1. ʻAʻole i lawa nā huaʻōlelo e hoʻokō ai i ka hana hōʻike. 2. Hoʻohana pinepine ʻia nā huaʻōlelo pololei ʻole no ka pōʻaiapili. 3. Kū pinepine e noʻonoʻo i ka huaʻōlelo. ʻO ka pono o ke kōkua ka hopena o kekahi manawa.	ʻAʻole i nui nā pilinaʻōlelo like ʻole i hoʻopuka ʻia. Nui nō nā hemahema pilinaʻōlelo.	Pinepine a ahuwale nā hemahema puana o ia mau hiʻohiʻona ʻōlelo o luna aʻe ala.	• Kākaʻikahi nā hiʻohiʻona poeko Hawaiʻi i hiluʻia ma luna aʻe ala. • Lohe nui ʻia ka hiʻohiʻona ʻōlelo ʻē. • He hana nui ka hoʻopuka manaʻo ʻana: he ʻāʻā ka leo.	Komo mau nā huaʻōlelo ʻōlelo ʻē ma ka ʻōlelo.	ʻAʻole lohe ʻia ke ʻano Hawaiʻi o ke kamaʻilio ʻana i wehewehe ʻia ma luna aʻe ala.

Appendix B: Hawaiian Oral Language Proficiency Assessment Rubric (English Version)

HAWAIIAN ORAL LANGUAGE PROFICIENCY ASSESSMENT RUBRIC

	Semantics		Phonology			Kuana'ike / Worldview	
	Communicative Skills	Vocabulary	Grammar	Pronunciation	Fluency	Language Steadfastness	Cultural and Linguistic Authenticity
3	• Speaks in complete sentences. • Ideas expressed are easily grasped by the listener. • Student's independent response includes most aspects of the assessment task (introduction, picture series). • Is able to independently direct his/her own communications. Speaks without relying on prompts or assistance.	• Word knowledge encompasses contexts of speech, which fulfill and go beyond the task. • Vocabulary is consistently used correctly. • Stops to search for words are rare if occurring at all.	Uses a wide variety of grammar patterns. Grammatical errors, if any, are infrequent.	Consistently pronounces hakalama, vowel blends, 'okina, kahakō, syllables, and phonemes correctly.	Speech embodies features of conversational Hawaiian language fluency: ease/comfort of speaking proper inflection, rhythm (speed and slowness as appropriate), proper pauses, absence of "um".	Steadfast adherence to Hawaiian language.	2 or more unique Hawaiian language features are present: 1. Hawaiian thought/ traditional knowledge ("to get on the car"; "holoholo" in place of "going fishing"; etc) 2. Language traditions/oratorical features (recites mo'okū'auhau, complementary pairs, opposites, etc...) 3. Idioms, famous sayings, proverbs 4. Use of traditional family terms correctly
2	• Speaks mostly at the phrase or sentence level. • Ideas expressed are mostly clear in meaning. • Some aspects of the task are included in the student's independent response. • The student requires some assistance in producing responses to the test items.	• Word knowledge is limited to the task at hand. • Vocabulary is not always used correctly. • Stops to search for words are sometimes necessary and usually result in finding a workable word choice.	Uses a variety of grammar patterns. Grammatical errors are present.	Mispronounces some aspects of hakalama, vowel blends, 'okina, kahakō, syllables, and phonemes.	• Features of conversational Hawaiian language fluency (listed above in row 3) are present along with some interference from foreign language features, e.g., "um".	Exhibits Hawaiian language steadfastness with occasional foreign language intrusion.	Inconsistently exhibits the above features of speaking Hawaiian in a Hawaiian way (1 instance).
1	• Speaks in brief and incomplete sentences, sometimes involving only one word or phrase. • Ideas expressed are unclear. • Few aspects of the task are included in the student's independent response. • Assistance and prompts are often required.	• Word knowledge is not sufficient to adequately fulfill the task. • Vocabulary is often used incorrectly. • Stops to search for words are frequent and necessary, and sometimes lead to the need for assistance.	Uses a limited number of grammar patterns. Grammatical errors are frequent.	Pronunciation errors are frequent and obvious.	• Features of conversational Hawaiian language fluency (listed above in row 3) are noticeably lacking. • Foreign language fluency features frequently interfere. • Student speaks haltingly ('a'ā ka leo).	Frequently interjects foreign language vocabulary.	Does not exhibit the Hawaiian language features listed in row 3 above.

7

Rubric-Based Scoring of Japanese Essays: The Effects on Generalizability of Numbers of Raters and Categories

James Dean Brown
Kimi Kondo-Brown
University of Hawai'i at Mānoa

Introduction

The purpose of the present study is to use generalizability theory (G-theory) to estimate the relative effects on generalizability of scores of the numbers of raters and categories. Previous studies have tackled the issues surrounding rubric development and validation for Japanese L2 writing. However, to our knowledge, no empirical investigations have focused on rubric-based scoring of Japanese L2 compositions in terms of the relative effects on generalizability of scores of the numbers of raters and categories. This study will use G-theory to do just that. Let us now turn to a brief literature review on (a) Japanese rubric development, (b) classical test theory reliability, and then (c) G-theory.

Japanese rubric development

Rubrics may be developed for the purpose of assessing the degree of achievement of learning outcomes specific to a course/program (criterion-referenced purposes) as well as for discriminating a candidate's performance against those of a large pool of candidates who have taken the same test (i.e., for norm-referenced purposes) (see Chapter 4 of this volume). While most of the literature that deals with Japanese L2 composition rubrics simply describes their structure and content and how to use them (e.g., Nihongo Kyooiku Gakkai, 1991, pp. 316–324; Ishida, 1992, pp. 153–155), a few studies also describe how the rubric in question was developed and/or examine the degree of agreement or reliability of the ratings obtained by the developed rubric (e.g., Kondo-Brown, 2002; Kondo-Brown & Brown, 2000; Morita, 1981; Tanaka, Tsubone, & Hajikano, 1998; Tanaka, Hajikano, & Tsubone, 1998). These studies will be reviewed below.

Brown, J. D., & Kondo-Brown, K. (2012). Rubric-based scoring of Japanese essays: The effects on generalizability of numbers of raters and categories. In J. D. Brown, (Ed.), *Developing, using, and analyzing rubrics in language assessment with case studies in Asian and Pacific languages* (pp. 169–184). Honolulu: University of Hawai'i, National Foreign Language Resource Center.

In Morita's (1981) study, the author analyzed the application of a nine-category rubric (with different numbers of points for each category) designed for rating Japanese L2 compositions. For this study, 86 Japanese L2 compositions were rated independently by two Japanese teachers. Morita investigated the percentage of agreement (i.e., of scores that were less than 5 points apart) between the two sets of ratings and found that the percentage was 88% for beginning students and 89% for intermediate students (p. 27).

In two studies led by Tanaka (Tanaka, Hajikano, & Tsubone, 1998; Tanaka, Tsubone, & Hajikano, 1998), the raters with and without teaching experience ($n=71$ for each group) ranked six compositions in terms of what they thought "good writing" was. Analysis with the Kendall coefficient of concordance indicated that the rankings for the non-experienced raters agreed at .62, while those for the experienced-teacher raters agreed at .71 (Tanaka, Hajikano, & Tsubone, 1998, p. 62). Using a survey that includes 22 rating criteria, the raters were asked to what degree they consider these criteria in determining *good writing*. A factor analysis was performed on the survey data and identified four factors at work: "accuracy (*seikakusa*)," "organization and form (*koosei* and *keishiki*)," "content (*naiyoo*)," and "richness (*yutakasa*)" (Tanaka, Tsubone, & Hajikano, 1998, p. 5). The *richness* includes such components as structural complexity and use of *Kanji* (Chinese characters). Based on these results, they recommend that a Japanese L2 composition rubric may include these four categories.

The Japanese L2 composition rubric used in Kondo-Brown (2002) and Kondo-Brown and Brown (2000) is a modified version of Jacobs, Zinkgraf, Wormuth, Harfiel, and Hughey's (1981) ESL composition profile (see Table 13 in Chapter 3 of this volume). The correlational and ANOVA analyses in the Kondo-Brown and Brown (2000) study indicated that trained teacher raters who scored Japanese L2 compositions using the rubric could produce highly correlated scores. In Kondo-Brown's (2002) study, where Multifaceted Rasch Model was applied using FACETS, the trained teacher raters using the rubric were found to be self-consistent in scoring L2 compositions. At the same time, the study observed significant differences in overall rater severity as well as a unique bias pattern specific to each rater. Based on these findings, Kondo-Brown (2002) suggested that, although the Japanese L2 composition rubric, which was developed based on the Jacob et al (1981) ESL composition profile, can help trained raters produce reliable ratings, multiple ratings are still recommended.

Clearly then, some studies have tackled the issues surrounding rubric development and validation for L2 Japanese writing. However, to our knowledge no empirical investigations have focused on rubric-based scoring of Japanese essays in terms of the effects on scoring generalizability of relative numbers of raters and categories. This study will us G-theory to do just that. Let us now turn to brief discussions of classical test theory reliability and then G-theory.

Classical test theory reliability

In using rubrics, we are concerned with reliability because we want to be sure that the rating scores we produce based on the rubric and the resulting decisions are consistent and fair. In classical test theory (CTT), internal consistency reliability is the most commonly used way to estimate the degree to which ratings are consistent. Internal-consistency reliability is commonly calculated using long established procedures for either interrater correlation (adjusted) reliability or for Cronbach alpha (for more on these statistics and how to calculate them, see Bachman, 2004, pp. 153–191; Brown, 2005a, pp. 169–198).

Interrater reliabilty is calculated by lining up the scores of two raters for a group of essays or interviews, and calculating the correlation coefficient for the relationship between the two sets of numbers. This can also be done for two sets of scores produced by one rater at two different times (say one week apart), in which case it is called *intrarater reliability*. Either interrater or intrarater reliability can be calculated in an *Excel*™ spreadsheet or a statistical analysis program like *SPSS*™ (for directions on how to do this in *Excel*™, see Brown, 2005a, pp. 139–145).

For purposes of reliability analysis, correlation coefficients typically range from .00 to 1.00 (if you happen to get a negative value that should be rounded to .00 for the purpose of reliability analysis). Under these conditions, a correlation coefficient for the scores of two raters can be interpreted as the proportion or percentage (by moving the decimal two places to the right) of reliable score variation for either of the two raters. The A correlation coefficient of .70 would indicate that 70% of variation in the first rater's scores was reliable, and by the same token, 70% of the variation in the second rater's scores can also be said to be reliable.

If you are averaging the two sets of scores (or adding them) before making a decision based on them, you would want to know the reliability of the two sets of ratings taken together. To estimate that, assessment specialists typically use the Spearman-Brown prophecy formula:

$$r_{xx'} = \frac{n \times r}{(n-1)r + 1}$$

where: $r_{xx'}$=two-rater reliability

r=correlation between the two sets of ratings

n=number of raters

For example, given the single rater reliability of .70, the Spearman-Brown prophecy formula would estimate the two-rater reliability as follows:

$$r_{xx'} = \frac{n \times r}{(n-1)r + 1} = \frac{2 \times .70}{(2-1).70 + 1} = \frac{1.40}{(1).70 + 1} = \frac{1.40}{1.70} = .8235294 \approx .82$$

So the estimated reliability for two raters taken together would be about .82. Thus 82% of the variation in ratings can be said to be reliable, and of course, by extension, 18% must be said to be unreliable.

Another approach for estimating the reliability of rubric-based ratings is known as Cronbach alpha; this procedure is explained for in its simplest two rater form in Brown (2005a, pp. 178–179). If more than two raters are employed, other procedures need to be used. The only reasonably easy way to calculate Cronbach alpha for three or more raters is to use a statistical program like *SPSS*™, where Cronbach alpha can be calculated (in version 19) by selecting *Analyze*, then selecting *Scale*, and then *Reliability analysis...*

Using the interrater correlations approach to reliability with three or more raters is explained in Brown (2005a, pp. 186–188). It should be noted that these procedures can also be used to investigate what the potential bang-for-the-buck would be if you were to increase the number of raters to 3, 4, 5, or even 10 raters. However, doing so only tells you the relative benefits of adding various numbers on one dimension, raters in this case. What if you also wanted to estimate the effects of increasing (or decreasing) the numbers on two dimensions, like the numbers of raters AND the numbers of rating categories? That is an area where generalizability theory is necessary and useful.

Generalizability theory

Generalizability theory (G-theory) was first proposed by Cronbach, Rajaratnam, and Gleser (1963) as an extension of `classical test theory reliability. G-theory uses analysis of variance procedures to separate and estimate the relative magnitude of the variance components (VCs) for various *facets* of measurement (Suen, 1990, pp. 41–42). These estimated VCs can then be used to investigate the potential effects of various increases or decreases in the numbers of these facets on the generalizability (which is analogous to reliability) of the scores. Design decisions, like how many raters and language categories should be used to get the best bang-for-the-buck, can be made based on more precise and flexible estimates of the effects on error of the facets being analyzed than those that were available in classical test theory. [For much more on G-theory, see Brennan (1983, 2001), Chiu (2001), and Shavelson & Webb (1991).]

The notion of applying G-theory in language testing first appeared in Bolus, Hinofotis, and Bailey (1982), but it was not actually applied until Brown and Bailey (1984). Other authors have provided overviews of the topic of G-theory. For example, Bachman (1997) briefly discusses the basic G-theory concepts, procedures, problems and solutions, while Brown and Hudson (2002, pp. 184–197) discussed criterion-related language testing applications of G-theory, and Bachman (2004, pp. 176–188) introduced some of the key G-theory notions.

G-theory has been quite widely applied in language testing research (Bachman, Lynch, & Mason, 1995; Brown, 1982, 1984, 1990, 1993, 1999, 2005b, 2007, 2008; Brown & Ahn, 2011; Brown & Bailey, 1984; Brown & Ross, 1996; Kozaki, 2004; Kunnan, 1992; Lee, 2005, 2006; Lee & Kantor, 2005; Lynch & McNamara, 1998; Molloy & Shimura, 2005; Sawaki, 2007; Schoonen, 2005; Shin, 2002; Stansfield & Kenyon, 1992; van Weeren & Theunissen, 1987; Xi, 2007; Yamamori, 2003; Yamanaka, 2005; Yoshida, 2004, 2007; Zhang, S., 2006; and Zhang, Y. 2003). Many of these studies included raters as one facet and some focused on applications of G-theory to the assessment of writing.

The purpose of the present study was to apply classical-theoryclassical test theory and G-theory analyses to the rubric-based scores of raters who scored Japanese compositions in five categories (*content, organization, vocabulary, language use,* and *mechanics*) with the goal of understanding the relative effects on generalizability of scores of the numbers of raters and categories. Not only would such an analysis be useful and revealing, but it would also be the first such study done for Japanese composition scores. To those ends, the following research questions were posed:

1. From a classical test theory (CTT) perspective, to what degree do the rubric-based Japanese composition scores provide suitable scores for our students in terms of difficulty and dispersion?
2. To what degree are the scores reliable as applied in this study with three raters?
3. From a G-theory point of view, what are the relative estimated variance components for persons, raters, categories, and their interactions for the Japanese composition scores?
4. And, to what degree do examinees, raters, categories, and their interactions contribute to the generalizability of the Japanese composition scores?
5. From a practical perspective, what numbers of raters and categories would be most effective given varying sets of circumstances?

Method

Participants

This study is based on the Japanese compositions written by 234 students. These students were attending the University of Hawai'i at Mānoa (UHM) and they had a wide range of Japanese proficiency levels. About 61% of the students were female, and they were mostly freshmen (83%) with widely varying majors. About 94% of the students were native speakers of English, and about 23% were Japanese heritage students with at least one Japanese-speaking parent. Approximately 94% had studied Japanese in high school for at least one year and 92% had never lived for any substantial amount of time in Japan. Almost 66% were placed in a beginning-level Japanese course as a result of other tests that they took at the same time as they wrote the compositions.

Materials

The 234 compositions consisted of 78 from each of three prompts (3 x 78=234). The prompts were descriptive in nature as follows: (a) describe how you like to spend your vacation; (b) describe yourself, your background, and your family members; and (c) describe Hawai'i to a friend in Japan. The shortest compositions were one or two lines but some were 20 lines or longer. The analytic rubric used in this study was a modified version of the Jacobs et al (1981) ESL composition shown in Table 13 in Chapter 3 of this book. The Jacobs et al (1981) rubric was originally designed for rating ESL compositions at Texas A & M University in five categories: content, organization, vocabulary, language use, and mechanics. In previous research that dealt with Japanese writing, various modified versions of Jacobs et al.'s (1981) ESL composition profile were used to measure Japanese L2 writing (e.g., Hirose & Sasaki, 1994; Kondo-Brown, 2002; Kondo-Brown & Brown, 2000; Pennington & So, 1993), as well as Japanese as a first language (L1) writing (e.g., Sasaki & Hirose, 1999).

The Japanese L2 composition rubric used for the present study was the same one used in previous studies (Kondo-Brown, 2002; Kondo-Brown & Brown, 2000). In earlier studies the three sets of total ratings obtained by trained raters using this rubric were highly correlated (Kondo-Brown & Brown, 2000) and self-consistent (Kondo-Brown, 2002). The rubric was developed by making a number of minor changes to the the Jacobs et al (1981) rubric so that it would be more appropriate for rating Japanese L2 compositions. For example, the original Jacobs et al. rubric was weighted with *content* getting 30%, *organization* 20%, *vocabulary* 20%, *language use* 25%, and *mechanics* 5%, while the adaptation used in this study had the same five categories equally weighted with 20 points each (scores of 7–20 were possible in each) (the actual rubric used in this study is shown in Table 13 in Chapter 3 of this volume).

A number of major and minor changes were also made in order to make the rubric appropriate for rating Japanese language compositions: (a) the description for *mechanics* in the revised scale takes out *capitalization* altogether from the description because capitalization does not exist in Japanese; (b) additions were made to *mechanics* in the revised rubric to include *Kanji* and *Kana* because these basic Japanese scripts are important in virtually all the second language Japanese writing rubrics covered in the literature review; (c) some grammar points mentioned in *language use* don't exist in Japanese (e.g., articles & prepositions) so they were removed from the description, while other grammar points were added (e.g., particles & inflections) because of their perceived importance in Tanaka, Tsubone, and Hajikano (1998); (d) *the consistency of writing style* was added to the *organization* section because of its perceived importance in Tanaka, Tsubone, and Hajikano (1998).

Scoring procedures

Three raters scored each of the 234 compositions. The raters were native speakers of Japanese with at least one graduate degree in a related field and experience teaching the language. Rater training on the scoring procedures took place before each scoring session for a total of three hours of such training. The first session consisted of the second author and the raters scoring 10 sample compositions at the same time. These compositions were just samples that were not otherwise used in the study. After doing the ratings, the scores were compared and discussed. The goal was to minimize differences in ratings. Each rater was asked to score the 234 compositions within two days, working their way systematically from the first prompt through the second on (on the first day) to the third (on the second day). Before doing the second-day ratings, an additional rater training session was conducted to discuss rating discrepancies that had arisen during the scoring of the first day compositions.

Results

Since all of the other results in this study can only be interpreted in terms of the distributions of scores as they are represented by the descriptive statistics, we will start with those. Table 1 shows the means, standard deviations (SD), lowest scores (Min), highest scores (Max), highest possible scores (Possible) for each rater and for the total scores (i.e., for all three raters combined with all five categories added up). Notice that the overall mean of 70.06 is fairly high, probably in part because the entire range of ratings is fairly high (from 40.33 to 99). Note also that the standard deviation is 11.04 and that there is room for approximately three standard deviations above and below the mean. The other three columns of numbers show the same statistics for each of the raters separately, and the results are fairly similar for the three of them. Notice also, however, that there are slight differences among the means: Rater 2 was the most severe, and Rater 1 was the most lenient with Rater 3 in between. Similarly, there were small differences in the standard deviations with Rater 1 having the smallest variation in scores, Rater 3 the largest variation, and Rater 2 in between.

Table 1. Descriptive statistics for total scores and individual raters

statistic	rater 1	rater 2	rater 3	total
Mean	71.68	68.76	69.73	70.06
SD	10.85	11.35	12.23	11.04
Min	40.00	50.00	36.00	40.33
Max	98.00	100.00	100.00	99.00
Possible	100.00	100.00	100.00	100.00

Table 2. Descriptive statistics for categories

statistic	content	organization	vocabulary	lang use	mechanics
Mean	14.07	13.80	13.94	14.70	14.18
SD	2.35	2.43	2.40	2.15	1.95
Min	8.00	7.70	8.00	8.30	7.70
Max	20.00	19.70	20.00	19.70	19.70
Possible	20.00	20.00	20.00	20.00	20.00

Table 2 shows the same descriptive statistics for the five categories (labeled across the top). Though the differences among these categories are small, Language Use had the highest mean and Organization had the lowest, while Organization appears to have the highest variation and Mechanics the lowest.

Table 3. Classical test theory inter-rater correlation coefficients for rater pairs, as well as two-rater and three-rater reliability estimates

type of reliability	content	organization	vocabulary	lang use	mechanics	total
raters 1 & 2	.831	.814	.859	.826	.875	.904
raters 2 & 3	.886	.836	.861	.820	.848	.902
raters 1 & 3	.811	.770	.859	.794	.859	.881
two-raters	.896	.870	.924	.885	.918	.937
three-raters	.928	.909	.948	.920	.944	.957
Cronbach alpha	.937	.923	.947	.927	.948	.984

Classical test theory reliability estimates are shown in Table 3. Across the top, labels are provided for the columns showing estimates for the five categories and the total scores. On the left side, rows are labeled for each pair of raters (1 & 2, 2 & 3, and 1 & 3) as well as for two-raters and three-raters. The reliability estimates for each pair were calculated using simple correlation coefficients, while the reliability estimates for two- and three-raters were calculated using the Spearman-Brown prophecy formula on the lowest correlation found among the pairs in each case (after Brown, 2005a, pp. 178–179). Notice that these reliability estimates range from moderate (in the .80s) to high (.90 and above), and that generally, the more raters the higher the reliability. Cronbach alpha (for all three raters and five categories combined) shows results similar to the three-rater reliabilities (though generally a bit higher than those for three raters).

G-Theory analyses

The first stage in G-theory analyses is called the generalizability study (or G-study). Based on analysis of variance (ANOVA), *variance components* (VCs) are derived for each of the facets and interactions in the study. For example, in the present rubrics-based ratings study, we were interested in the relative effects of persons crossed with raters crossed (*see Chapter 4 for more on crossed versus nested studies*) with categories ($p \times r \times c$) and their interactions. Using the GENOVA G-theory analysis program (available free of charge for download at http://www.education.uiowa.edu/casma/GenovaPrograms.htm), we calculated the $p \times r \times c$ ANOVA results as shown in first four columns of Table 4. We also calculated variance components and their standard errors as shown in the last two columns of Table 4.

Table 4. ANOVA for G-Study ($p \times r \times c$) with estimated variance components and their standard errors

effect	df	SS	MS	VC	SE
persons	233	17108.7442	73.43	4.6380782	0.4517994
raters	2	205.6587	102.83	0.0754414	0.0623218
categories	4	60.7066	15.18	0.0028414	0.0147098

continued...

Table 4. ANOVA for G-Study (p x r x c) with estimated variance components and their standard errors *(cont.)*

effect	df	SS	MS	VC	SE
pr	466	1347.5413	2.89	0.4692167	0.0379760
pc	932	1408.0935	1.51	0.3217313	0.0240530
rc	8	97.7345	12.22	0.0498768	0.0233485
prc	1864	1017.0655	0.55	0.5456360	0.0178633
total	3509				

The last part of this G-study involves interpreting the VCs for each facet and interaction in terms of relative magnitude. The easiest way to explain this is to convert the VCs into percentages of the total variance as shown in Table 5. Clearly the largest VC is for persons, as it should be in a norm-referenced test like the one analyzed here. Raters, categories, and their interaction (rc) contributed negligible amounts of variance, with 1.24%, .05%, and .82, respectively, while the two-way interactions for pr and pc accounted for considerably more variance, with 7.69% and 5.27%, respectively, and the three-way prc interaction accounted for 8.94%. What this means is that the persons VC is spreading people out a great deal as would be expected, but the pr, pc, and pcr interactions are showing the extent to which raters and categories are inconsistent across persons, and each other. This finishes the first G-study stage.

Table 5. Variance components and percentages of variance for persons, raters, categories and their interactions

effect	VC	% var
persons	4.6380782	76.00
raters	.0754414	1.24
categories	.0028414	0.05
pr	.4692167	7.69
pc	.3217313	5.27
rc	.0498768	0.82
prc	.5456360	8.94
total	6.1028218	100.00

Decision study

The second stage is called a decision study (D study). Here the G-study VCs are used to calculate generalizability coefficients (analogous to classical test theory reliability coefficients) for various testing conditions. In this particular study, with its p x r x c design, it is appropriate to examine generalizability coefficients for various numbers of raters and categories. The aim of the D study is to investigate various potential test designs to determine which will be most generalizable in a revised version of the assessment procedures and rubric given the practical constraints on the possible numbers of raters, numbers of rubric categories, and so forth. It is also necessary to take into account issues like test administration time, cost of raters, student fatigue, etc.

The general formula for calculating generalizability coefficients is as follows:

$$E\rho^2 = \frac{\hat{\sigma}_p^2}{\hat{\sigma}_p^2 + \hat{\sigma}_e^2}$$

That is, the generalizability coefficient is the ratio of persons variance ($\hat{\sigma}_p^2$) to persons variance plus error variance ($\hat{\sigma}_p^2 + \hat{\sigma}_e^2$). D-studies can be done for relative decisions (i.e., norm-referenced) or absolute decisions (i.e., criterion-referenced).

In the case of tests designed for relative decisions (i.e., norm-referenced tests designed for making decisions like admissions decisions or like the placement decisions in this study), the error is referred to as lower-case delta error as shown in the following formula:

$$E\rho^2(\delta) = \frac{\hat{\sigma}_p^2}{\hat{\sigma}_p^2 + \hat{\sigma}_e^2(\delta)}$$

Recall that, in this study, there are three facets: persons (p), categories (c), and raters (r), and four interactions are possible pc, pr, rc, and prc. Since only interactions involving p contribute to error in relative decisions only the pc, pr, and prc interactions are used in calculating the lower-case delta error term as follows (the n values in the denominators will be used later in this discussion to adjust for varying numbers of raters and categories):

$$\hat{\sigma}_e^2(\delta) = \frac{\hat{\sigma}_{pr}^2}{n_r} + \frac{\hat{\sigma}_{pc}^2}{n_c} + \frac{\hat{\sigma}_{prc,e}^2}{n_r n_c}$$

Substituting $\frac{\hat{\sigma}_{pr}^2}{n_r} + \frac{\hat{\sigma}_{pc}^2}{n_c} + \frac{\hat{\sigma}_{prc,e}^2}{n_r n_c}$ for the $\hat{\sigma}_e^2(\delta)$ in the generalizability coefficient for relative decisions equation above:

$$E\rho^2(\delta) = \frac{\hat{\sigma}_p^2}{\hat{\sigma}_p^2 + \frac{\hat{\sigma}_{pr}^2}{n_r} + \frac{\hat{\sigma}_{pc}^2}{n_c} + \frac{\hat{\sigma}_{prc,e}^2}{n_r n_c}}$$

For example, to calculate the generalizability coefficient for three raters and five categories, we insert the VC values for $\hat{\sigma}_p^2$, $\hat{\sigma}_{pr}^2$, $\hat{\sigma}_{pc}^2$, and $\hat{\sigma}_{prc}^2$ (4.6380782, .4692167, .3217313, and .5456360, respectively) into the equation and place the numbers 3 where nr is found and 5 where nc is found. The result is .947 as follows:

$$E\rho^2(\delta) = \frac{4.6380782}{4.6380782 + \frac{.4692167}{3} + \frac{.3217313}{5} + \frac{.5456360}{3(5)}} = .947473595 \approx .947$$

Table 6. Generalizability coefficients (for relative decisions, NRT) with different numbers of categories and raters

		categories														
		1	2	3	4	5	6	7	8	9	10	11	12	13	14	15
raters	1	.776	.837	.859	.871	.878	.883	.887	.889	.891	.893	.894	.895	.896	.897	.898
	2	.848	.897	.915	.924	.929	.933	.936	.938	.939	.940	.941	.942	.943	.944	.944
	3	.875	.919	.935	.943	**.947**	.951	.953	.955	.956	.957	.958	.959	.960	.960	.961
	4	.890	.931	.945	.952	.957	.960	.962	.964	.965	.966	.967	.968	.968	.969	.969
	5	.898	.937	.951	.958	.963	.966	.968	.969	.970	.971	.972	.973	.973	.974	.974
	6	.904	.942	.956	.962	.967	.969	.971	.973	.974	.975	.976	.976	.977	.977	.978
	7	.909	.946	.959	.965	.969	.972	.974	.975	.977	.977	.978	.979	.979	.980	.980
	8	.912	.948	.961	.967	.971	.974	.976	.977	.978	.979	.980	.981	.981	.982	.982
	9	.914	.950	.963	.969	.973	.976	.978	.979	.980	.981	.982	.982	.983	.983	.984
	10	.916	.952	.964	.970	.974	.977	.979	.980	.981	.982	.983	.983	.984	.984	.985
raters	11	.918	.953	.965	.972	.975	.978	.980	.981	.982	.983	.984	.984	.985	.985	.986
	12	.919	.954	.966	.973	.976	.979	.981	.982	.983	.984	.985	.985	.986	.986	.986
	13	.921	.955	.967	.973	.977	.980	.981	.983	.984	.985	.985	.986	.986	.987	.987
	14	.922	.956	.968	.974	.978	.980	.982	.983	.984	.985	.986	.986	.987	.987	.988
	15	.923	.957	.969	.975	.978	.981	.983	.984	.985	.986	.986	.987	.987	.988	.988

The values in Table 6 were calculated using the same equation and similar calculations but different values for n_r and n_c. To read Table 6, just look across the top for the number of categories that should be included in a revised version of these assessment procedures and down the left side for the number of raters. For example, under the present assessment conditions, five rubric categories were used and three raters, and the resulting generalizability coefficient is .947 (in bold italics), but perhaps raters are expensive in a particular institute and so they would prefer to use six categories and only two raters for a generalizability of .933, or in another institution, perhaps raters are expensive and time is of the essence, so they decide to use only two categories and two raters for a generalizability of .897 (or about .90). Clearly then, Table 6 indicates what the generalizability would be with different numbers of rater and categories so that decisions can be made about how best to go about revising the rubric and assessment procedures under the conditions in specific instructional contexts so that the scores will be acceptably dependable in future versions of the rubric and assessment procedures (more about this in the next section).

Discussion and conclusion

The primary purpose of this section will be to provide direct answers to the research questions posed at the end of the Introduction section. From a classical test theory (CTT) point of view, the rubric-based scores on the Japanese composition test are not too low for the students at UHM with a mean of 70.06 out of 100, and a range of scores from 40.33 to 99. Though they would be better centered if the mean were 50, the current mean of about 70 seems more humane in terms of how the students would feel about their performance than a test with a lower mean. This is especially true in light of the fact that the scores are well dispersed through the range of about 40 to 99 as indicated by the standard deviation of 11.04. In addition, the scores assigned by the raters based on this Japanese composition rubric were very reliable, producing a CTT interrater reliability of .957 for three raters. All in all, from a CTT point of view, the assessment procedures, the rubric, and the raters all appear to be functioning well for norm-referenced placement purposes.

In G-theory terms, the variance components reported in Table 5 show that the largest VC is clearly the 4.6380782 for persons. The VCs for raters, categories, and the rater-by-category interaction (rc) contributed negligible amounts of variance, with VCs of .0754414, .0028414, and .0498768, respectively. What does this mean? It means that the VC for persons is more than 60 times larger than the VC for raters, more than 1630 times larger than the VC for categories, and more than 90 times larger than the VC for the interaction of raters and categories. This is as it should be in a norm-referenced test like the one analyzed here. We typically want to spread people out along a continuum of abilities. In contrast, we do not necessarily want the raters to be spread out all over the scale, nor do we want categories to produce widely different scores from each other, nor in fact do we want the raters to vary unsystematically from each other across the categories. So far, all of these expectations have been met. This may be clearer to some readers if they consider the fact that a relatively high percentage of persons variance (76%) indicates the variance is where we want and need it to be for norm-referenced decisions, and that relatively low percentages of variance were found for raters (1.24%), categories (.05%), and raters-by-categories (.82%) (recall that these percentages were also shown in Table 5).

However, the relatively high VCs for the persons-by-raters interaction (.4692167), persons-by-categories interaction (.3217313), and persons-by-raters-by-categories interaction (.5456360) indicate that these interactions contribute to the variance to degrees that we should consider seriously, accounting for 7.69%, 5.27%, and 8.94% of the variance, respectively. The persons-by-raters interaction indicates the degree to which raters are inconsistently differing from each other (lower or higher) in scoring different persons. The persons-by-categories interaction indicates the degree to which scores for categories are inconsistently differing from each other (lower or higher) for different persons. The persons-by-raters-by-categories interaction indicates the degree to which scores for categories are inconsistently differing from each other (lower or higher) and doing so inconsistently for different persons. Clearly then, such interactions indicate inconsistency, which is why they are considered sources of error in calculating generalizability coefficients, which are in turn designed to estimate the proportion of dependable, or consistent, variance.

From a practical perspective, Table 6 can serve as a sort of what-if table for exploring the effects of different numbers of raters and categories on measurement generalizability so that the Japanese composition rubric and assessment procedures can be revised on the basis of data and analyses (rather than on intuitions) with the goal of making them more generalizable in the future. Looking again at Table 6, it is clear that, under the present assessment conditions of five rubric categories and three raters, the generalizability is estimated to be .947. The what-if questions for revision can go well beyond that simple observation. For example, what if we used five categories but only used two raters? (.929) Or one rater? (.878) Or if we used five categories but increased the number of raters to four? (.957) Or five raters? (.963). The same sorts of questions can be asked for categories. For instance, what if we used three raters but only used four categories? (.943) Or three categories? (.935) Or two? (.919) Or even one? (.875) But such what-if questions don't need to be only on one dimension or the other. We can ask what the generalizability would be for any combination of numbers (up to 15) of raters or categories. This is what makes G-theory and the resulting D study very useful indeed.

It is also true that the table can be used the other way around to answer questions like how many raters and categories do we need to get at least .95 generalizability? There are a number of possible answers to that sort of question (i.e., nine raters and two categories, five raters and three categories, four raters and four or five categories, three raters and six through 15 categories). Thus this table can be used as a very flexible tool to consider various possible changes in the design and what their effects on generalizability would likely be. Generally speaking, it appears in Table 6 that adding categories (after 5) or adding raters (after 5) does not provide very much bang-for-the-buck. But various combinations of numbers of rubric categories and raters within five of each seem to result in considerable differences in the generalizability. Naturally, the ultimate decision must take into account additional conditions in the assessment procedures and practices of the particular institution involved. For example, conditions such as resources and time, the importance of the decision, the number of other pieces of information used in the decision, and so forth may influence choices in numbers of raters and categories along with the information provided in Table 6. All of these are important considerations in designing assessment procedures and interpreting the resulting scores. Hopefully, this study will make such tasks a bit easier at least for rubrics-based tests like the Japanese composition test studied here.

References

Bachman, L. F. (1997). Generalizability theory. In C. Clapham & D. Corson (Eds.), *Encyclopedia of languages and education Volume 7: Language testing and assessment* (pp. 255–262). Dordrecht, Netherlands: Kluwer Academic.

Bachman, L. F. (2004). *Statistical analyses for language assessment*. Cambridge, UK: Cambridge University.

Bachman, L. F., Lynch, B. K., & Mason, M. (1995). Investigating variability in tasks and rater judgments in a performance test of foreign language speaking. *Language Testing, 12*(2), 239–257.

Bolus, R. E., Hinofotis, F. B., & Bailey, K. M. (1982). An introduction to generalizability theory in second language research. *Language Learning, 32*, 245–258.

Brennan, R. L. (1983). *Elements of generalizability theory*. Iowa City: ACT Publications.

Brennan, R. L. (2001). *Generalizability theory*. New York: Springer.

Brown, J. D. (1982). *Testing EFL reading comprehension in engineering English*. Unpublished dissertation at the University of California at Los Angeles.

Brown, J. D. (1984). A norm-referenced engineering reading test. In A.K. Pugh & J.M. Ulijn (Eds.), *Reading for professional purposes: Studies and practices in native and foreign languages*. London: Heinemann Educational.

Brown, J. D. (1990). Short-cut estimators of criterion-referenced test consistency. *Language Testing Journal, 7*, 1, 77–97.

Brown, J. D. (1993). A comprehensive criterion-referenced language testing project. In D. Douglas & C. Chapelle (Eds.), *A new decade of language testing research* (pp. 163–184). Washington, DC: TESOL.

Brown, J. D. (1999). Relative importance of persons, items, subtests and languages to TOEFL test variance. *Language Testing, 16*(2), 216–237.

Brown, J. D. (2005a). *Testing in language programs: A comprehensive guide to English language assessment* (New edition). New York: McGraw-Hill.

Brown, J. D. (2005b). Statistics corner—Questions and answers about language testing statistics: Generalizability and decision studies. *Shiken: JALT Testing & Evaluation SIG Newsletter, 9*(1), 12–16. Available online at http://jalt.org/test/bro_21.htm. [accessed Dec. 10, 2006].

Brown, J. D. (2007). Multiple views of L1 writing score reliability. *Second Language Studies, 25*(2), 1–31. Available online at http://www.hawaii.edu/sls/sls/wp-content/uploads/2011/06/BrownWritingGstudy.pdf [accessed April 2, 2011].

Brown, J. D. (2008). Raters, functions, item types, and the dependability of L2 pragmatic tests. In E. Alcón Soler & A. Martínez-Flor (Eds.), *Investigating pragmatics in foreign language learning, teaching and testing* (pp. 224–248). Clevedon, UK: Multilingual Matters.

Brown, J. D., & Ahn, R. C. (2011). Variables that affect the dependability of L2 pragmatics tests. *Journal of Pragmatics, 43*(1), 198–217.

Brown, J. D., & Bailey, K. M. (1984). A categorical instrument for scoring second language writing skills. *Language Learning, 34*, 21–42.

Brown, J. D., & Hudson, T. (2002). *Criterion-referenced language testing.* Cambridge, UK: Cambridge University.

Brown, J. D., & Ross, J. A. (1996). Decision dependability of item types, sections, tests, and the overall TOEFL test battery. In M. Milanovic & N. Saville (Eds.), *Performance testing, cognition and assessment* (pp. 231–265). Cambridge, UK: Cambridge University.

Chiu, C. W.-T. (2001). *Scoring performance assessments based on judgments: Generalizability theory.* Boston: Kluwer Academic.

Cronbach, L. J., Rajaratnam, N., & Gleser, G. C. (1963). Theory of generalizability: A liberalization of reliability theory. *British Journal of Statistical Psychology, 16*, 137–163.

Hirose, K., & Sasaki, M. (1994). Explanatory variables for Japanese students' expository writing in English: An exploratory study. *Journal of Second Language Writing, 3*(3), 203–229.

Ishida, T. (1992). *Nyuumon nihongo tesutohoo [Introduction to Japanese testing method].* Tokyo: Taishuukan Shoten.

Jacobs, H. L., Zinkgraf, S. A., Wormuth, D. R., Hartfiel, V. F. & Hughey, J. B. (1981). *Testing ESL composition: A practical approach.* Rowley, MA: Newbury House.

Kondo-Brown, K. (2002). An analysis of rater bias with FACETS in measuring Japanese L2 writing performance. *Language Testing, 19*, 1–29.

Kondo-Brown, K. and Brown, J. D. (2000). *The Japanese placement tests at the University of Hawai'i: Applying item response theory.* NFLRC NetWork #20. Honolulu: Second Language Teaching & Curriculum Center, University of Hawai'i.

Kozaki, Y. (2004). Using GENOVA and FACETS to set multiple standards on performance assessment for certification in medical translation of Japanese into English. *Language Testing, 21*(1), 1–27.

Kunnan, A. J. (1992). An investigation of a criterion-referenced test using G-theory, and factor and cluster analysis. *Language Testing, 9*(1), 30–49.

Lee, Y.-W. (2005). *Dependability of scores for a new ESL speaking test: Evaluating prototype tasks.* TOEFL Monograph MS-28. Princeton, NJ: ETS.

Lee, Y.-W. (2006). Dependability of scores for a new ESL speaking assessment consisting of integrated and independent tasks. *Language Testing, 23*(2), 131–166.

Lee, Y.-W, & Kantor, R. (2005). *Dependability of ESL writing test scores: Evaluating prototype tasks and alternative rating schemes.* TOEFL Monograph MS-31. Princeton, NJ: ETS.

Lynch, B. K., & McNamara, T. F. (1998). Using G-theory and many-facet Rasch measurement in the development of performance assessments of the ESL speaking skills of immigrants. *Language Testing, 15,* 158–180.

Molloy, H., & Shimura, M. (2005). An examination of situational sensitivity in medium-scale interlanguage pragmatics research. In T. Newfields, Y. Ishida, M. Chapman, & M. Fujioka (Eds.) *Proceedings of the May. 22–23, 2004 JALT Pan-SIG Conference* Tokyo: JALT Pan SIG Committee (pp. 16–32). Available online at www.jalt.org/pansig/2004/HTML/ShimMoll.htm. [accessed Dec. 10, 2006].

Morita, F. (1981). Sakubun no hyooka [Evaluating compositions]. *Nihongo Kyooiku [Journal of Japanese Language Teaching], 43,* 17–33.

Nihongo Kyooiku Gakkai [The Society of Teaching Japanese as a Foreign Language]. (Ed.). (1991). *Nohongo tesuto handobukku* [Japanese language testing handbook]. Tokyo: Taishuukan Shoten.

Pennington, M. C., & So, S. (1993). Comparing writing process and product across two languages: A study of 6 Singaporean university student writers. *Journal of second language writing, 2,* 41–63.

Sasaki, M. & Hirose, K. (1999). Development of an analytic rating scale for Japanese L1 writing. *Language Testing 16,* 457–478.

Sawaki, Y. (2007). Construct validation of analytic rating scales in a speaking assessment: Reporting a score profile and a composite. *Language Testing, 24*(3), 355–390.

Schoonen, R. (2005). Generalizability of writing scores: An application of structural equation modeling. *Language Testing, 22*(1), 1–30.

Shavelson, R. J., & Webb, N. M. (1981). Generalizability theory: 1973–1980. *British Journal of Mathematical and Statistical Psychology, 34,* 133–166.

Shin, S. (2002). Effects of subskills and text types on Korean EFL reading scores. *Second Language Studies* (Working Papers), 20(2), 107–130. Available online at http://www.hawaii.edu/sls/sls/wp-content/uploads/2011/06/ShinSunyoungs-G-study.pdf. [accessed Dec. 10, 2006].

Stansfield, C. W., & Kenyon, D. M. (1992). Research of the comparability of the oral proficiency interview and the simulated oral proficiency interview. *System, 20,* 347–364.

Suen, H. K. (1990). *Principles of test theories.* Hillsdale, NJ: Lawrence Erlbaum.

Tanaka, M., Hajikano, A., & Tsubone, Y (1998). Daini gengo to shite no nihongo ni okeru sakubun hyooka [Criteria for writing by non-native speakers of Japanese: Factors affecting the evaluation of "good writing]. *Nihongo Kyooiku [Journal of Japanese Language Teaching], 99,* 60–71.

Tanaka, M., Tsubone, Y., & Hajikano, A. (1998). Dainigengo to shite no nihongo ni okeru sakubun hyooka kijun: Nihongo kyooshi to ippan nihonjin no hikaku [Evaluation criteria for writing by non-native speakers: A comparison of survey results for Japanese teachers and non-teachers]. *Nihongo Kyooiku [Journal of Japanese Language Teaching], 96,* 17–33.

Van Weeren, J., & Theunissen, T. J. J. M. (1987). Testing pronunciation: An Application of generalizability theory. *Language Learning, 18*(1), 109–122.

Xi, X. (2007). Evaluating analytic scoring for the TOEFL® Academic Speaking Test (TAST) for operational use. *Language Testing, 24*(2) 251–286.

Yamamori, K. (2003). Evaluation of students' interest, willingness, and attitude toward English lessons: Multivariate generalizability theory. *The Japanese Journal of Educational Psychology, 51*(2), 195–204.

Yamanaka, H. (2005). Using generalizability theory in the evaluation of L2 writing. *JALT Journal, 27*(2), 169–185.

Yoshida, H. (2004). *An analytic instrument for assessing EFL pronunciation.* Unpublished Ed.D. dissertation. Philadelphia, PA: Temple University.

Yoshida, H. (2007). Exploring the assessment of English pronunciation using GENOVA and FACETS. *JACET Kansai Journal, 9,* 27–40.

Zhang, S. (2006). Investigating the relative effects of persons, items, sections, and languages on TOEIC score dependability. *Language Testing, 23*(3), 351–369.

Zhang, Y. (2003). Effects of persons, items, and subtests on UH ELIPT reading test scores. *Second Language Studies, 21*(2), 107–128. Available online at http://www.hawaii.edu/sls/sls/wp-content/uploads/2011/06/ZhangYao.pdf. [accessed April 2, 2011].

Section IV:
Conclusion

8
Conclusions on Rubric-Based Assessment

James Dean Brown
University of Hawai'i at Mānoa

Introduction

This book was divided into four sections: an introduction, two main sections, and a conclusion. The first section consisted of Chapter 1 which introduced the book with a brief overview of the rubrics-based assessment literature as well as an overview of the chapters in this book. In the process, the chapter cited some of the more useful books on rubrics in the general education literature and categorized a number of articles in second language studies that discussed or used rubrics.

The second section covered the issues involved in developing, using, and analyzing rubric-based assessment. Chapter 2 examined the central issues and strategies that are important in developing rubrics, revising them, and using rubrics to assess student language performance. Chapter 3 discussed the different types of rubrics used for language performance assessment and explained the most common ways rubrics are used in language instruction. This chapter also described three case studies that showcased different types of rubrics and pedagogical uses of them. Chapter 4 addressed the many issues that arise in doing basic statistical analyses including the different kinds of scales that rubrics create. This chapter also covered a variety of different statistical analysis techniques including the relatively simple classical test theory descriptive statistics, correlational analyses, reliability indices, and standard errors of measurement, as well as more advanced statistical procedures in generalizability theory (including generalizability and decision studies for relative and absolute decisions, phi(lambda), and signal-to-noise ratios) and multifaceted Rasch measurement (including fit statistics, vertical rulers, probability curves, and bias analysis).

The third section provided three major case studies in Asian and Pacific languages. Chapter 5 investigated the reliability and validity of the Kaiaka Reo Year Eight Māori language writing test administered to year eight students in Māori immersion schools in New Zealand. Chapter 6 reported on the development, piloting, analysis, and revision of a set of rubric-based Hawaiian oral language assessment procedures administered to students from seven Hawaiian Language Immersion Program schools located on four different islands in Hawai'i. Chapter 7 reported on a

---

Brown, J. D. (2012). Conclusions on rubric-based assessment. In J. D. Brown, (Ed.), *Developing, using, and analyzing rubrics in language assessment with case studies in Asian and Pacific languages* (pp. 187–193). Honolulu: University of Hawai'i, National Foreign Language Resource Center.

study that analyzed the rubric-based scores of three raters who independently assessed Japanese-as a second language compositions in five language categories (content, organization, vocabulary, language use, and mechanics) including a number of different statistical analyses like descriptive statistics, inter-rater reliability analysis, and generalizability theory analyses.

The fourth section is this Chapter 8, which summarizes the book briefly, then provides a table to help readers find which chapters covered which rubrics-related topics, and three additional tables that readers can use to quickly find whichever statistical topics, specific statistics, or example rubrics they might like to locate in this book.

What topics does this book cover?

This book has covered a number of topics related to rubric design, development, use, analysis, and research. Table 1 shows the general rubrics-related topics that were covered in the book and which chapters include them. Table 2 covers the main statistical topics in this book and the chapters that include them, and Table 3 lists the specific statistics included in this volume and where they can be found. Statistical topics are topics wherein statistical concepts (like types of scales, descriptive statistics, generalizability theory, etc.) are discussed in broad terms. In contrast, rubrics-related statistics are the actual statistics themselves (like the mean, standard deviation, variance components, generalizability coefficient, etc.) including explanations of how to calculate and interpret the numbers that result from these statistical analyses.

Note that the asterisks (*) in the tables mean that the chapter provides a definition and some discussion of the topic. Where I have put "ex," it means that the chapter provides an example of the concept or statistic in an actual research report (these usually include a definition and further explanation as well).

While the book has no index, readers can use these tables to explore which topics and statistics are covered overall in the book and which topics and statistics are covered in each chapter. These tables can also help readers who are looking for a specific topic or statistic to find the chapters that cover or include it.

Table 1.   General Rubrics-related topics in this book

topic	chapter						
	1	2	3	4	5	6	7
rubric defined	*		*				
rubrics in language teaching	*		*				
rubrics literature review	*		*				
abstracts of this book's chapters	*						
holistic versus analytic rubrics		*					
task-dependent/task-independent rubrics			*				
primary-trait rubrics			*				
rubric-like instruments			*				
steps in rubric development		*			ex	ex	ex
planning a rubric development project		*			ex	ex	ex
designing a rubric		*			ex	ex	ex
planning the assessment project		*			ex	ex	

topic	chapter						
	1	2	3	4	5	6	7
rater training		*			ex		ex
using a rubric		*			ex	ex	ex
evaluating rubric reliability and fairness		*			ex	ex	ex
evaluating rubric quality		*			ex	ex	ex
planning feedback based on rubrics		*				ex	
revising for pedagogically useful ratings		*				ex	
internet resources for creating rubrics		*					
pedagogical uses of rubrics			*			ex	
improving the consistency and efficiency of grading			*				
providing feedback and supporting student learning			*			ex	
guiding instruction			*			ex	
generating a record of student achievement			*				
communicating with others outside the classroom			*				
provides one or more case studies			*		*	*	*
rubric and rating validity					ex		

Table 2. Rubrics-related statistical topics in this book

statistical topic	chapter						
	1	2	3	4	5	6	7
types of scales (nominal, ordinal, interval, ratio)				*			
descriptive statistics				*	ex	ex	
classical test theory reliability							ex
generalizability theory				*			ex
crossed versus nested facets				*			ex
generalizability study				*			ex
decision study				*			ex
multifaceted Rasch analysis				*	ex	ex	
fit statistics				*	ex	ex	
vertical ruler				*	ex	ex	
probability curve				*	ex	ex	
item characteristic curve					ex		
partial credit scoring					ex	ex	
rater severity					ex	ex	
category difficulty					ex	ex	
scale step analysis					ex		

Table 3. Rubrics-related statistics in this book

statistics	1	2	3	4	5	6	7
Mean				*	ex	ex	
Median						ex	
Midpoint						ex	
Standard deviation				*	ex	ex	
Minimum				*	ex	ex	
Maximum				*	ex	ex	
Range				*	ex	ex	
Pearson product-moment orrelation coefficient				*		ex	
Point-biserial correlation coefficient						ex	
interrater & intrarater reliability				*			ex
Spearman-Brown prophecy formula				*			ex
Standard error of measurement				*			
Variance components				*			ex
Generalizability coefficient				*			ex
Error component for relative decisions				*			ex
Dependability estimate				*			
Error component for absolute decisions				*			
Phi(lambda)				*			
Signal-to-noise ratios				*			
Logit				*	ex	ex	
Root mean square standard error (RMSE)				*		ex	
Separation				*		ex	
Reliability				*	ex	ex	
Chi-square				*		ex	
# Misfit				*		ex	
Infit mean square					ex		
Outfit mean square					ex		
Standardized z					ex		

What example rubrics does this book provide?

Five of the chapters in this book provide a total of 22 example rubrics as listed in Table 4. These rubrics were designed for foreign or second language teaching/learning contexts (for Japanese and English as a second or foreign language) or first language revitalization contexts (for Hawaiian and Maori). Nonetheless, with small modifications, all of the example rubrics could easily be adapted and used in a wide range of foreign, second, and first language revitalization teaching and learning contexts.

Notice that the labels at the top of Table 4 indicate that the table provides five types of information about each rubric: the Chapter in which it is found, the rubric (identified by Table or Figure number, or Appendix letter), the type of rubric it is, the focus of the rubric, and additional description of the rubric. Clearly, the rubrics listed in Table 4 come in many shapes and forms including analytic, holistic, and primary trait rubrics, as well as checklist and numerical scale rubric-like devices. Among these are instruments designed for assessing an even greater array of skill areas including writing reports, compositions, essays, letters, narratives, and other writing tasks, as well as speaking, singing, listening, and given oral presentations. Examples are even provided of task-dependent and task-independent rubrics for assessing the mixed-skills involved in more complex tasks.

Table 4. Example rubrics in this book

chapter	rubric	type	focus	description
1	Table 1	holistic	writing reports	rubric for scoring written reports with scores on one axis
1	Table 2	analytic	writing reports	rubric for scoring written reports with language categories on one axis & scores on the other
2	Table 1	holistic	writing compositions	holistic version of the scale for rating composition tasks
2	Table 2	analytic	writing compositions	analytic scale for rating composition tasks
2	Table 4	holistic	writing essays	draft holistic scale for rating essays written by examinees with a wide range of abilities
2	Table 5	analytic	speaking	labeling and completing an analytic speaking rubric
2	Table 8	analytic	oral presentations	oral presentation rubric created on the Rubistar website in four minutes
3	Table 1	holistic	singing	a holistic rubric for singing in Japanese
3	Table 2	analytic	writing tasks	a generic analytic rubric for Japanese writing tasks
3	Table 3a	holistic	mixed-skill task	task-dependent rubric
3	Table 3b	holistic	mixed-skill task	task-independent rubric
3	Table 4	primary-trait	writing narratives	NAEP primary-trait rubric for narrative writing
3	Table 5	checklist	oral presentations	a checklist used for peer review of an oral presentation
3	Table 6	numerical scale	writing letters	a numerical scale used for a Japanese classroom unit test
3	Table 7	holistic	speaking	sample holistic speaking rubric for beginning-level college Japanese students

continued...

Table 4.	Example rubrics in this book *(cont.)*			
chapter	rubric	type	focus	description
3	Table 8	analytic	speaking	sample analytic speaking rubric for beginning-level college Japanese students
3	Table 10	holistic	speaking	task-independent rubric for young learners of Japanese
3	Table 11	holistic	speaking	sample task-dependent rubric for young learners of Japanese
3	Table 13	analytic	writing compositions	rubric for scoring Japanese L2 compositions in a college placement test
5	Figure 3	analytic	writing	Kaiaka Reo: analytical scale–description of Maori writing performance levels–Tuhituhi Year Eight
6	Appendix A	analytic	speaking	Hawaiian oral language proficiency assessment rubric (ʻōlelo Hawaiʻi)
6	Appendix B	analytic	speaking	Hawaiian oral language proficiency assessment rubric (English version)

Conclusion to the conclusion

Rubrics provide an essential set of tools for language teachers and researchers in today's world of communicative approaches with their notional, functional, task-based, problem solving, etc., syllabuses. Over the course of many years, language teachers were able to rationalize and content themselves with receptive test item formats like true-false, multiple-choice, and matching. And, those receptive item formats are fine for some purposes. As the label implies, receptive item formats are best suited to assessing *receptive* language skills like reading and listening. They can also be used to test *passive* knowledge of things like grammar, vocabulary, phonemes, and so forth. However, receptive item formats are not suitable for testing the *productive* language skills of writing and speaking, the *active* knowledge of grammar, vocabulary, phonemes, etc., or the interactions of any of those productive skills or active knowledge.

Typically, language teachers and researchers are ready and able to devise ways to collect language samples of productive skills and active knowledge from students in the written forms like essays, emails, and so forth or in the oral forms of interviews, role plays, group work, and so forth. These language samples may simply require students to fill-in words, phrases, utterances, and so forth or may require more elaborate task performances (sometimes requiring the use of one, two, three, or even four skills at the same time for task success). These language samples may also involve self-assessments, peer-assessments, or more elaborate student projects, portfolios, and so forth. As a field, we know how to get students to demonstrate their productive language skills and active knowledge.

However, problems often start when it comes time to do something with those language samples. What sorts of scores or feedback can teachers generate for the language samples? One answer to that question is provided by rubrics in their various forms. Rubrics are perfect for scoring written or oral language samples, or giving students verbal feedback either on their language production or on what their specific score(s) mean. This book has shown that rubrics are relatively easy to devise, they are relatively easy to use for scoring, and because they are relatively concrete in their descriptions of expected language behaviors, they lend themselves to communicating with students exactly what is expected of them as well as the degree to which those expectations have been met.

In short, rubrics provide a set of tools that allow teachers and researchers to assess productive skills and active knowledge, but rubrics also provide tools that can be used to promote efficient communication between teachers and students about what the teachers are looking for in the students' productive language abilities. That potential for fostering teacher-student communication is one of the most important features of rubrics. However, we should never minimize the importance of rubrics in effectively assessing productive language abilities and active knowledge when we need that information for research purposes or for admissions decisions, placement into course levels, fostering learning during courses, or grading students during and after the course is completed. Rubrics are not magical, but they certainly can help.

NATIONAL FOREIGN LANGUAGE RESOURCE CENTER
University of Hawai'i at Mānoa

ordering information at nflrc.hawaii.edu

Pragmatics & Interaction
Gabriele Kasper, series editor

Pragmatics & Interaction ("P&I"), a refereed series sponsored by the University of Hawai'i National Foreign Language Resource Center, publishes research on topics in pragmatics and discourse as social interaction from a wide variety of theoretical and methodological perspectives. P&I welcomes particularly studies on languages spoken in the Asian-Pacific region.

L2 LEARNING AS SOCIAL PRACTICE: CONVERSATION-ANALYTIC PERSPECTIVES
PALLOTTI, GABRIELE, & WAGNER, JOHANNES (EDS.)

This volume collects empirical studies applying Conversation Analysis to situations where second, third and other additional languages are used. A number of different aspects are considered, including how linguistic systems develop over time through social interaction, how participants 'do' language learning and teaching in classroom and everyday settings, how they select languages and manage identities in multilingual contexts and how the linguistic-interactional divide can be bridged with studies combining Conversation Analysis and Functional Linguistics. This variety of issues and approaches clearly shows the fruitfulness of a socio-interactional perspective on second language learning.

380pp., ISBN 978-0-9800459-7-0 $30.

TALK-IN-INTERACTION: MULTILINGUAL PERSPECTIVES
HANH THI NGUYEN & GABRIELE KASPER (EDITORS), 2009

This volume offers original studies of interaction in a range of languages and language varieties, including Chinese, English, Japanese, Korean, Spanish, Swahili, Thai, and Vietnamese; monolingual and bilingual interactions; and activities designed for second or foreign language learning. Conducted from the perspectives of conversation analysis and membership categorization analysis, the chapters examine ordinary conversation and institutional activities in face-to-face, telephone, and computer-mediated environments.

430pp., ISBN 978-0-8248-3137-0 $30.

Pragmatics & Language Learning
Gabriele Kasper, series editor

Pragmatics & Language Learning ("PLL"), a refereed series sponsored by the National Foreign Language Resource Center, publishes selected papers from the biannual International Pragmatics & Language Learning conference under the editorship of the conference hosts and the series editor. Check the NFLRC website for upcoming PLL conferences and PLL volumes.

PRAGMATICS AND LANGUAGE LEARNING VOLUME 11
Kathleen Bardovi-Harlig, César Félix-Brasdefer, & Alwiya S. Omar (Editors), 2006

This volume features cutting-edge theoretical and empirical research on pragmatics and language learning among a wide-variety of learners in diverse learning contexts from a variety of language backgrounds and target languages (English, German, Japanese, Kiswahili, Persian, and Spanish). This collection of papers from researchers around the world includes critical appraisals on the role of formulas in interlanguage pragmatics and speech-act research from a conversation analytic perspective. Empirical studies examine learner data using innovative methods of analysis and investigate issues in pragmatic development and the instruction of pragmatics.

430pp., ISBN 978-0-8248-3137-0 $30.

PRAGMATICS AND LANGUAGE LEARNING VOLUME 12
Gabriele Kasper, Hanh thi Nguyen, Dina R. Yoshimi, & Jim K. Yoshioka (Editors), 2010

This volume examines the organization of second language and multilingual speakers' talk and pragmatic knowledge across a range of naturalistic and experimental activities. Based on data collected on Danish, English, Hawai'i Creole, Indonesian, and Japanese as target languages, the contributions explore the nexus of pragmatic knowledge, interaction, and L2 learning outside and inside of educational settings.

364pp., ISBN 978-09800459-6-3 $30.

NFLRC Monographs
Richard Schmidt, series editor

Monographs of the National Foreign Language Resource Center present the findings of recent work in applied linguistics that is of relevance to language teaching and learning (with a focus on the less commonly taught languages of Asia and the Pacific) and are of particular interest to foreign language educators, applied linguists, and researchers. Prior to 2006, these monographs were published as "SLTCC Technical Reports."

RESEARCH AMONG LEARNERS OF CHINESE AS A FOREIGN LANGUAGE
Michael E. Everson & Helen H. Shen (Editors), 2010

Cutting-edge in its approach and international in its authorship, this fourth monograph in a series sponsored by the Chinese Language Teachers Association features eight research studies that explore a variety of themes, topics, and perspectives important to a variety of stakeholders in the Chinese language learning community. Employing a wide range of research methodologies, the volume provides data from actual Chinese language learners and will be of value to both theoreticians and practitioners alike. *[in English & Chinese]*

180pp.; 978-0-9800459-4-9 $20.

MANCHU: A TEXTBOOK FOR READING DOCUMENTS (SECOND EDITION)
Gertraude Roth Li, 2010

This book offers students a tool to gain a basic grounding in the Manchu language. The reading selections provided in this volume represent various types of documents, ranging from examples of the very earliest Manchu writing (17th century) to samples of contemporary Sibe (Xibo), a language that maybe considered a modern version of Manchu. Since Manchu courses are only rarely taught at universities anywhere, this second edition includes audio recordings to assist students with the pronunciation of the texts.

418pp.; ISBN 978-0-9800459-5-6 $36.

TOWARD USEFUL PROGRAM EVALUATION IN COLLEGE FOREIGN LANGUAGE EDUCATION
John M. Norris, John McE. Davis, Castle Sinicrope, & Yukiko Watanabe (Editors), 2009

This volume reports on innovative, useful evaluation work conducted within U.S. college foreign language programs. An introductory chapter scopes out the territory, reporting key findings from research into the concerns, impetuses, and uses for evaluation that FL educators identify. Seven chapters then highlight examples of evaluations conducted in diverse language programs and institutional contexts. Each case is reported by program-internal educators, who walk readers through critical steps, from identifying evaluation uses, users, and questions, to designing methods, interpreting findings, and taking actions. A concluding chapter reflects on the emerging roles for FL program evaluation and articulates an agenda for integrating evaluation into language education practice.

240pp., ISBN 978-0-9800459-3-2 $30.

SECOND LANGUAGE TEACHING AND LEARNING IN THE NET GENERATION
Raquel Oxford & Jeffrey Oxford (Editors), 2009

Today's young people—the Net Generation—have grown up with technology all around them. However, teachers cannot assume that students' familiarity with technology in general transfers successfully to pedagogical settings. This volume examines various technologies and offers concrete advice on how each can be successfully implemented in the second language curriculum.

240pp., ISBN 978-0-9800459-2-5 $30.

CASE STUDIES IN FOREIGN LANGUAGE PLACEMENT: PRACTICES AND POSSIBILITIES
Thom Hudson & Martyn Clark (Editors), 2008

Although most language programs make placement decisions on the basis of placement tests, there is surprisingly little published about different contexts and systems of placement testing. The present volume contains case studies of placement programs in foreign language programs at the tertiary level across the United States. The different programs span the spectrum from large programs servicing hundreds of students annually to small language programs with very few students. The contributions to this volume address such issues as how the size of the program, presence or absence of heritage learners, and population changes affect language placement decisions.

201pp., ISBN 0-9800459-0-8 $20.

CHINESE AS A HERITAGE LANGUAGE: FOSTERING ROOTED WORLD CITIZENRY
Agnes Weiyun He & Yun Xiao (Editors), 2008

Thirty-two scholars examine the socio-cultural, cognitive-linguistic, and educational-institutional trajectories along which Chinese as a Heritage Language may be acquired, maintained and developed. They draw upon developmental psychology, functional linguistics, linguistic and cultural anthropology, discourse analysis, orthography analysis, reading research, second language acquisition, and bilingualism. This volume aims to lay a foundation for theories, models, and master scripts to be discussed, debated, and developed, and to stimulate research and enhance teaching both within and beyond Chinese language education.

280pp., ISBN 978–0–8248–3286–5 $20.

PERSPECTIVES ON TEACHING CONNECTED SPEECH TO SECOND LANGUAGE SPEAKERS
James Dean Brown & Kimi Kondo-Brown (Editors), 2006

This book is a collection of fourteen articles on connected speech of interest to teachers, researchers, and materials developers in both ESL/EFL (ten chapters focus on connected speech in English) and Japanese (four chapters focus on Japanese connected speech). The fourteen chapters are divided up into five sections:

- What do we know so far about teaching connected speech?
- Does connected speech instruction work?
- How should connected speech be taught in English?
- How should connected speech be taught in Japanese?
- How should connected speech be tested?

290pp., ISBN 978–0–8248–3136–3 $20.

CORPUS LINGUISTICS FOR KOREAN LANGUAGE LEARNING AND TEACHING
Robert Bley-Vroman & Hyunsook Ko (Editors), 2006

Dramatic advances in personal-computer technology have given language teachers access to vast quantities of machine-readable text, which can be analyzed with a view toward improving the basis of language instruction. Corpus linguistics provides analytic techniques and practical tools for studying language in use. This volume provides both an introductory framework for the use of corpus linguistics for language teaching and examples of its application for Korean teaching and learning. The collected papers cover topics in Korean syntax, lexicon, and discourse, and second language acquisition research, always with a focus on application in the classroom. An overview of Korean corpus linguistics tools and available Korean corpora are also included.

265pp., ISBN 0–8248–3062–8 $25.

NEW TECHNOLOGIES AND LANGUAGE LEARNING: CASES IN THE LESS COMMONLY TAUGHT LANGUAGES
Carol Anne Spreen (Editor), 2002

In recent years, the National Security Education Program (NSEP) has supported an increasing number of programs for teaching languages using different technological media. This compilation of case study initiatives funded through the NSEP Institutional Grants Program presents a range of technology-based options for language programming that will help universities make more informed decisions about teaching less commonly taught languages. The eight chapters describe how different types of technologies are used to support language programs (i.e., Web, ITV, and audio- or video-based materials), discuss identifiable trends in elanguage learning, and explore how technology addresses issues of equity, diversity, and opportunity. This book offers many lessons learned and decisions made as technology changes and learning needs become more complex.

188pp., ISBN 0-8248-2634-5 $25.

AN INVESTIGATION OF SECOND LANGUAGE TASK-BASED PERFORMANCE ASSESSMENTS
JAMES DEAN BROWN, THOM HUDSON, JOHN M. NORRIS, & WILLIAM BONK, 2002

This volume describes the creation of performance assessment instruments and their validation (based on work started in a previous monograph). It begins by explaining the test and rating scale development processes and the administration of the resulting three seven-task tests to 90 university level EFL and ESL students. The results are examined in terms of (a) the effects of test revision; (b) comparisons among the task-dependent, task-independent, and self-rating scales; and (c) reliability and validity issues.

240pp., ISBN 0-8248-2633-7 $25.

MOTIVATION AND SECOND LANGUAGE ACQUISITION
ZOLTÁN DÖRNYEI & RICHARD SCHMIDT (EDITORS), 2001

This volume—the second in this series concerned with motivation and foreign language learning—includes papers presented in a state-of-the-art colloquium on L2 motivation at the American Association for Applied Linguistics (Vancouver, 2000) and a number of specially commissioned studies. The 20 chapters, written by some of the best known researchers in the field, cover a wide range of theoretical and research methodological issues, and also offer empirical results (both qualitative and quantitative) concerning the learning of many different languages (Arabic, Chinese, English, Filipino, French, German, Hindi, Italian, Japanese, Russian, and Spanish) in a broad range of learning contexts (Bahrain, Brazil, Canada, Egypt, Finland, Hungary, Ireland, Israel, Japan, Spain, and the US).

520pp., ISBN 0-8248-2458-X $30.

A FOCUS ON LANGUAGE TEST DEVELOPMENT: EXPANDING THE LANGUAGE PROFICIENCY CONSTRUCT ACROSS A VARIETY OF TESTS
THOM HUDSON & JAMES DEAN BROWN (EDITORS), 2001

This volume presents eight research studies that introduce a variety of novel, non-traditional forms of second and foreign language assessment. To the extent possible, the studies also show the entire test development process, warts and all. These language testing projects not only demonstrate many of the types of problems that test developers run into in the real world but also afford the reader unique insights into the language test development process.

230pp., ISBN 0-8248-2351-6 $20.

STUDIES ON KOREAN IN COMMUNITY SCHOOLS
DONG-JAE LEE, SOOKEUN CHO, MISEON LEE, MINSUN SONG, & WILLIAM O'GRADY (EDITORS), 2000

The papers in this volume focus on language teaching and learning in Korean community schools. Drawing on innovative experimental work and research in linguistics, education, and psychology, the contributors address issues of importance to teachers, administrators, and parents. Topics covered include childhood bilingualism, Korean grammar, language acquisition, children's literature, and language teaching methodology. [in Korean]

256pp., ISBN 0-8248-2352-4 $20.

A COMMUNICATIVE FRAMEWORK FOR INTRODUCTORY JAPANESE LANGUAGE CURRICULA
Washington State Japanese Language Curriculum Guidelines Committee, 2000

In recent years, the number of schools offering Japanese nationwide has increased dramatically. Because of the tremendous popularity of the Japanese language and the shortage of teachers, quite a few untrained, non-native and native teachers are in the classrooms and are expected to teach several levels of Japanese. These guidelines are intended to assist individual teachers and professional associations throughout the United States in designing Japanese language curricula. They are meant to serve as a framework from which language teaching can be expanded and are intended to allow teachers to enhance and strengthen the quality of Japanese language instruction.

168pp., ISBN 0–8248–2350–8 $20.

FOREIGN LANGUAGE TEACHING AND MINORITY LANGUAGE EDUCATION
Kathryn A. Davis (Editor), 1999

This volume seeks to examine the potential for building relationships among foreign language, bilingual, and ESL programs towards fostering bilingualism. Part I of the volume examines the sociopolitical contexts for language partnerships, including:

- obstacles to developing bilingualism
- implications of acculturation, identity, and language issues for linguistic minorities.
- the potential for developing partnerships across primary, secondary, and tertiary institutions

Part II of the volume provides research findings on the Foreign language partnership project designed to capitalize on the resources of immigrant students to enhance foreign language learning.

152pp., ISBN 0–8248–2067–3 $20.

DESIGNING SECOND LANGUAGE PERFORMANCE ASSESSMENTS
John M. Norris, James Dean Brown, Thom Hudson, & Jim Yoshioka, 1998, 2000

This technical report focuses on the decision-making potential provided by second language performance assessments. The authors first situate performance assessment within a broader discussion of alternatives in language assessment and in educational assessment in general. They then discuss issues in performance assessment design, implementation, reliability, and validity. Finally, they present a prototype framework for second language performance assessment based on the integration of theoretical underpinnings and research findings from the task-based language teaching literature, the language testing literature, and the educational measurement literature. The authors outline test and item specifications, and they present numerous examples of prototypical language tasks. They also propose a research agenda focusing on the operationalization of second language performance assessments.

248pp., ISBN 0–8248–2109–2 $20.

SECOND LANGUAGE DEVELOPMENT IN WRITING: MEASURES OF FLUENCY, ACCURACY, AND COMPLEXITY
Kate Wolfe-Quintero, Shunji Inagaki, & Hae-Young Kim, 1998, 2002

In this book, the authors analyze and compare the ways that fluency, accuracy, grammatical complexity, and lexical complexity have been measured in studies of language development in second language writing. More than 100 developmental measures are examined, with detailed comparisons of the results across the studies that have used each measure. The authors discuss the theoretical foundations for each type of developmental measure, and they consider the relationship between developmental measures and various types of proficiency measures. They also examine criteria for determining which developmental measures are the most successful and suggest which measures are the most promising for continuing work on language development.

208pp., ISBN 0–8248–2069–X $20.

THE DEVELOPMENT OF A LEXICAL TONE PHONOLOGY IN AMERICAN ADULT LEARNERS OF STANDARD MANDARIN CHINESE
Sylvia Henel Sun, 1998

The study reported is based on an assessment of three decades of research on the SLA of Mandarin tone. It investigates whether differences in learners' tone perception and production are related to differences in the effects of certain linguistic, task, and learner factors. The learners of focus are American students of Mandarin in Beijing, China. Their performances on two perception and three production tasks are analyzed through a host of variables and methods of quantification.

328pp., ISBN 0–8248–2068–1 $20.

NEW TRENDS AND ISSUES IN TEACHING JAPANESE LANGUAGE AND CULTURE
Haruko M. Cook, Kyoko Hijirida, & Mildred Tahara (Editors), 1997

In recent years, Japanese has become the fourth most commonly taught foreign language at the college level in the United States. As the number of students who study Japanese has increased, the teaching of Japanese as a foreign language has been established as an important academic field of study. This technical report includes nine contributions to the advancement of this field, encompassing the following five important issues:

- Literature and literature teaching
- Technology in the language classroom
- Orthography
- Testing
- Grammatical versus pragmatic approaches to language teaching

164pp., ISBN 0–8248–2067–3 $20.

SIX MEASURES OF JSL PRAGMATICS
Sayoko Okada Yamashita, 1996

This book investigates differences among tests that can be used to measure the cross-cultural pragmatic ability of English-speaking learners of Japanese. Building on the work of Hudson, Detmer, and Brown (Technical Reports #2 and #7 in this series), the author modified six test types that she used to gather data from North American learners of Japanese. She found numerous problems with the multiple-choice discourse completion test but reported that the other five tests all proved highly reliable and reasonably valid. Practical issues involved in creating and using such language tests are discussed from a variety of perspectives.

213pp., ISBN 0–8248–1914–4 $15.

LANGUAGE LEARNING STRATEGIES AROUND THE WORLD: CROSS-CULTURAL PERSPECTIVES
Rebecca L. Oxford (Editor), 1996, 1997, 2002

Language learning strategies are the specific steps students take to improve their progress in learning a second or foreign language. Optimizing learning strategies improves language performance. This groundbreaking book presents new information about cultural influences on the use of language learning strategies. It also shows innovative ways to assess students' strategy use and remarkable techniques for helping students improve their choice of strategies, with the goal of peak language learning.

166pp., ISBN 0-8248-1910-1 $20.

TELECOLLABORATION IN FOREIGN LANGUAGE LEARNING: PROCEEDINGS OF THE HAWAI'I SYMPOSIUM
MARK WARSCHAUER (EDITOR), 1996

The Symposium on Local & Global Electronic Networking in Foreign Language Learning & Research, part of the National Foreign Language Resource Center's 1995 Summer Institute on Technology & the Human Factor in Foreign Language Education, included presentations of papers and hands-on workshops conducted by Symposium participants to facilitate the sharing of resources, ideas, and information about all aspects of electronic networking for foreign language teaching and research, including electronic discussion and conferencing, international cultural exchanges, real-time communication and simulations, research and resource retrieval via the Internet, and research using networks. This collection presents a sampling of those presentations.

252pp., ISBN 0-8248-1867-9 $20.

LANGUAGE LEARNING MOTIVATION: PATHWAYS TO THE NEW CENTURY
REBECCA L. OXFORD (EDITOR), 1996

This volume chronicles a revolution in our thinking about what makes students want to learn languages and what causes them to persist in that difficult and rewarding adventure. Topics in this book include the internal structures of and external connections with foreign language motivation; exploring adult language learning motivation, self-efficacy, and anxiety; comparing the motivations and learning strategies of students of Japanese and Spanish; and enhancing the theory of language learning motivation from many psychological and social perspectives.

218pp., ISBN 0-8248-1849-0 $20.

LINGUISTICS & LANGUAGE TEACHING: PROCEEDINGS OF THE SIXTH JOINT LSH-HATESL CONFERENCE
CYNTHIA REVES, CAROLINE STEELE, & CATHY S. P. WONG (EDITORS), 1996

Technical Report #10 contains 18 articles revolving around the following three topics:
- Linguistic issues—These six papers discuss various linguistic issues: ideophones, syllabic nasals, linguistic areas, computation, tonal melody classification, and wh-words.
- Sociolinguistics—Sociolinguistic phenomena in Swahili, signing, Hawaiian, and Japanese are discussed in four of the papers.
- Language teaching and learning—These eight papers cover prosodic modification, note taking, planning in oral production, oral testing, language policy, L2 essay organization, access to dative alternation rules, and child noun phrase structure development.

364pp., ISBN 0-8248-1851-2 $20.

ATTENTION & AWARENESS IN FOREIGN LANGUAGE LEARNING
RICHARD SCHMIDT (EDITOR), 1996

Issues related to the role of attention and awareness in learning lie at the heart of many theoretical and practical controversies in the foreign language field. This collection of papers presents research into the learning of Spanish, Japanese, Finnish, Hawaiian, and English as a second language (with additional comments and examples from French, German, and miniature artificial languages) that bear on these crucial questions for foreign language pedagogy.

394pp., ISBN 0-8248-1794-X $20.

VIRTUAL CONNECTIONS: ONLINE ACTIVITIES AND PROJECTS FOR NETWORKING LANGUAGE LEARNERS
Mark Warschauer (Editor), 1995, 1996

Computer networking has created dramatic new possibilities for connecting language learners in a single classroom or across the globe. This collection of activities and projects makes use of email, the internet, computer conferencing, and other forms of computer-mediated communication for the foreign and second language classroom at any level of instruction. Teachers from around the world submitted the activities compiled in this volume—activities that they have used successfully in their own classrooms.

417pp., ISBN 0-8248-1793-1 $30.

DEVELOPING PROTOTYPIC MEASURES OF CROSS-CULTURAL PRAGMATICS
Thom Hudson, Emily Detmer, & J. D. Brown, 1995

Although the study of cross-cultural pragmatics has gained importance in applied linguistics, there are no standard forms of assessment that might make research comparable across studies and languages. The present volume describes the process through which six forms of cross-cultural assessment were developed for second language learners of English. The models may be used for second language learners of other languages. The six forms of assessment involve two forms each of indirect discourse completion tests, oral language production, and self-assessment. The procedures involve the assessment of requests, apologies, and refusals.

198pp., ISBN 0-8248-1763-X $15.

THE ROLE OF PHONOLOGICAL CODING IN READING KANJI
Sachiko Matsunaga, 1995

In this technical report, the author reports the results of a study that she conducted on phonological coding in reading kanji using an eye-movement monitor and draws some pedagogical implications. In addition, she reviews current literature on the different schools of thought regarding instruction in reading kanji and its role in the teaching of non-alphabetic written languages like Japanese.

64pp., ISBN 0-8248-1734-6 $10.

PRAGMATICS OF CHINESE AS NATIVE AND TARGET LANGUAGE
Gabriele Kasper (Editor), 1995

This technical report includes six contributions to the study of the pragmatics of Mandarin Chinese:

- A report of an interview study conducted with nonnative speakers of Chinese; and
- Five data-based studies on the performance of different speech acts by native speakers of Mandarin—requesting, refusing, complaining, giving bad news, disagreeing, and complimenting.

312pp., ISBN 0-8248-1733-8 $20.

A BIBLIOGRAPHY OF PEDAGOGY AND RESEARCH IN INTERPRETATION AND TRANSLATION
Etilvia Arjona, 1993

This technical report includes four types of bibliographic information on translation and interpretation studies:

- Research efforts across disciplinary boundaries—cognitive psychology, neurolinguistics, psycholinguistics, sociolinguistics, computational linguistics, measurement, aptitude testing,

- language policy, decision-making, theses, dissertations;
- Training information covering program design, curriculum studies, instruction, school administration;
- Instruction information detailing course syllabi, methodology, models, available textbooks; and
- Testing information about aptitude, selection, diagnostic tests.

115pp., ISBN 0–8248–1572–6 $10.

PRAGMATICS OF JAPANESE AS NATIVE AND TARGET LANGUAGE
GABRIELE KASPER (EDITOR), 1992, 1996

This technical report includes three contributions to the study of the pragmatics of Japanese:
- A bibliography on speech act performance, discourse management, and other pragmatic and sociolinguistic features of Japanese;
- A study on introspective methods in examining Japanese learners' performance of refusals; and
- A longitudinal investigation of the acquisition of the particle ne by nonnative speakers of Japanese.

125pp., ISBN 0–8248–1462–2 $10.

A FRAMEWORK FOR TESTING CROSS-CULTURAL PRAGMATICS
THOM HUDSON, EMILY DETMER, & J. D. BROWN, 1992

This technical report presents a framework for developing methods that assess cross-cultural pragmatic ability. Although the framework has been designed for Japanese and American cross-cultural contrasts, it can serve as a generic approach that can be applied to other language contrasts. The focus is on the variables of social distance, relative power, and the degree of imposition within the speech acts of requests, refusals, and apologies. Evaluation of performance is based on recognition of the speech act, amount of speech, forms or formulæ used, directness, formality, and politeness.

51pp., ISBN 0–8248–1463–0 $10.

RESEARCH METHODS IN INTERLANGUAGE PRAGMATICS
GABRIELE KASPER & MERETE DAHL, 1991

This technical report reviews the methods of data collection employed in 39 studies of interlanguage pragmatics, defined narrowly as the investigation of nonnative speakers' comprehension and production of speech acts, and the acquisition of L2-related speech act knowledge. Data collection instruments are distinguished according to the degree to which they constrain informants' responses, and whether they tap speech act perception/comprehension or production. A main focus of discussion is the validity of different types of data, in particular their adequacy to approximate authentic performance of linguistic action.

51pp., ISBN 0–8248–1419–3 $10.

www.ingramcontent.com/pod-product-compliance
Lightning Source LLC
Chambersburg PA
CBHW080336170426
43194CB00014B/2581